KU-267-770

Management Consulting

—

Philip A. Wickham

·1227166

LIBRARY

ACC. No.
01047952.

DEPT.

CLASS No.
658·46 WIC

UNIVERSITY
COLLEGE CHESTER

FINANCIAL TIMES
PITMAN PUBLISHING

To Louise, for the same reasons

FINANCIAL TIMES
MANAGEMENT
LONDON • SAN FRANCISCO
KUALA LUMPUR • JOHANNESBURG

*Financial Times Management delivers the knowledge,
skills and understanding that enable students,
managers and organisations to achieve their ambitions,
whatever their needs, wherever they are.*

London Office:
128 Long Acre, London WC2E 9AN
Tel: +44 (0)171 447 2000
Fax: +44 (0)171 240 5771
Website: www.ftmanagement.com

A Division of Financial Times Professional Limited

First published in Great Britain in 1999

© Financial Times Professional Limited 1999

The right of Philip A. Wickham to be identified as Author
of this Work has been asserted by him in accordance
with the Copyright, Designs and Patents Act 1988.

ISBN 0 273 63811 4

British Library Cataloguing in Publication Data
A CIP catalogue record for this book can be obtained from the British Library

All rights reserved; no part of this publication may be reproduced, stored
in a retrieval system, or transmitted in any form or by any means, electronic,
mechanical, photocopying, recording, or otherwise without either the prior
written permission of the Publishers or a licence permitting restricted copying
in the United Kingdom issued by the Copyright Licensing Agency Ltd,
90 Tottenham Court Road, London W1P 0LP. This book may not be lent,
resold, hired out or otherwise disposed of by way of trade in any form
of binding or cover other than that in which it is published, without the
prior consent of the Publishers.

10 9 8 7 6 5 4 3 2 1

Typeset by 🐦 Tek-Art, Croydon, Surrey
Printed and bound in Great Britain by Clays Ltd, St Ives plc

The Publishers' policy is to use paper manufactured from sustainable forests.

Contents

PART 3 Making the project happen: developing project management skills

Preface

Consulting is one of the most interesting, exciting and challenging of management roles. For those who can meet its demands, it is one which can bring great financial, professional and intellectual rewards.

The skills a consultant develops are highly valuable. Consultancy demands a focus on thorough and insightful analysis, the achieving of well-defined objectives, a concern with utilising resources productively and communicating ideas in a way which influences people. The value of skills like these is not confined just to the narrow delivery of a formal consulting project. They are valuable in management generally. Work in non-profit situations can also benefit from a recognition of the benefits a consulting approach can bring. For this reason, a consulting project offers a valuable learning opportunity for students of business and management. It provides a chance to develop skills that will be of use whatever career path is pursued.

The management skills good consultants bring to their projects are rich and varied and draw from a broad range of business disciplines. The consultant must offer an ability to analyse information, to lead and manage projects, often of great complexity, and to build productive relationships with people. The consultant must integrate these abilities into a professional approach to taking advantage of new business opportunities and positively meeting business challenges.

This book aims to offer comprehensive support to students who wish to develop these skills through the undertaking of a consulting exercise as part of their learning programme. It will be of value to undergraduates and full time postgraduates. Its insights and practical advice will also be valuable for post-experience students and students undertaking part-time programmes. The book will also be of use to students undertaking work-based and distance learning programmes.

Although the book is primarily aimed at students of management, it recognises that students studying many other disciplines face management challenges. It will be of interest to students studying general management and specialist management areas such as marketing, human resource management, operations management and finance. It will also be of interest to students who are studying technical disciplines (such as engineering, computing and information technology) who expect consulting and offering advice to managers to be an important element in their professional life.

In addition to those on formal learning programmes, the book will also offer insights to practising managers who are eager to learn, particularly those who wish to capitalise on the growing demand for an internal consultancy approach to management tasks in rapidly changing organisations.

Effective consulting, like any form of good management, knits together intellectual understanding and performance abilities. A consulting exercise is most profitable as a learning experience if it does three things. First, if it offers an opportunity to develop a deep conceptual understanding of the critical issues all businesses face in today's increasingly competitive world. Second, if it provides a means of applying that understanding to take advantage of real business situations. Third, and most importantly, if it allows the learning gained to be applied to future management practice. With this in mind, this book is structured into six parts.

Part 1 of the book deals with the context in which the consulting project provides a learning experience. It considers how the consulting project is best approached as an opportunity to develop transferable skills. In particular it explores the adoption of an active learning strategy. Such a strategy is the best way to meet the three objectives outlined above. This part aims to act as a route map for the book. It considers management consulting in broad terms. It highlights the challenges management consulting presents and the skills that can be used to meet them and then directs the reader to the part of the book that addresses those issues.

Part 2 of the book is concerned with the consulting project as a practical management task. It deals with the ways in which consultants create value for their client businesses (hence the basis on which consultancy can be *sold* to clients), the types of project that consultants undertake and the consulting *process*, the stages through which a consulting project moves and the management issues these stages raise.

Part 3 addresses the actual running of the consulting exercise as a formal management project. It addresses the way project management issues such as objective definition, planning and budgeting relate to consulting and how they can be approached effectively.

Knowing how to deliver a project is only the start, though. It is critical that a project be *right* for the business and the situations it faces. Part 4 of the book is concerned with developing the analytical skills that are necessary to identify the opportunities, understand the capabilities and rationalise the challenges a wide variety of businesses face. It ensures that the consultant develops projects that are profitable for, and attractive to, modern businesses.

Being able to identify the right way forward for a business and knowing how to direct it there with a specific project is a sure foundation for a consultant. What makes the consultant really effective, though, is an ability to bring people along with them when they are delivering that project. Part 5 of the book examines the interpersonal and influence skills that enable consultants to see their ideas become reality. In particular, it offers practical advice in developing leadership, motivational, team-working, communication and influencing skills.

Part 6 of the book deals with how the successes of the consulting exercise can be built upon and the skills developed might be used. It offers advice on relating the outcome of the consulting project as a valuable and differentiating point of the curriculum vitae. It explores professional consulting as a career option and how exploiting consulting skills can make careers in general management more successful.

A live consulting project can be one of the most interesting, challenging and rewarding aspects of a programme of management study. This book aims to help you make the best of it and make the best out of it.

Philip A. Wickham

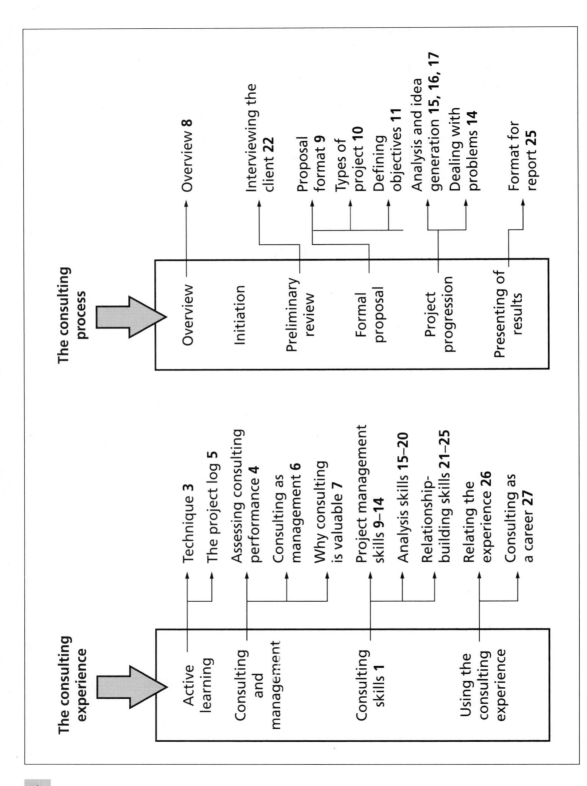

Figure P.1 Map of ideas in the book and the relevant chapters

A note on the layout
of this book

The management of a consulting project calls on a variety of skills. Effective delivery can be supported by a number of management techniques. This book aims to give an insight into these skills and techniques in a way which makes their use practical and guides practice in using them.

Consultants must integrate their skills. The tasks that make up a consulting project cannot be split so that one skill can be used in isolation from the others. People skills must be used to support analysis. Good project management enables relationships to be built. Effective analysis ensures that the project progresses towards delivering the desired outcomes on time and on budget.

A consulting project does not call on skills in a sequential way. One does not follow another. However, a book must, by its very nature, relate them in a linear manner. So there is no one 'right' way to detail the skills and techniques a consultant might use. All that can be hoped is that the organisation of the book is coherent, consistent and logical. I hope this book achieves this. The structure has been found to be successful as the basis of a lecture series on management consulting.

Students who wish to use this book actively to support the consulting exercise will want to work their way through the book in a linear way, especially if it supports a lecture course. But they will also find that they will need to dip in and draw out ideas from different parts at different times if they are actually engaged in a live consulting exercise.

To assist the student to use this book actively and help him or her find ideas when needed, the map opposite (Figure P.1) is offered. The map is divided into two parts. The first part deals with the consulting experience, what it is, what it offers and how it might be used. The second deals with the consulting process. For each theme in the consulting experience the map highlights the chapters which explore that aspect of the experience. For each stage in the consulting process, the map directs the reader to the chapters where important ideas are related and which provide support for the successful achievement of that stage.

Of course, the guidance provided by the map is not exhaustive. Emphasis is on those ideas which experience suggests students find particularly valuable at that stage. The map is just a way in to the text at an informative point. The text contains cross-references to other chapters in which related ideas are covered, or which expand on the original material.

In recognition of the fact that managing a business management consulting programme for students presents challenges to the management education, the Appendix provides practical guidance on designing, running and assessing such projects.

The book aims to be comprehensive and self-contained. A number of pointers are given in the text to the excellent books and journal articles which develop further the ideas presented here. These works are listed in Suggestions for further reading at the end of the book. The interested student is encouraged to increase his or her understanding by exploring these original works.

Chris Floyd
A profile of consulting success

A powerful and motivating way to assist in developing a rewarding career is to identify someone who has pursued a path you would like to follow and to adopt this as a 'road map' for the way you might develop. If this person works for the same organisation, he or she can become a mentor and provide ongoing support and encouragement. Mentoring is a technique of growing importance in personal development.

As a way of setting the context for the value of the skills described in this book we can look at the career of Chris Floyd, a successful consultant with leading consulting firm Arthur D. Little. This provides an example of what can be achieved through learning effective consulting skills together with active practice in developing them.

At an age when most managers are only just starting to think about the possibility of a move into a senior position, Dr Chris Floyd has already had several years' experience as a European Director of Arthur D. Little's UK Northern office. Arthur D. Little is one of the world's leading management and technology consultancies. Chris is one of the directors responsible for Arthur D. Little's 150 UK staff and the head of the firm's Northern UK office. He is a leading member of the company's Global Technology and Innovation Management Practice, and specialises in using technology to develop competitive advantage and enhance strategic performance.

He has worked with a large number of leading international companies operating in sectors as diverse as packaging, biotechnology, advanced materials, household appliances, control instrumentation and ceramics. He is an adviser on technology management to the European Commission. He is also the author of *Managing Technology for Corporate Success* (Gower, 1997), a leading source of ideas for the effective management of technology-focused consulting projects.

Consulting offers a rich variety of management challenges. Chris is an example of what can be achieved if those challenges are met. His first degree was in engineering and, after taking a technical higher degree and gaining experience as a structural engineer, he decided to concentrate on management. He joined a small consulting company specialising in new product development and undertook a part-time MBA in parallel with this. This presented the opportunity of a fast learning curve. Chris had to learn quickly to combine his technical knowledge with a fundamental understanding of clients' businesses, and the opportunities and issues they faced. He had to manage complex projects, and develop communication and influencing skills to ensure that the client understood the consulting recommendations and was motivated to implement them.

An active approach to learning enabled Chris to develop analysis, project management and relationship-building skills quickly and effectively. With these skills in place, he moved on to join Arthur D. Little. He continued to develop his skills and enjoyed a fast-track career with the company.

Chris feels the secret of his success is that he has never stopped learning. As a result, his career is, in many ways, only just beginning.

The learning context

1

The skills of the consultant

Learning outcomes

The learning outcomes from this chapter are:
- to recognise the nature of consulting as a management task;
- to appreciate the skills effective management consultants bring to the job;

and in particular:
- to recognise the importance of the *project management skills* necessary to keep the consulting project on schedule and on budget;
- to recognise the importance of the *analysis skills* needed to understand the client business, identify the opportunities it faces and develop strategies to exploit them;
- to recognise the importance of the *relationship-building skills* needed to relate ideas to positively influence decision makers and to make the project happen in real organisations.

1.1 What a business consultant does

Management consulting is, as its title suggests, a management *activity*. But it is a special form of management. Many would regard it as one of the most exciting of management challenges. It is certainly one of the most demanding. The upside of this is that it can also be one of the most rewarding. Not just financially (though the rewards here can be high indeed for good consultants), but also in terms of task enjoyment, satisfaction with achievements and intellectual stimulation.

A management consultant is rewarded for going into an organisation and undertaking a special project on its behalf. Usually the organisation is a profit-motivated commercial venture. But it does not have to be. Consultants are also (and increasingly) called upon to offer their services to non-profit organisations such as charities. Governmental and non-governmental organisations, whether local, national or international, also make frequent calls on the skills of management consultants.

The types of project undertaken by consultants are as varied as management itself. They may involve the proffering of technical expertise. They may be 'softer' and aim at generating cultural change within the organisation. They may have the objective of resolving internal conflicts within the organisation. They may be concerned with helping the organisation build relationships with outside parties. They may aim to help the organisation gain some critical resource. They can be focused on some specific issue which has been recognised by the organisation's management and has been well defined. Often, though, they are of a broad 'business development' nature. Most will involve gathering and analysing information and sharing discoveries with the organisation. Usually the management consulting project is undertaken over a relatively short time scale – say weeks or, at most, a few months. Increasingly, however, projects with a longer timescale (up to a year or more) are in demand.

In short, a management consultant offers his or her management abilities, expertise and insights to the client business in order to *create value for it*. Consulting activity is something that the client business decides to buy in. It represents a *factor* that managers decide they need in order to progress their business and improve its performance. As a factor that is bought in, consulting activity competes with all the other factors a business must buy in if it is to grow: money for investment, people and their skills, raw materials and the equipment necessary to deliver what the business offers. The client will only find the service the consultant is offering attractive if it is something that the business cannot provide for itself. Further, it must be the *best* investment option on offer given all the other things the business could buy in.

This means a consultant must understand a number of things from the outset. Clearly, the consultant must know why what he or she is offering will be of value to the client business. Although important, this is not enough. Consultants must also know why what they are offering represents a good *investment opportunity* for the business given all the other investment opportunities available. This forms the basis of what the consultant can 'sell' to the business. As with any form of selling to organisations, the selling is most effective when the underlying *buying process* is appreciated. Organisations do not buy – individuals within them do. The way in which individuals react, interact and influence each other must be taken into account when delivering a consulting exercise. In short, the consultant must recognise what he or she will enable the business to do in its marketplace, why the business cannot do this for itself and how the individuals who make up the business can unify around the project.

Although Management Consultancy is seen as a specialist management role the consultant must have the skills of a general manager. He or she must not only be able to undertake specific (and often technical projects). He or she must also be able to market what they offer (not forgetting that marketing includes product development as well as promotion), sell the product to clients and manage a relationship with them. This is a challenge. But if it is met effectively the rewards can be great. Consultants often enjoy fast-track careers. Experience in consulting provides such a fast 'learning curve' that they quickly mature as managers and can take on high-level roles, even when quite young. For the ambitious manager, investing in developing the skills that make a consultant effective offers great rewards.

1.2　The effective consultant's skill profile

Consulting represents a particularly challenging management task for a number of reasons. First, the consultant is not working within his or her 'own' organisation. He or she is, in the first stages of the consulting exercise at least, an 'outsider'. In some ways this offers advantages. It may allow the consultant to ask questions and make recommendations that an 'insider' feels they cannot. Managers within a business tend to adopt the organisation's way of seeing things – a kind of 'groupthink' which limits the way both problems and opportunities are seen. A consultant may see things in a different way. He or she might well see opportunities in a fresher, more responsive way. Because the consultant ultimately leaves the organisation he or she can afford a more dispassionate approach. Painful 'home truths' may be recognised more readily (or at least not denied!) by the consultant. For this reason, the consultant will be in a stronger position to advocate difficult courses than someone who does not wish to compromise an open-ended and long-term position within the business.

On the other hand, being an outsider presents some challenges. It means that the consultant must actively build relationships and create a sense of trust. Established managers can often take these for granted. Consultants may formally be employed by an organisation, but often they must operate some distance from it. The employing organisation offers support in a variety of ways but the consultant is 'out on his or her own' in a way the conventional manager is not. The consultant must be both self-supporting and self-starting.

The consultant is often involved in projects which are 'strategic'. Strategic projects have significant consequences and affect the future of the whole business. They can cut across the interests of the managers of established parts or functions within the business. Managers may resist what they see as interference in 'their' areas and challenges to 'their' interests. (These issues are explored at length in the studies by Guth and MacMillan (1986) and Wooldridge and Floyd (1990).) Managing such projects demands an ability to deal with such organisational politics in a firm, sensitive and responsible way.

All managers must offer a value-adding service to their organisations. However, a consultant is able to offer a service in a way which is *explicit*. What a consultant offers is subject to scrutiny which is much more intense and continuous than the scrutiny to which an established manager is exposed. An effective (and politically astute) consultant must be willing to let the client management take credit for successes while often being prepared to take the blame for mistakes.

In order to meet the challenge of managing the consulting project the consultant must develop a skill profile which allows him or her to call upon abilities in three key areas:

◆ an ability to manage the consulting exercise as a *formal project*;

◆ an ability to manage the *analytical skills* necessary to gain an understanding of the client business and the possibilities it faces;

◆ an ability to *communicate ideas* and *positively influence* others.

These three areas represent distinct types of management skill. Learning and using them can be supported by a variety of concepts and techniques. These concepts and techniques are drawn from a wide range of management disciplines and traditions. However, it should not be forgotten that the effective consultant can not only call upon skills in each of these areas but integrate them into a seamless whole of management practice.

We can picture these three skill areas working together as illustrated in Figure 1.1.

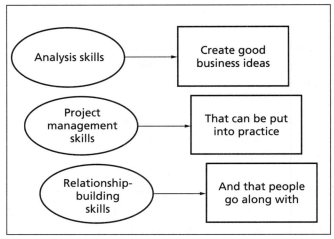

Figure 1.1   **The skills of the consultant**

The next three sections provide an overview of these consulting skill areas. These reviews are an introduction. They will leave unanswered many questions about the type of challenges these skills can be used to address, how the skills may be developed and how they can be used. It will be the task of the following sections in this book to explore these questions in depth.

1.3 Project management skills

A consulting exercise is a self-contained project within a business environment. The best results are achieved if the consulting exercise is managed as such. Important project management skills include the following.

An ability to define objectives and outcomes

An objective states what the project is going to achieve for the client. However not every statement is a good objective. A stated objective must be subject to a critical review. Is it well defined? Will the organisation know when it has achieved the objective? Is the objective achievable, given the external market conditions that face the business? Is it realistic, given the business's internal resources?

How is the objective to be phrased? Will it be readily and clearly understood by those who will play a part in achieving it? Is the objective one that all involved in the business can commit to? If not, why not? How will this matter? These questions will be explored fully in Chapter 11.

An ability to develop formal plans

A plan is a course of action specified in order to achieve a certain objective. Critical aspects of planning include defining tasks, ordering them and understanding the resource implications of the task sequence; in particular, identifying who will be responsible for carrying the tasks out and the financial implications of their activities.

A plan must be properly articulated and communicated if it is to work. A variety of project planning techniques are discussed in Chapter 12.

An ability to sequence and prioritise tasks

Even a simple plan will demand that a number, often a considerable number, of tasks be carried out by different people at different times. Those tasks must be co-ordinated within the shape of the overall project. Timetabling will be important. It will only be possible to carry out some tasks after others have been carried out first. Some tasks may be performed alongside each other. Some tasks must be given priority over others if resources are to be used effectively. Prioritisation must be done both *by* individuals and *between* individuals on the project team.

A project in which task order and priority have been well defined will be delivered in a shorter time period and at lower cost than one which has not. A number of formal (though practical and quite easy to use) methods have been developed to assist managers organise complex task sequences. These are reviewed in Chapter 12.

An ability to manage the financial resources that are to be invested in the consulting project

All management activity demands that money be spent. As a minimum, managers and other workers must be paid for their work. The purchase of external goods (market research, for example) may also be required. With some projects capital expenditure may be expected. For example, the consultant may take responsibility for the purchase of a major piece of equipment or building or investment in an expensive promotional campaign. Keeping track of that expenditure is a critical management responsibility. Profiles of expected expenditure – budgets – must be set before the project starts so that the resource requirements may be understood. These budgets must be managed. Actual expenditure must be monitored against anticipated expenditure. A project, no matter how good its outcomes, runs the risk of disappointing the client if it turns out to be more expensive that anticipated.

Most consulting projects undertaken by students do not demand the management of large financial sums. However, clients have been known to make money available to the student team – especially if a project is going well and they are keen to expand its possibilities. It is far from uncommon for a client who is pleased with the outcomes of a consulting exercise to ask members of the student team who have delivered it to come in on a full-time basis and implement its recommendations.

For these reasons developing an awareness of budget management issues and recognising the skills necessary for managing them are valuable parts of the consulting learning experience. An effective approach to managing the budget for a consulting project is discussed in Section 12.5.

An ability to recognise the human expertise necessary to deliver the project

A particularly important aspect of recognising the human expertise necessary to deliver a project is to recognise how the various members of the consulting team can specialise their roles. It is often said that people are a business's greatest asset. After all, it is only people who can make one business different from another.

Consultants must work as part of a team. At any one time professional consultants will be members of at least two teams: one based with their own employing business and one at the client business. Student consultants are also likely to be members of a team made up of other students. This team will be an adjunct to the management team at the client business.

Productive team working is crucial for consulting success. (This is an issue discussed in detail in Chapter 23.) One area where team working and project management skills meet is in deciding who will do what. Not every member of the team can or should attempt to undertake every task. It is unlikely, given people's individual preferences, that they would wish to. A lot of value can be created by differentiation activities and allowing an individual in the team an opportunity to specialise his or her contribution. The range of individual roles in the project is considered in Section 12.2.

An ability to manage personal time

Time is the most precious of resources. We never seem to have enough of it. All managers must learn to use their time well. This is no less so for the student consultant. The consulting exercise will not be the only thing on the agenda. Other courses must be attended, tutorials prepared for and examinations revised for. A little time for a social life would also be nice!

The management of personal time is an important aspect of project management. Time management skills are discussed in detail in Chapter 13. They are worth investing in. Not only do they allow time to be used productively, they also mean that last-minute panics are avoided. This reduces stress. Relaxed management is more effective, engenders confidence, makes learning easier and much more enjoyable.

1.4 Analysis skills

A consulting exercise must do something for the client business. It must offer the business the chance of moving from where it is 'now' to somewhere 'new and better'. This demands both an analysis of the business's current situation and an analysis of the opportunities open to it. Analysis involves taking information about the business and its situation and then processing that information so that effective decisions may be made from it.

The management consultant's analysis skills may be considered at two levels. At one level there are skills which enable information in general to be manipulated and used. These are skills which all people use all the time. However, a consultant must hone them to a high level. At a more technical level there are skills which facilitate the analysis of business activity. Consultants must be specialists in understanding a business, its strengths and weaknesses, its situation and the opportunities and threats it presents. To do so requires the application of more specific concepts and techniques.

General analysis skills are often subsumed into management 'intuition'. They are just what experienced managers do on the basis of what they know. Just because they are not necessarily explicit does not mean they are not important. In fact, this is evidence of *deep learning* (deep learning is a technique that can be learned – *see* Chapter 3). General analysis skills include the following.

An ability to identify what information is available in a particular situation

Decision makers demand information. The more information that is taken into account the more confidence there can be in the decision made. A good decision maker is active in auditing the information that is available to be used in a decision-making situation. In many cases this will involve background research and reviews of published information. However, at an immediate level it will demand effective questioning of those with experience of the business and its situation to get them to share the information they have (and which they may not even know they have!). This process involves both problem definition and questioning skills. Problem definition is reviewed in Chapter 16. Questioning skills are a critical communication skill and are considered in Section 22.3.

An ability to identify what information is needed in a particular situation

Often in a decision-making situation it is not a lack of information which presents a problem. Quite the reverse in fact: it is that too much is available. The consultant always walks a tightrope between not gaining enough information and so making uninformed decisions and having so much that focused decision making is impaired, between what the two of the founders of modern systems thinking, Kast and Rosenzweig (1985), have called 'extinction by instinct' and 'paralysis by analysis'. The practical implications of this issue are explored in a 1995 paper by Anne Langley.

Having identified what information is available in a situation a consultant must decide which information is pertinent to the decision in hand. The information that is needed to make the decision an effective one must be distinguished from that which is merely a distraction. The balance will lie in the nature of the decision, its significance to the consulting project and the business, and the type of information available.

An ability to process that information to identify the important relationships within it

Information on its own is not much use. It must be processed in order to identify the important relationships within it. Critically, what the information is really saying about the business and the opportunities open to it must be revealed. For example, consumer demand figures suggest a market is growing. Does this present an opportunity for your client's business? Or does it just make life easier for competitors? Will it attract new ones into your client's market? For example a report in the *Financial Times* suggests an important competitor of your client is failing. Does this suggest an easier time for your client or does it herald a tougher time for your client's sector as a whole? An innovative new product of the client business is making a real impact in the market. Good. But will it lead to cash flow problems? Drawing conclusions such as these demands an understanding of patterns of relationships and causal linkages that connect businesses, their customers and their environments together. Creative approaches to analysis are discussed in Chapter 15.

An ability to draw meaning from that information and use it to support decision making

Once connections have been made and conclusions drawn it is necessary to identify the impact of those conclusions on the courses of action open to the client business and their significance to the consulting project.

This processing of information has both 'private' and 'public' aspects. The private aspect involves a detached and reflective consideration of what the information means and what, in consequence, is the best option for the business. The public aspect demands using information to make the case for a particular course of action, to advocate particular options, to convince others of the correctness of that course and to meet objections. These two aspects do, of course, go hand in hand.

The 'intuitive' side of analysis is often supplemented by the use of formal techniques which can help business decision making. Some of the more important consulting analysis skills are in the areas dealt with in the following sections.

An ability to recognise the business's profile of strengths, weaknesses and capabilities

All businesses are different. They develop strengths which allow them to deliver certain sorts of value to particular customers in a special and valuable way. They have weaknesses which leave them open to attack by competitors. A variety of conceptual frameworks can be used to guide the exploration of a firm's strengths, capabilities and weaknesses.

An ability to recognise the opportunities and challenges the environment offers the business

A business's environment presents a constantly shifting kaleidoscope of possibilities. Some offer new opportunities to serve customers better and so grow and develop the business. Others expose weaknesses which, at best, leave the business in a position where it will fail to reach its potential and, at worst, will cause its decline. An ability to evaluate the opportunities and threats the business is offered by its markets is a fundamental prerequisite to devising rewarding consulting projects and defining their objectives.

An ability to assess the business's financial situation

Financial performance is not the only measure of a business's success. But it is fundamental. It is only through a sound financial performance that a business can reward its stakeholders. An analysis of a company's financial situation offers a route to understanding its performance in its marketplace, the risks to which it is exposed and the resources it has available to invest in the future. Financial analysis is easiest and most rewarding when undertaken with the guidance of formal ratio methods.

All of these methods of analysis will be considered in detail in Chapter 17.

An ability to evaluate the business's markets and how they are developing

A market is the total of demand for a particular good or service. A particular business gains sales through having a share of that market. The growth of the business will be sensitive to the development of its markets. If the market is growing new business opportunities may present themselves. But new competitors may be being attracted to them as well. If the market is in decline then business pressures may be building. If the market is fragmenting then new niches may be opening up and innovation may be rewarded.

An analysis of trends in the business's markets, combined with a consideration of the firm's capabilities, can be used to define consulting project outcomes which make a real contribution to the business's development.

The techniques which can be used to explore market conditions and the opportunities they present will be considered in Chapter 18.

An ability to assess the business's internal conditions

A business is only able to exploit market opportunities if it has the internal conditions which allow it to meet them head-on. The business must have internal conditions which are flexible and responsive to new possibilities and have the resources needed to innovate in an appropriate way. The business must have the capacity to grow in response to those possibilities or be able to get hold of the resources it will need to invest in growth. These resources include human skills as well as productive capacity.

An ability to analyse the way in which decision making occurs within the business

Understanding the possibilities open to a business and devising ways in which those possibilities can be exploited is only the first half of the consultant's responsibilities. If the consultant is to offer real value to a business then he or she must also help the business make those possibilities a reality.

One of the few, perhaps the only, unquestionable truth about organisational life is that businesses rarely recognise good ideas instantly and pursue them without question. Usually a consultant must convince the client business that what he or she is suggesting is a real opportunity. To do this an effective consultant must understand decision making in the business, and use this knowledge to his or her advantage. This demands knowing who is involved in the decision-making process and the role different individuals play. It also means a sensitivity to who will gain (and who might lose) if particular ideas are put into practice. The consultant must be aware that not all objections are purely rational. Analysing the decision-making processes in the client business is a first stage in building relationships with individuals in the business. Models which assist in this analysis are discussed in Chapters 19 and 20.

1.5 Relationship-building skills

Analysis skills offer an insight into where the client business might go. Project management skills offer an ability to deliver the project necessary to move the business forward. However, these skills are only of very limited use if the client firm's management and influential outsiders cannot be convinced that this is the right way to go and that they should offer their support to the project and the direction it offers. Gaining this support demands relationship-building skills.

Some critical relationship-building skills include the following.

An ability to build rapport and trust with the client

Rapport is hard to define – but it is easy to recognise. Two people have a rapport when they communicate with ease and work together effectively. It is clear that they have a trust in each other and a commitment to each other. Rapport is not confined to face-to-face communication. It is a feature of all communication. Rapport can be built through written and verbal communications as well. It is not just subject to what is said. How things are said matters as well.

Rapport is very important in 'lubricating' the consultant's activities within the organisation. Developing rapport demands practice. It is a skill which can be developed through active learning. Guidance and some hints on how to build rapport are given in Chapter 22.

An ability to question effectively

Questioning is one of the fundamental communication skills. Questioning is not only a way to get information (though this is important). It is also a way to build rapport and to control the direction of a conversation. Effective questioning skills are an important plank in any manager's leadership strategy. They are especially important for the consultant. Questioning is so important that it is discussed in a separate section (22.3).

An ability to communicate ideas succinctly and precisely

A consultant brings a special level of expertise to a business. He or she must offer something the business cannot offer itself. This may mean that the consultant is working in an area with a high technical content, for example finance or marketing. Areas such as these and many others have a language all their own. The consultant must be cautious about using this language directly to the client. After all, the client is not interested in the consultant's knowledge of a technical area but in his or her ability to use that knowledge in a way which creates value for his or her business.

A consultant has most impact when he or she talks the same language as the client. Ideas must be related in a way which is succinct and precise and uses no more technical jargon that the client is comfortable with. Converting technical ideas into plain language is not always easy. But it is important and is a skill of its own which can be developed with practice.

An ability to negotiate objectives and outcomes

A consulting project must have definite objectives and outcomes. The value the project is expected to deliver to the client business must be explicit. However, the consultant and the client do not always agree, in the first instance at least, on what those outcomes should be. The client may not have a clear idea of what is wanted for the business. If he or she does have a definite idea it may be beyond the scope of what the consultant is in position to realistically offer. It may be that the consultant is not convinced that what the client is demanding as an outcome is absolutely right for the business. Such disagreements can often occur with student consulting projects where the client's expectations are very high and there is a need to reconcile commercial with educational outcomes.

Whatever the source of any disagreement, the project outcomes must be defined and agreed by consultant and client. This is a process of negotiation that results in the formal project brief.

The need to negotiate is not an admission that there is necessarily a conflict between the client and the consultant. Rather, it is a recognition that the consultancy exercise will work best when both client and consultant have clear expectations as to what will result from the consulting exercise and what the responsibility of both parties will be in achieving them. The consultant must be aware that disappointment in consultancy (for both client and consultant team) results more from unclear expectations than from poor outcomes.

Ways to approach negotiating the outcomes of the project are considered in Chapter 11.

An ability to convince through verbal, written and visual mediums

In business, having good ideas is not enough. Ideas must be used to encourage people to follow them as courses of action. They must be used to encourage the business's managers to implement plans and its backers to make supportive investment decisions. Ideas must be communicated in a way which convinces people that they are good and are worth implementing. This conviction comes as much from the 'how' of communication as from the 'what', that is, from the form of the communication as well as its content.

Conviction results if ideas are communicated in a manner which is appropriate to the audience; for example if the communication uses the right language, is of the right length and adopts a proper style. This applies to communication in any situation and whether the medium is verbal, visual or written.

An ability to use information to make a case for a particular course of action

Of course, ideas must have some substance if they are to deliver real value. Communication of ideas must be backed up with information. This includes both facts and interpretation of facts. The logic of that interpretation must be clear. Different people in the client business will seek and will be convinced by different corroborating information, at different levels and presented in different ways. Some information will be included in an initial communication. Other parts may be kept back as a response to questions and challenges.

Knowing when to use particular information, and how to use it to convince, is an important communication skill for the consultant, especially as a consultant's ideas are likely to be under close scrutiny by the client business, certainly more so than those of internal managers. Convincing with information and well-structured, well-communicated arguments is a theme developed in Chapter 25.

An ability to develop selling strategies

Effective selling calls for a definite, well-developed and quite well-understood set of skills. Selling of goods and services is a specialist management activity. However, all managers are involved in selling their ideas all the time. Consultants must certainly sell their ideas. But they must also sell themselves and their own organisations as *providers* of ideas. This is a particular challenge for consultants involved in general management rather than some specialist area. A business may readily accept that it lacks technical knowledge in product development, information technology or finance. However, few businesses will readily admit to being deficient in general management skills.

The consultant can draw on a variety of formal selling skills. These must be used appropriately though. Consultancy, as a 'product', does not usually respond to a 'hard sell' approach. Rather, a formal selling approach should be used as the tactic in a well-thought through selling strategy. This strategy should aim to communicate what the consultant can genuinely offer the client and be used to build a long-term, mutually rewarding relationship.

An ability to work effectively as a member of a team

Many consulting tasks (especially those of major significance) require a team effort. As a minimum they will demand that the consultant and client work together. Usually they will involve an extended management team in the client business. Often the consulting task will have significant resource implications and will be complex to deliver. The scope of its demands will go beyond the capabilities of one individual, certainly in time and perhaps in technical knowledge. Delivering the project will require the consultant to work as part of a team.

Good team working is essential for business success and not just in consulting. It is a skill in itself. It demands many things. It requires, for example, a careful definition of individual roles in relation to the team as a whole. It also requires well-honed interpersonal, motivation and conflict-resolution skills. Most of all, perhaps, it demands a willingness to align the interests of the individuals who make up the team with the overall task the team must address. This requires an ability to advocate individual interests and yet, when necessary, to compromise individual concerns for the interests of the group as whole.

If the team is to develop a productive coherence through which its members can make individual contributions then it must be actively managed. Chapter 23 considers the issues involved in and the skills needed for team working. These will be considered with the support of conceptual thinking about the dynamics of team working.

An ability to demonstrate leadership

Leadership is an ability to focus and direct the individuals in an organisation in a way which brings the whole organisation benefits. Leadership is perhaps the most valuable commodity a senior manager can offer his or her organisation. Leadership draws together a variety of relationship skills, not least articulation of vision, motivation and communication, into a coherent behavioural strategy.

It should not be thought that a consulting team can have only one, permanent leader and that the remainder of the team must be followers. Such an assumption lies behind many intragroup conflicts. Leadership is not an inherent and fixed property of an individual. It is situational; that is, it arises out of the conditions of a particular situation in which people interact in a particular way. Leadership may shift between members as the project evolves and the situation changes. The individual who shows leadership for the team may not be the same as the person who shows leadership towards the client business or towards people from outside the team offering support to the project. In professional consulting, as in business generally, leadership up the formal reporting hierarchy, from subordinate to superior, may be as important as traditional leadership down it.

A consulting project is one of the best opportunities a student will be given to recognise the nature and value of leadership, and to develop leadership skills. The nature of leadership skills important for the consultant are discussed in Chapter 24.

The project management, analysis and relationship skill areas do not work in isolation. They must operate in conjunction and in balance with each other. Relationship building must be based on a proficient analysis of the business and the people in it. Project management must be aimed at delivering negotiated outcomes. Good project management skills offer a base on to which can be built a trust that outcomes will be delivered. And so on.

Team discussion point	You have undertaken a consulting exercise with a local travel firm. The firm is very pleased with the outcomes of the project and by way of thanks offers your group a free holiday together. Consider this holiday as a project. What project management, analysis and relationship-building skills must the group use if you are to make the holiday enjoyable for all?

Hint

Consider the various stages of the 'project':

◆ deciding where to go, when to go and how long to stay;

◆ deciding what needs to be taken and packing your luggage;

◆ travelling to your destination;

◆ enjoying the activities available on the holiday;

◆ returning home.

What skills will be called on at each stage?

Summary of key ideas

The effective consultant offers the client firm a way to add value that it cannot do on its own. To do this the consultant must call on three areas of management skill:

◆ *analysis skills* – an ability to know where to go and how to get there;

◆ *relationship building skills* – an ability to take people along with you;

◆ *project management skills* – an ability to make it happen!

These are general management skills. Consulting presents a steep learning curve. This means it is a challenge. However, the rewards are high. An effective consultant can expect to take on highly responsible roles at an early stage in his or her career.

Figure 1.2   The consultant must always convince the client that the service on offer is of real value!

Source: Copyright © 1998 United Feature Syndicate, Inc. Reproduction by permission.

2

Learning outcomes from this book

Learning outcomes

The learning outcomes from this chapter are:

◆ to appreciate the *opportunities* the consulting exercise offers as a learning experience;

◆ to recognise the types of *skill* the consulting exercise presents an opportunity to develop;

◆ to understand how those the skills developed on the consulting exercise can be *transferred* to management challenges in the future.

2.1 The consulting process as a management challenge

Consulting is a management exercise which presents a rich variety of challenges and experiences. However, all consulting exercises tend to follow a common pattern of basic activities. The consulting exercise represents a process through which value is created for the client. This process has a number of distinct stages. These are discussed in detail in Chapter 8. However, a brief preview is useful at this stage so that an understanding of the type of learning opportunity they present can be created.

The key stages in the consulting process are:

1 making an initial contact with the client;

2 initiating the consulting project;

3 analysing the client business;

4 defining the objectives of the project;

5 making a formal proposal to the client;

6 progressing the project;

7 communicating the findings;

8 following up.

(*See also* Figure 2.1.)

Each of these stages demands project management, analysis and relationship-building skills in different measures. Consultants have to earn a living. They must attract the client with what they have to offer. Consultants must market themselves. This is not an activity used just to gain the consulting contract. Consultants must constantly market what they have to offer to the client. This is a process of engagement that is fundamental to building a good working relationship with the client. As with any business, a formal approach to marketing and promotion can pay dividends. The consultant must develop a marketing mix for what he or she offers, and what his or her business offers: a 'product' – the exact nature of the service on offer and why it will be valuable to the client; a 'price' – what it will cost the client; a 'place' – a means of getting the service to the client and a 'promotion' – a way of informing potential clients what is on offer.

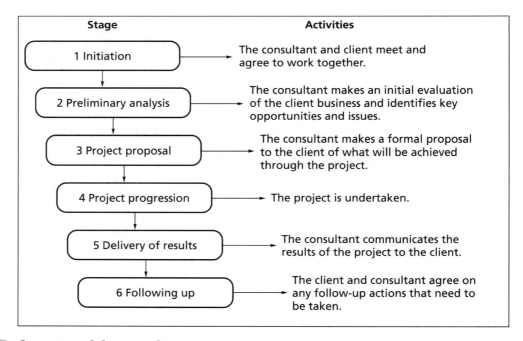

Stage	Activities
1 Initiation	The consultant and client meet and agree to work together.
2 Preliminary analysis	The consultant makes an initial evaluation of the client business and identifies key opportunities and issues.
3 Project proposal	The consultant makes a formal proposal to the client of what will be achieved through the project.
4 Project progression	The project is undertaken.
5 Delivery of results	The consultant communicates the results of the project to the client.
6 Following up	The client and consultant agree on any follow-up actions that need to be taken.

Figure 2.1 Overview of the consulting process

Initial contact is important. First impressions can be used to build a productive partnership. If the relationship gets off to a bad footing, the consulting exercise may not get sold at all. Even if it does, it may be difficult to build the rapport and trust which will be necessary to make the project work. The initial contact must be turned into a project which offers an opportunity for both partners in the consulting process.

The consulting project must be designed to meet the needs of the client business. It must help it capitalise on opportunities and avoid threats. Understanding these requires a detailed analysis of the client business. This analysis must be conducted so that proper decisions about the nature of the consulting exercise can be made. It is unwise to assume that the client has actually performed such an analysis, at least in an explicit way.

This consulting project will be defined in terms of its *objectives*. Defining and negotiating objectives demands effective use of analysis and relationship-building skills. The objectives must be communicated back to the client through the formal brief. This brief is not just a piece of communication. It is an opportunity for the consultant to sell him or herself. (The consultant must remember that the consulting exercise may be a competitive pitch and the client may be selecting a consultant on the basis of the formal proposal!) In any case, it is a chance to keep control of the project and develop the relationship with the client.

Once objectives have been agreed the project must be progressed towards delivering the desired outcomes. Progression means defining and undertaking specific tasks and managing the resources involved in the project. These resources are financial, human, information and time. This task is made much easier if project management skills such as planning and resource management can be called upon. The consulting team must also learn to work together in a productive and satisfying way. It is also highly likely that further analysis will be needed as the project is progressed.

As soon as the consulting team has rationalised its proposal it must be presented to the client. This calls upon the effective use of good communication skills. If the client is to accept the recommendations, positive persuasion must be used. After the formal project is completed, the consultant may need to follow up – to see how the implementation of the recommendations made is going – and to offer further advice. This is not just good practice; it is a way of maintaining and developing the relationship that has been built. More work and recommendations may well follow!

In summary, the consulting exercise presents a management experience which is challenging, in terms of both the wide range of skills it calls upon and the depth to which specific skills must be applied. The consulting exercise offers an opportunity to apply existing skills and develop new ones. It provides a theatre in which human relationship skills can be rehearsed and a forum in which analysis skills can be practised. For the student of business the consulting exercise offers a valuable opportunity to put knowledge gained in a classroom environment into practice. Such practice is an essential element of an active learning strategy. This practice not only reinforces knowledge, it dramatically increases confidence in using it. Relevant knowledge combined with confidence in using it is a formidable cocktail in a business environment. It is a highly valuable and transferable skill.

2.2 Key learning outcomes from the consulting project

Every consulting project has different features. However, all consulting projects offer an opportunity to hone a broad range of management skills. These management skills are valuable. They can be used to great effect in a wide variety of consulting situations. They can also be used in management other than in a formal consulting project. They are equally effective as the basis for general management practice.

This book is designed to work with you in gaining the effective delivery of a consulting project. It aims to support you in delivering the project outcomes in an effective, enjoyable and rewarding way. Its guidance will help ensure that the project outcomes will be valuable for the business you work with. Most importantly, though, it aims to enable you to use the consulting experience as the basis of developing skills which will be of value in the future.

The experience of the project will be a means for you to develop your managerial performance. This will be of value in two ways. First, the delivery of the project will in itself provide evidence of your management ability. Second, if the project is approached with a positive approach and an active learning strategy in mind, the experience will enhance your ability to deal with new management challenges in the future. Both of these will be of value in your professional career.

This book aims to help you achieve some definite learning outcomes that will help you deliver the consulting exercise and which will be transferable to your future management career. In particular, if you use this book to support active learning on a consulting project you will:

◆ recognise the importance of sound analytical thinking when approaching business opportunities and challenges;
◆ recognise the need for a pro-active approach to taking advantage of those business opportunities and responding to challenges;
◆ recognise the rewards that are to be gained from effective team working;
◆ develop an appreciation of the importance of effective communication in a business situation;

◆ develop an understanding of the project management techniques which will enable you to plan and deliver projects on time and on budget;

◆ recognise your own skill profile, identify your strengths and areas where you have an opportunity to develop further;

◆ develop confidence in presenting and promoting your own business ideas.

This list is not exhaustive. There are many other things which might be learned from undertaking a consulting project. This list should be regarded as the minimum the experience offers.

2.3 Active learning and developing transferable skills

We all learn all the time. Sometimes learning is a formal process demanding a specific commitment of time and attention. At other times it is a passive process that just simply seems to happen. Think about a sport you are interested in or a musician you enjoy listening to. How much do you know about them? Would you feel confident to give a presentation to your friends about them? For how long could you go on talking? Five minutes, ten, thirty? Longer even? Reflect on how much you actually know about the subject. Yet at what stage did you actually sit down and 'learn' the information you might include in such a talk? It is not unlikely that you have never done so. And yet you have learned a lot about something that interests you. Learning, if we are motivated to learn, is remarkably easy. And enjoyable!

Management, as a discipline, has built up a body of valuable insights. These insights make management easier and more effective. If a manager is to take advantage of these they must be learned. However, management is more like a craft than an abstract discipline. It exists to be practised. This practice builds on the insights that have been gained. Learning about management can be interesting. Performing it, and performing it well, is thrilling. The link between learning about management concepts and a rewarding management performance is provided by *active learning*.

Active learning consists of a cycle of activity. This cycle involves stages of analysis, experience, reflection and planning. This active learning cycle will be discussed fully in Chapter 3. At this stage we just need to recognise that it offers a means to understanding how we learn and a way to make learning more effective. Active learning ensures that we make the best use of the learning experience and that we take maximum advantage to both build on successes and learn from mistakes.

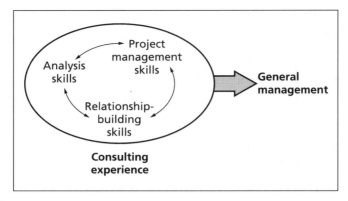

Consulting
experience

| Figure 2.2 | Transferability of consulting skills |

Skills are developed through practice in particular situations. Clearly, once a skill has been developed in a particular situation it can prove to be useful in a variety of new and different situations in the future. Such a skill is said to be *transferable*. Management consulting presents a challenge which is both broad and deep. It calls upon a wide variety of skills and demands they be used well. At heart, good consultants are just very effective managers. The skills a consultant develops need not be confined just to the practice of consulting itself. They are transferable to a wide variety of other business situations (*see* Figure 2.2).

Consultants usually make a move into general management at some point in their career either within a consulting firm or in a general business sector. Quite often they are recruited by businesses for which they have worked. The management skills a consultant has developed and which he or she can use in a general management role enable them to take on quite senior positions while still relatively young. Many very effective managers approach their tasks from the perspective of being internal consultants offering their insights in the same way, and at the same level of effectiveness, as an outside consultant would.

Achieving the learning outcomes offered by using this book to support a consulting exercise approached in a positive fashion with an active learning mindset will enable you to reach a higher, and more rewarding, level of managerial competence faster, whatever management role you decide to take on.

Team discussion point

What career options have you considered so far? How would achieving the learning outcomes specified in Section 2.2 to help you to:

◆ approach a recruitment interview with an organisation offering that career option;

◆ be more successful in that career?

Summarise your conclusions in a short presentation to the remainder of your group.

Summary of key ideas

◆ A consulting exercise offers an opportunity to develop a wide range of management skills and insights.

◆ These are defined in terms of specific and valuable learning outcomes.

◆ The skills developed are transferable to a great variety of rewarding management roles and challenges.

◆ The best way to take advantage of the consulting experience is to approach it in a positive way with an active learning mindset.

3

An active learning strategy

Learning outcomes
The learning outcomes from this chapter are:

◆ to understand what an *active learning strategy* is;

◆ to appreciate the *benefits* an active learning strategy offers;

◆ to recognise the four stages of the *experiential learning cycle*;

◆ to be able to *apply* an active learning approach to the consulting project.

3.1 Active learning and the experiential learning cycle

Managers, as human beings do, desire some outcomes more than others. In management, a desired outcome is called an *objective*. Managers work to achieve their objectives. They are directed towards them and motivated by them. When faced with a particular situation, the manager must evaluate that situation and make a decision as to what course of action to take so that the outcomes are the preferred ones and the objectives wanted are achieved.

Learning is a process which enables a manager to make the right decisions in light of the particular aspects of a situation and desired objectives. Sometimes a manager will use a particular idea or concept to help him or herself make sense of a situation and formulate a course of action. Such a formal approach to decision making is very important in management. At other times, and quite frequently, a manager will make decisions without using formal concepts. The decision making appears to be on an 'intuitive' basis. What is really happening here is that the concepts the manager is using to evaluate the situation and formulate the decision are so well known and understood by him or her that he or she feels no need to bring the concepts up to the conscious mind before they are used.

Understanding an idea at such a level is a result of what is known as *deep learning*. This means that any knowledge gained is understood in such a way that not only can it be recalled but it can be called upon almost intuitively to make sense of some situation, it can be used to develop a real understanding of that situation and it can be used to support effective decision making in response to it (*see* Figure 3.1).

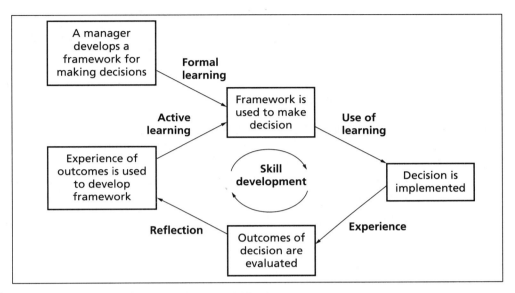

Figure 3.1   **Dynamic learning of management skills**

Deep learning is particularly important in sustaining relationship skills. For example, as we will discover in Chapter 24, there are a number of rules and guidelines on how to behave if one wishes to demonstrate effective leadership. At first, you will find yourself using these guides in a very conscious manner. It may be obvious to other people that you are using them (especially if they themselves know the rules as well). With practice, though, they will become 'second nature'. You will be able to call upon them without having to bring them into the conscious mind. Eventually, you will find that you are developing your own leadership style and in effect have modified the original behaviour rules to suit your own situation and approach. At this point, they achieve their full value. Your leadership style is not only natural but also a tool you can use almost instinctively to manage situations more effectively. Not having to worry about the rules, you can get on with achieving your objectives.

Active learning is an approach which aims to make the most out of any learning experience by encouraging the learning to occur at a deep level. It is a philosophy of learning developed by Kolb in 1978. Active learning turns conscious learning of formal ideas into effective management tools that support good practice as quickly and efficiently as possible.

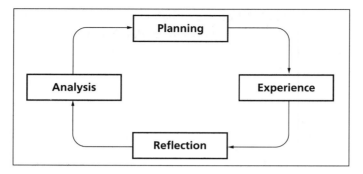

Figure 3.2 The experiential learning cycle

Active learning is a very natural way to learn. It reflects the way we learn in a general sense from our experiences. Approaching it in a conscious manner just makes it more efficient. A good way to approach active learning is through the experiential learning cycle. This cycle has four stages. These are illustrated in Figure 3.2. To understand its power as an approach to effective learning we shall explore each stage in depth.

3.2 Analysis

Analysis is the process through which we make sense of a situation. It is what we engage in before making a decision. Though this process sounds rather formal we should not forget that we use analysis all the time.

When we cross a road, for example, we analyse the situation by looking to make sure that there are no cars coming. You may remember as a child being taught a phrase to encourage you to 'look left, then right, then left again'. As adults, we do not even think about doing this. However, the fact that we are still using such a rule becomes evident when we go to a country where the driving is on the other side of the road to that we are used to. We can easily find ourselves looking the wrong way. For a while we have to make a conscious decision to check in the right direction before stepping out into the road. We must relearn the rule.

There are different levels of analysis. Some are relatively informal, others are more formal. Some use quite simple rules, others very complex ones. The way in which particular rules are used in order to achieve an analysis are referred to as the *analysis strategy*. The type of analysis strategy adopted depends on six factors.

◆ The complexity of the situation faced

In essence, complexity relates to how much information must be processed in order to make sense of the situation. Some situations do not present much information to be analysed. A decision by the consulting team to meet the client on a particular date only requires an understanding of the importance of meeting and a time when all who will be present are free.

Many business situations are much more complex, though. The decision to present the business as an investment opportunity to a venture capitalist, for example, demands a thorough understanding of the factors which determine the competitive potential of the business, the opportunities its marketplace presents, the nature of the investments it wishes to make, the risks these present, the ways in which venture capitalists make decisions and how these might be influenced.

In complex situations the analysis adopts one of, or a combination of, two strategies. The first is to break the information set down into a series of simpler sub-sets. The second is to examine the information to see if a simplifying pattern can be seen; to see the wood through the trees, as it were.

◆ Experience of the decision maker

If the decision maker has extensive experience of a particular type of situation then his or her response to that situation tends to become intuitive. In effect, learning how particular outcomes result from specific decisions has occurred at a deep level. Experience of one type of situation can often be used as the basis of decision making in new situations. The strategy here is to see how the features of the new situation compare with those of known situations and how this knowledge may be used to guide action. Some caution is advised, though. It is easy to see similarities when they don't exist. Inappropriate actions can result.

◆ The formal knowledge the decision maker can call upon

Some analysis is best undertaken using a formal approach. For example, if we want to make sense of the financial situation of a business then knowledge of the principles of business finance and the analysis methods it offers are useful. If we wish to analyse a business's markets then the tools offered by the discipline of marketing provide valuable insights.

The use of formal approaches to decision making is particularly valuable in management. Indeed, the recognition that we lack a formal approach to analysing a situation can be a spur to learning.

◆ The significance of the decision

Some decisions are of little consequence. The impact of the actions they advocate are limited. Other decisions are of major importance. The actions that will follow from them are likely to have a major impact on the business. The likely impact of the decision will influence the analysis that goes into supporting that decision. One of the reasons organisations have vertical hierarchies is so that important decisions can be pushed 'up' to senior managers whereas less important ones can be pushed 'down' to less experienced people.

Consultants usually work with the senior people in an organisation. Even if the project involves working with more junior people, any recommendations made will be subject to review and possible sanction by senior people. The patterns of decision making in real organisations can be quite complex, however. The notion that people at the 'top' make the important decisions and people 'below' put them into practice is dangerously simplistic. Quite junior people may influence senior ones. Middle-ranking people may block the decisions of those above. Various groups may work against each other through political infighting. A good consultant needs to be aware of these subtleties and take them into account when progressing the consulting project.

◆ The cognitive style of the decision maker

Cognitive style refers to the fundamental way in which a person sees the world and processes information about it. Some decision makers, for example, tend to see the 'big picture' and ignore the details. Other people are good at keeping their eye on the details but can fail to integrate them into a unified whole. Some people operate in such a way that the verbal mode is dominant. They are receptive to speech and can take in spoken information easily and quickly. Others operate in a visual mode. They prefer to see information presented in the form of pictures and diagrams.

Recognising the cognitive style of a decision maker, both oneself and others, can be very useful. If we understand our own style we can use it to make learning more efficient and easier. If we understand the cognitive style of others, this offers an important clue when we are developing a strategy to influence them. The cognitive style of managerial decision makers is considered in Section 15.5.

◆ Pressure to justify the decision to others

Decisions are rarely made in isolation. Decision makers working in organisations will usually be called upon to justify the decisions they have made. Some organisations expect even small decisions which are of limited consequence to be justified up the management hierarchy. Others will push even quite major decision-making responsibility down the hierarchy. The decision-making style an organisation adopts will depend on its culture. Some organisations prefer an informal style of decision making. Managers will be expected to use their experience and come across as 'intuitive'. Other organisations will adopt a more formal style of decision making and justification. Documentary proposals may be demanded which give evidence of the application of formal decision support tools, such as investment return and risk assessment.

It is important that a consultant appreciates the decision-making style an organisation advocates. If the consultant taps into it in a sympathetic way then he or she will improve the chances that the ideas offered will become reality. This important theme is expanded on in Chapters 19 and 20.

These six factors (presented in diagram form in Figure 3.3) influence which analysis strategy will be adopted. Chapter 15 in Part 4 of this book, which is dedicated to developing analysis skills, examines the details of the analysis strategies that can be called on to assist decision making.

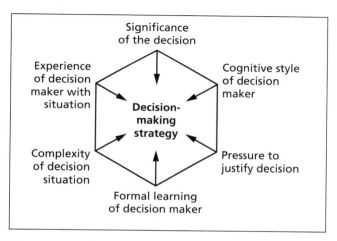

Figure 3.3 Factors influencing the analysis of decisions

3.3 Experience

The experience stage is the one in which the learner actually engages with specific situations, makes decisions, implements them and experiences the resulting outcomes. Experience is about using the knowledge you have. It is the actual *doing* stage of the learning cycle.

Management is an activity which combines conceptual understanding with ability to put ideas into practice. A programme of formal learning presents a good opportunity to develop conceptual understanding. A live consulting project presents an opportunity to put ideas into practice. It does so in a way which is both 'safe' and monitorable. The experience is safe because the decisions and actions that result from them are contained within the boundaries of a learning experience. This is not to say that they are of no consequence, though. They can often be of great value to the business which is the subject of the consulting exercise. The experience is monitorable because it occurs within the support structure of a formal learning programme with well-defined learning outcomes and a focused assessment procedure.

In short, a live consulting project provides a chance to see your ideas happen. It is an opportunity to see how you can achieve successes and develop an understanding of why you enjoy them. It is also an opportunity to make mistakes and to learn from them.

3.4 Reflection

Reflection represents an examination of a decision and an evaluation of the effects resulting from that decision: its *outcomes*. This has two main parts. The first is considering the decision taken and seeing how it relates to the outcomes that have occurred. The second is considering the desirability of those outcomes and whether they are the outcomes one would seek again in the future. Typical questions to ask yourself at the reflection stage include:

◆ What was the decision I implemented?

◆ What actions did this lead me to take?

◆ What effects did those actions have?

◆ What were the resulting outcomes?

◆ How did those effects produce the outcomes?

◆ How sophisticated is my understanding of how those actions were linked to the outcomes?

◆ What factors outside my control also contributed to the outcomes?

◆ Might I bring some or all of those factors under my control in the future?

◆ How did those outcomes impact on those around me?

◆ What feedback (positive or negative) did people around me provide on my actions?

◆ Could I use more feedback in the future?

◆ How satisfying did I find the outcomes personally?

◆ Might I aim for slightly different outcomes in the future?

Reflection should be an active process. It demands a communication with self. It is advisable to put a little time aside to engage in reflection. It can be useful to actually make notes (words or mind maps can be used) as an aid to reflection.

Such notes can be included in the project log (*see* Chapter 5). Reflection can be engaged in as both a private activity or a group activity. It is always useful to get other people's opinions and get a different perspective on the relationship between your actions and the resulting outcomes.

The key requirement is that reflection be honest. Successes should be noted (and, of course, enjoyed). On the other hand, mistakes (both your own and other people's) should also be recognised and used as a positive chance to learn.

3.5 Planning

Planning is the stage which makes use of the investment in analysis, action and reflection. It is concerned with deciding what moves to make in the future. Planning is the process of making a decision as to the best way to approach a situation the next time it is encountered. It has three aspects to it.

The first is a decision as to what outcomes might be desired from that situation. This will include consideration of how satisfying the outcomes achieved last time were and the impact they had on other people. The second is using the analysis undertaken to build understanding of what actions to take in order to achieve the desired outcomes.

Like analysis, planning is a process that varies greatly in both formality and complexity. It might be the planning of the actual consulting exercise, in which case it will call upon the formal planning techniques discussed in Chapter 12. But planning also comes into tackling specific tasks within the project itself. Presenting the final report will also demand planning. If it is to be done successfully a number of questions must be answered. What message is being sent? How should that message be structured? How will the client react to it? How do I *want* them to react to it? And so on. Even a relatively simple task like asking the client for some information will be more successful if some planning goes into it first. Ask, for example: will the client have this information? Can it be obtained elsewhere? How can I use the contact to build my relationship with the client? And so on.

By way of a summary, the planning stage should build on the reflection stage by seeking answers to the critical questions:

◆ What went right last time? Why? How can I repeat that success this time?
◆ What went wrong last time? Why? How can I avoid that failure this time?

Experiential learning is a cycle. Active learning is iterative and continuous. It occurs by repeatedly passing around the cycle. One experience builds into the next through the links of reflection, planning and analysis. Active learning may seem rather complex. It is not. It is merely the way we learn when we learn naturally. With a little practice you will find you are engaged in active learning without knowing it, apart from recognising that your learning has become easier, faster and more enjoyable. Active learning has itself become deep learning.

Team discussion point	Identify an area of knowledge or expertise that you have developed. This might be an interest or hobby. Consider how you went about learning this. How much formal learning took place? On reflection, did you use active learning even if you didn't recognise it at the time?
	Give a brief presentation on your reflections to the rest of your team.

Summary of key ideas	◆ Management in general, and consulting in particular, is a discipline which demands that conceptual understanding and performance skills are integrated.
	◆ Consultants need to make sure that they have learned the conceptual basis of all the skills they call upon – project management, analytical and relationship building at a *deep level*. This ensures that such skills can be called on to meet the management challenges consultants face.
	◆ The best and most efficient way to make learning deep is to use the experiential learning cycle. This has four stages:
	– *analysis*: recognising how the situation and the actions of the decision maker interact to produce outcomes;
	– *experience*: putting ideas into practice and seeing what outcomes emerge;
	– *reflection*: evaluating the outcomes to assess their impact and desirability;
	– *planning*: deciding on the approach to take in a situation based on the first three stages.
	◆ Active learning is an easy and natural way to learn more effectively.

4

Strategies for assessing the performance of consultants

Learning outcomes

The learning outcomes from this chapter are:

◆ to appreciate *assessment strategies* used for evaluating consulting exercises;

◆ to recognise the way in which the assessment procedure can be *used* positively to guide the consulting exercise;

◆ to appreciate the fact that consulting is a *team activity* and that rewards must be earned on a team basis.

4.1 The assessment of consulting exercises

Assessment is a necessary part of any learning experience. It should not be thought of as a hurdle or something set up to trip the unwary student. The assessment procedure can be positive force that drives the learning opportunity forward and directs it in the right way. Assessment focuses the mind on the critical elements of the learning experience. It motivates the student to approach learning as an opportunity.

Assessment is not just a feature of academic life. Managers face constant assessment. This may take the form of informal reviews or more formal structured evaluations. It may be linked to the business's financial performance through bonus payments. For a consultant running his or her own business, customers and the marketplace offer immediate assessment.

Consultants are assessed by their performance in gaining and running consulting projects and delivering their agreed outcomes on time and on budget. Specific elements that will be considered in the assessment of a consultant's performance will be:

- selling the consulting exercise to clients and gaining new business;
- defining projects and agreeing objectives to the satisfaction of the client;
- delivering outcomes in a way that meets (or better exceeds) the client's expectations;
- contributing to the growth and development of the consultant's own business organisation.

The assessment of a student consulting exercise must reflect these concerns. It provides an assessment that is realistic. In doing so it highlights the important elements of the learning experience. It will ensure that the skills developed on the exercise are genuinely transferable to a professional context.

This assessment is individual. Ultimately, of course, a manager's organisation is assessed by the highly competitive marketplace for management skills. And this is an assessment of the firm as a whole. The manager succeeds or fails as a member of a team. Team working must be recognised as an element of assessment and effective team working rewarded.

4.2 Assessment of the project proposal

The project proposal is a critical part of the consulting process. The proposal defines the scope, objectives and outcomes of the project. It is the formal declaration of what the project will achieve for the client. It is critically important that what the project aims to achieve is both unambiguous and understood by the client and consultant team. What makes the client satisfied with what a consultant delivers is not so much the outputs but the outputs relative to expectations. A good consulting exercise will still disappoint if the client's initial expectations were too high. This can be very frustrating for the consultant team, especially when the outputs delivered are, on their own terms, good.

So the project proposal is more than just a statement of what the project will achieve. It provides a tool for managing the client's expectations.

Some of the elements that will be examined for assessment purposes are:

- Are the objectives well defined?
- Are the outputs ones which the client will appreciate and value?
- Are they appropriate, given the opportunities and challenges the client business faces?
- Are they realistic, given the resources available to the consultant team?
- Are they achievable, given the skills and abilities of the consulting team?

◆ Are they phrased in a way which will have an impact on, and which is comprehensible to, the client?

◆ Do they reflect real discussion between the client and consultant team?

The project proposal need not be a long document. Many would argue that it should be no longer than one page. However, despite being short, the project proposal is the platform on which the consulting exercise is built. For this reason it is worth while investing a good deal of time, energy and thought in the proposal.

A good proposal gets the exercise off to a strong start. A weak one will hamper the project at the outset. There is a real danger it will never catch up! The format for the project proposal is discussed at length in Chapter 9.

4.3 Assessment of the final report

The final report is the means by which the consultancy team deliver their findings and recommendations to the client. It is the product a consultant offers. It is through the final report that the consultant is judged.

The final report is usually presented in a written format and may be backed up with a presentation using visual aids. There are as many forms of final report as there are types of consulting project. Approaches to layout and format are discussed in Chapter 25.

There are a number of elements by which the final report might be evaluated. These include:

◆ *Background research*. Is the report based on a full and proper evaluation of the business, its situation and its environment?

◆ *Evidence of understanding and insights*. Does the report reflect a genuine understanding of the issues the business is trying to address and a positive attempt to come up with innovative solutions?

◆ *Effective use of conceptual frameworks to generate insights and under-standings*. Have the theories and formal models that are available to guide business thinking and to assist in innovation been called on and used properly?

◆ *Quality of recommendations*. Are the recommendations innovative? Are they right for the business?

◆ *Actionability of recommendations*. Are the recommendations practical and do they make a call to action for the business?

◆ *Organisation of the report.* Is it easy to find important information and findings? Does the report build an argument for the final recommendations in a logical and coherent manner?

◆ *Quality of presentation.* Does the report look professional? Is it free of spelling and grammatical errors?

◆ *Use of language to sell ideas.* Is the language appropriate for the client? Does it strike the right tone? Will it motivate the client to implement the recommendations?

◆ *Use of visual devices.* Are visual devices, diagrams and charts used to good effect in aiding communication?

The critical element that underlies all evaluation, though, must be:

◆ Does the final report actually deliver what the project proposal said would be delivered?

That is:

◆ Have the original objectives been met and have the stated outcomes been achieved? If not will the client be disappointed by the result?

4.4 Assessment of the project log

The project log is a personal record of the project. Its function and layout are discussed fully in Chapter 5. Its main use is as a place where reflection on the learning experience can be undertaken.

Some important elements in the assessment will be:

◆ Is it a true and accurate record of the project?

◆ Does it reflect attention to the objectives and outcomes of the project as a whole and specific stages within it?

◆ Is there reflection on positive experiences, an attempt to understand what made them successful and how that success may be repeated in the future?

◆ Is there reflection on negative experiences, an attempt to understand what went wrong and how the mistake can be avoided in the future?

◆ Is there reflection on the dynamics of the team and how team members work together?

◆ Is there reflection on your own style of management, how you approach motivating other members of the team and how you might develop your leadership style?

Remember, there are no marks to be lost through being honest about the project and your performance on it in the project log. There are marks to be gained if you offer evidence that you are using the project as a positive opportunity to learn actively.

Every live consulting programme is different. Your tutor will advise you about the details of the assessment procedure planned for learning experience.

Team discussion point	Business consulting projects are group exercises. The grade obtained from the exercise is often awarded either wholly, or partly, on a group basis. Inevitably not every member of the group will make the same contribution. This is a consequence of differentiating tasks, the reason for forming a team in the first place.

As a result, though, some will feel they have made a greater contribution than is needed to gain the 'average' group mark and that they have 'carried' those who have (in their own opinion at least) made a less substantive contribution; one which would not, on its own, have earned the average group mark.

Yet, at the end of the day, every member of the group will earn the same group mark. How do you feel about this? Do you think it is fair?

You might like to consider the following questions in your discussion:

1 In a business situation do the members of teams always make an equal contribution?

2 To what extent does the team as a whole have a responsibility to encourage the underperforming member?

3 What are the responsibilities of the team leader in rewarding the above-average performer?

4 What are the responsibilities of the team leader in directing and motivating the underperforming member?

5 Do the answers to Questions 3 and 4 change if the leader has 'emerged' out of the group rather than been formally appointed by the group?

6 How will you as a group deal with the issue if an underperformer emerges? Can you agree a strategy now?

Summary of key ideas

◆ Assessment is intended to focus the mind on learning outcomes and encourage their achievement. It is *not* a hurdle to be passed.

◆ A three-part assessment procedure achieves the following requirements for the consulting exercise:

1 A project proposal defining project objectives and outcomes. This can be used to 'sell' the project to the client and then manage expectations.

2 A final report detailing findings and recommendations, and communicating them impactfully to the client.

3 A project log which acts as a record of the project and facilitates active learning.

◆ These are activities in which a professional consultant would engage.

5

Keeping a project log

Learning outcomes

The learning outcomes from this chapter are:

◆ to recognise how a *project log* can help the effective delivery of the consulting project;

◆ to know what to *include* in the log;

◆ to be able to select a log *format* that is right for you and your project.

5.1 The function of the project log

A log is a day-by-day record of the consulting project. It summarises the activities, analysis, observations and experiences that occur as the project unfolds. Most professional consultants keep a private log of the consulting projects they undertake. Keeping a log may be part of the assessment procedure for a student consulting exercise (*see* Chapter 4). Even if it is not, the fact that professional consultants use one suggests there may be advantages in keeping a personal log in any case.

Why should this be so? Keeping a log takes time. It requires a commitment on the part of the consultant. We should always ask the same questions about any activity that demands a significant input on the part of the manager. First: what value is this activity adding? Second: is the value added worth the effort?

These questions must be demanded of the keeping of a consulting project log. This section will make the case that the value created through the keeping of a project log more than justifies the effort needed for its upkeep. This does, of course, depend on exactly how much information goes into keeping the log. This is subject to its format. We will deal with the question of what format to use in detail in Section 5.3.

The main benefits the log offers are as follows.

◆ It aids project planning activities

A consulting project, like any other project, needs managing in its own terms. Formal project management techniques are valuable. (These are discussed in detail in Chapter 12.) The consultant must have a detailed and up-to-date schedule of the tasks that need to be undertaken. This demands an understanding of how activities support each other and depend on each other. Once this schedule is in place it provides a series of milestones or benchmarks against which the delivery of the project can be monitored. These benchmarks have a 'what' and 'when' aspect: *what* must have been done and *when* it must have been done by. The log offers a ready device for monitoring the what and when of these outcomes and for triggering remedial action if an expected outcome does not happen.

◆ It provides a summary for information collected

In order to deliver the consulting exercise effectively it will be necessary to collect information. The amount of information needed will depend on the nature of the project. This information can often be quite extensive. It is not likely that it will be in the form of a neat summary. Articles and reports will be sourced. Statistics and facts will be identified. The log provides a good place to keep key data, a summary of the information collected and references back to primary sources. Ready access to this will make analysis and compiling the final report much easier.

◆ It provides a secure location for notes taken when communicating

A consulting exercise demands both extensive and wide-ranging communications. As the exercise is undertaken a large number of notes will need to be taken as a result of these communications. These will arise from taking minutes in meetings, taking details from telephone conversations and recording the details of interviews.

It is tempting to not take detailed notes when engaging in communication with others. It is quite natural to assume that we will retain all the points made during communication in our memory. This is illusory. Our memories are not particularly good. Although we think we can retain everything, details are quickly forgotten. Important and valuable points slip from our grasp. Taking written notes helps in two ways. First, the very act of writing something down helps reinforce it in our memory. Second, it provides a hard source to refer back to when our memories need refreshing. Using the log as a place to keep these notes means they can be found later (odd scraps of paper are always lost). It should also be added that taking notes is a good way to assist in *active listening* (*see* Section 22.4).

◆ It provides a forum for analysis

Analysis is an important part of decision making. Approaches to analysis are discussed in Part 4 of this book. Analysis acts on information. Information must be processed before it becomes meaningful. Analysis takes a number of forms. It can be calculations performed on numerical data. It might be statistical manipulation aimed at identifying trends. It could be developing a visual representation, such as a graph, so that relationships become clear. It might be generation of a mind map to aid inventiveness and encourage innovation. Whatever its form, analysis must be an active process.

Active analysis is best undertaken in a written or visual form. The project log provides a good place to undertake analysis notes. First, using the log encourages analysis to be undertaken where and when it is necessary. This is better than leaving analysis until later. Doing analysis as the opportunity arises means that its insights are immediately available to guide the project and direct the need for more information. Analysis is usually more productive if the information to be processed is fresh in the mind and the motives for performing the analysis are clear and pressing. The motive for undertaking is the need to know something. If the analysis is sophisticated and is better left to a later time the log can still be used to make a note about the need to do the analysis.

If a piece of analysis is undertaken by the group as a whole, or by one group member on behalf of the group as a whole, then copies may be included in other group members' logs.

You should not forget that any analysis performed may well be included in the final report to the client. If it is included in the log it will act as at least a first draft that can be accessed easily. This will mean that you will not need to redraft it when writing the final report.

◆ It encourages reflection on the consulting experience

The consulting project is an opportunity to learn. Learning is most effective (and easiest) if it is undertaken actively. Active learning involves a cycle of analysis, practice and reflection (*see* Chapter 3). The log, if used properly, can help the development of an active learning strategy. It does this by encouraging reflection and facilitating analysis.

A few questions that you might consider reflecting on within the log include the following:

◆ What outcomes have been achieved at this stage of the project?

◆ How do these compare to the project plan?

◆ How did they compare with my own expectations? (The answer to this question may not be the same as that to the previous one!)

◆ How might they compare with other people's expectations? (In particular: other members of the group; the client; the project assessors.)

◆ What has gone well to this stage?

◆ What made it a positive experience?

◆ What might have gone better?

◆ Why were these aspects not such a positive experience?

◆ How might this experience be improved in the future?

◆ It acts as a permanent record of the consulting exercise

Our memories are not perfect. In some instances it is useful to be able to refer back and find out when something happened, what was undertaken or what was said or agreed at a particular point. The log can be used to store this information. This enables quick and productive review of the project as an aid to reflection on it. The log can be used to establish how much time was spent on a particular activity undertaken on behalf of the project. This can be useful for planning new projects. Information in the log can be used to resolve some of the disputes which inevitably occur when working in teams.

◆ It provides a long-term learning resource

Active learning never ends. The future tends to throw new situations at us. But this does not, of course, mean that our learning from previous situations is of no value. Far from it. We can only build on the experience we have. The project log can provide us with information that we might use to plan our responses to new challenges. It can offer a guide to personal strengths and the areas that might be developed in the future. It can offer insights into what types of task we enjoy doing (and why). In this respect, many students, for example, find it very useful as a source of points to discuss at job interviews.

LIBRARY, UNIVERSITY COLLEGE CHESTER

5.2 What to include

The discussion in the previous section gives an indication of the kind of information that can feature in the log. At this stage it is useful to summarise what might be included.

Key headings include:

◆ the date;

◆ the stage of the project;

◆ the status of the project (actual outcomes relative to objectives);

◆ a summary of activities undertaken since the last entry;

◆ the objectives of those activities;

◆ minutes of meetings held;

◆ details of information gathered;

◆ notes from communications;

◆ details of analysis undertaken.

And, in addition to these 'routine' headings:

◆ active learning reflections on the consulting experience.

Of course, the length of the inclusions under each heading will vary. Not every heading will be needed for every day's entry. Detailed reflection on active learning may not be a priority for *every* entry, especially if the project is at a very busy stage and entries are being made every day. Time should be taken at a convenient point to reflect on what has been learned.

Text is the main form of written communication and is very useful. However, many people also like to explore ideas using mind maps and other creative devices. The log is a good place to develop and keep these.

5.3 Suggested formats

The project log is a working tool which the consultant uses to assist in delivering the consulting project. It is a private document. It is not intended to be shown to the client. It is a flow of ideas, comments, notes and reflections. It does not matter if it is rough and untidy in appearance. What matters is that it works as a store of notes on the project and a stimulus to reflection, not that it be polished and presentable.

Project Log – Date: 13 June 1998

Key achievements to date:
· first meeting with client;
· initial analysis undertaken;
· team have met to develop first draft of proposal.

Objectives for next stage:
· agree proposal with client;
· move on to next stage of anlaysis.

Note: Meeting to be held next Wednesday – make sure all team know about it. Especially John, who missed last meeting!

Analysis
Client does not seem clear on what he wants. We must get a clear idea by the end of the meeting. Two strategies: (1) we explore options fully and hope that a decision comes out of the meeting; (2) we need to put forward clear proposals – tell him what he needs. It seems we must chose between the 'expert' and 'doctor–patient' modes described by Edgar Schein – task for self: get book out of library tonight to review. After this we must decide who will be doing what.

John
John is starting to be a bit of a problem. He has missed meetings and when he has attended he has not been prepared. I think I need to apply a bit of leadership!

Mind map on how to deal with John

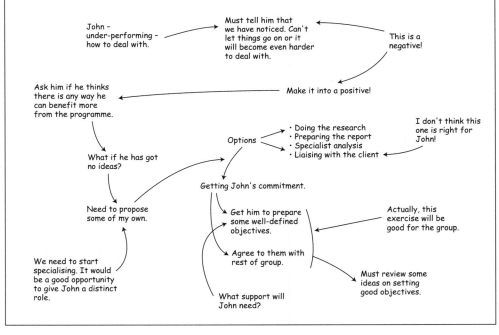

Figure 5.1   **An example of a page from a project log**

The project log should not be completely unorganised, though. You want to be able to find ideas later. A variety of formats have proved to be effective for organising the project log. You should select one that works for you. You may like the idea of a standardised form which prompts entries under the points discussed above. An example of how this might be filled in is given (*see* Figure 5.1). The blank form may be photocopied when needed. This approach is good because it disciplines thinking about the project. A loose-leaf binder allows pages to be inserted as they are required. It also allows other pieces of information such as notes from meetings to be included. You can add pages if you need more room for later reflection.

On the other hand, you may feel that the standardised format is restrictive. You might prefer the latitude to create entries as and when they are necessary in the way you think fit. In this case a bound notebook is best. It is permanent and pages cannot be lost. Notes from meetings can be added as the meetings happen. Leave some room for later reflection though. Odd pages can always be glued in between the bound leaves.

Increasingly, some people like the idea of using an electronic notebook for the project log. These are good for generating presentable versions of the log. However, they may tempt one to revise and refine notes to produce a polished document rather than let them stand as honest and immediate reflection on experienced events (which is what they are meant to be). Electronic notebooks can also prove to be slow and may be quite invasive as a way of making notes in a meeting.

Whatever format you choose, remember the function of the log is to aid active learning, not to be a history of the project.

Team discussion point	In private, consider the formats available for a project log. Decide on one which you think will work for you.
	Present your format to the rest of the group. Say what you think are its strong points. Invite (positive!) criticism, to identify what might be its weak points. After each group member has done this consider your choice of format. Can it be improved by making some modification? Does another format look better?
	Select the format you will use for the project. Don't forget, it is an individual choice. It is not necessary that every member of the group use the same format.

The project log is an invaluable tool for the consultant.

◆ It provides a summary for information collected.

◆ It provides a secure location for notes taken when communicating.

◆ It acts as a permanent record of the consulting exercise.

◆ It encourages reflection on the consulting experience.

◆ It provides a forum for analysis.

The log should include details on the stages of the project, events and communications that take place. It should consider these in relation to the objectives set and the outcomes achieved. It is also a place where information important for the project may be noted and analysis undertaken. Critically, the log is a place where reflection on outcomes, both positive and negative, may be made.

The log is a private document. It need not be polished for presentation. Experiment with formats and find one that works for you.

Business consulting
in practice

___

6

What, exactly, is business consulting?

Learning outcomes

The main learning outcomes from this chapter are:
◆ to understand the nature of business consulting as a management role;
◆ to appreciate the nature of the client–consultant role relationship;
◆ to recognise the responsibilities of the consultant.

6.1 Consulting and management roles

The nature of management is subject to a great deal of discussion. A traditional approach defines management in terms of the *functions* the manager undertakes. Henri Fayol, a management thinker of the first decades of the twentieth century, for example, decided there were five such basic functions. These are planning, organising, staffing, directing and controlling.

◆ Planning

Planning is concerned with deciding a future direction for the business and defining the courses of action and projects needed to move the organisation in that direction. Planning varies greatly in its formality. A simple project with few tasks and low resource requirements will only demand a minimum of consideration and documentation. A major project with complex, and perhaps risky, outcomes will require a considerable degree of time and effort in its planning. Its implementation will involve complex communication networks drawing together a large number of managers. Formal planning techniques may be advantageous if project organisation is to be effective. Different businesses differ in approach to planning and the degree to which it is formalised. As well as the nature and complexity of the project and the significance of its outcomes, organisational style, culture and individual management traits will also be important determinants in the approach to planning.

◆ Organising

The organising function relates to the overall structure of the business. Roles, responsibilities and reporting relationships are defined for individuals and subgroups. In strategic terms this means ensuring that the organisation's structure is appropriate for its strategy and environmental situation. This is sometimes referred to as the strategy-structure-process fit. This is a topic reviewed well by Van de Ven and Drazin (1985).

◆ Staffing

Staffing is the function that is concerned with making sure that the business has the right people in place. It ensures that its people have the right skills in order to undertake the projects the business needs to carry out to be successful. In modern organisations the staffing function is often integrated into a broader human resource management function. Key elements of the human resource strategy are recruitment and training. Additional elements will include establishing remuneration and staff motivation policies.

◆ Directing

Directing relates to the process of encouraging people to undertake the tasks necessary to deliver the project outcomes the business needs. Originally it referred to the management function of instruction or delegation to subordinates. A modern interpretation would be broader and would include a manager's responsibilities as a leader and motivator of teams.

◆ Controlling

Managers use resources. Resources, be they money, people or productive assets, must be utilised in the best way possible. Controlling is the function that is concerned with making sure that the right resources are in place, that they are being used effectively and that their use is properly accounted for.

Traditionally, controlling was largely about *budgeting*, that is financial control. Now a broader interpretation would regard it as the process of focusing the business towards its goals through the implementation of an appropriate *strategy*. This strategy will direct the utilisation of all the business's resources.

This traditional approach to the nature of management has been criticised because it offers an idealised image of what the manager actually does. It pictures the manager as 'above' the organisation, co-ordinating its activities in a detached way, progressing it towards some well-defined, rational end. In fact, most organisations are not like this at all. Managers cannot detach themselves from their organisations; they are very much part of them. They must work with limited information and make decisions using intuition as much as formal analysis. The ends they work towards may be motivated as much by implicit and emotional drives as explicit and rational ones. Organisations produce managers as much as managers produce organisations.

The Canadian management theorist, Henry Mintzberg, spent a long period observing how managers actually worked. In his groundbreaking 1973 book, *The Nature of Managerial Work*, he suggested that a more productive approach was to look at the roles managers actually undertake rather than the functions they are supposed to undertake. He suggested that there are ten such roles which fall into three groups: interpersonal roles, informational roles and decisional roles.

Interpersonal roles relate to the ways in which managers interact with other organisational members. It is through interpersonal roles that managers draw their power and authority. The three key interpersonal roles are the figurehead, the leader and the liaison.

◆ The figurehead

The figurehead role is the one in which the manager represents his or her organisation, or the part of it for which he or she is responsible, in a formal manner. This role draws on the responsibilities defined in a job description, though traditional activities, informal elements and unwritten expectations may also play an important part in characterising the figurehead role.

◆ The leader

The leader role refers to the manager's interaction with subordinates. It is the role the manager is playing when he or she is delegating tasks, motivating people to undertake them and supporting them in achieving them.

◆ The liaison

Many managers have a responsibility for representing the business to the outside world. Sales people, procurement managers and finance specialists in particular have important responsibilities in this way. The liaison role is the one in which managers interact with people from other organisations. The critical responsibility is one of gaining some resource for the business such as, for the management roles noted, customer goodwill, essential productive factors or investment capital.

Managers must make decisions on behalf of their organisations. To do so they must make use of available information on both the internal state of the business and what is happening in its environment. *Informational roles* are concerned with obtaining and manipulating the information the business needs. The three critical informational roles are the monitor, the disseminator and the spokesman.

◆ The monitor

The monitor role is that which leads the manager to identify and acquire information on behalf on the organisation. It may also involve the processing and storage of that information so that it is readily available for use by decision makers. Analysis is a critical task for the monitor. The production of sales statistics, accounts and market intelligence are important tasks for the monitor.

◆ The disseminator

Managers do not work in isolation. Information must be shared with others in the organisation. The disseminator role is concerned with making sure that available information is passed on within the organisation to information processors and decision makers. Dissemination occurs through a variety of means. Reports, meetings and presentations represent formal means of dissemination. Unofficial 'grapevines' are often a very influential way of disseminating information informally.

◆ The spokesman

The spokesman is also involved in disseminating information, but to the outside world rather than internally. Important spokesman roles are taken on by sales and marketing staff who tell customers about what the company has on offer, purchasing managers, who let suppliers know what the company needs and financial managers, who let investors know about the company's status and future prospects.

The third class of roles, *decisional roles*, are involved in identifying a future direction for the organisation, defining the projects needed in order to get it there and dealing with those things which tend to knock it off the path it must follow while getting there.

◆ The entrepreneur

The entrepreneur role is concerned with shaping and making decisions which lead the organisation forward in a significant way. Mintzberg uses the term entrepreneurial in a broader sense than an economist might. Any manager can take on the entrepreneurial role, not just those who set up and own businesses. An entrepreneurial decision is one which aims to exploit an opportunity, or address a threat. Such a decision may be significant, but it is not pressing at the time. It encompasses the activities of conventional entrepreneurs and what have come to be known as *intrapreneurs*, managers who take an entrepreneurial approach within an established business.

The entrepreneurial role demands that information be taken from those undertaking the informational roles and then used to identify new opportunities and new ways of doing things. To make entrepreneurial decisions really happen will demand effective use of the interpersonal roles. The entrepreneurial decision maker takes resources and makes good use of them, even if it means that decision maker may be exposed to risk. Critically, the entrepreneurial role is concerned with driving change. The organisation is not the same after the entrepreneurial decision maker has finished with it.

◆ The disturbance handler

Organisations tend to establish and then follow set patterns of behaviour. They find their own ways of doing things and then stick to them. This is known as organisational inertia. A fixed pattern of working will produce satisfactory results provided that there is no change in either the organisation's internal state or its external condition. If change does occur, the organisation's way of doing things may no longer produce the desired results. Such a change is known as a disturbance.

Disturbances can arise from internal events such as intergroup conflicts or the loss of a critical person from the organisation. External disturbances usually result from the organisation losing access to an essential resource. This might be loss in sales income from an important customer or group of customers. The cause of this may be a customer moving to a competitor or going out of business altogether. The loss of an important input from a supplier also represents a disturbance. Disturbances can also arise if an investor loses faith in the business and pulls out investment capital.

The opportunities and threats the entrepreneurial decision maker addresses are long term. Disturbances, on the other hand, demand immediate attention. The business will fail if they are not dealt with promptly. A disturbance is often referred to as a management crisis. Organisational inertia conditions management's response to a crisis. Often, the first reaction of managers when faced with a crisis is to try and replace the missing resource and so keep the organisation in its original state. Maintaining the status quo when the organisation has been knocked off track by a disturbance is the responsibility of the disturbance handler.

The kinds of project the disturbance handler undertakes will depend on the type of disturbance affecting the organisation. Disturbance handlers may attempt to resolve intergroup conflicts. If a critical resource such as a customer, supplier or investor is lost then they will lead the search for a suitable replacement.

Disturbance handling is not a continuous role. It comes into play only when a crisis happens. Some managers may be predisposed to deal with certain crises as a consequence of their roles: sales managers, for example, will be in the front line if an important customer is lost; purchasing managers will lead the way in finding a new supplier. If the crisis is significant enough conventional relationships can be driven into a state of flux. Recrimination and organisational politics can arise. Eventually new roles and even new leaders may emerge. Leaders often come to the fore in a crisis.

Sometimes the projects undertaken to deal with disturbances will be successful. The organisation may be able to return to its original state. Often, though, the crisis will be too great and the organisation's ability to respond too limited. In this case the organisation will need to make functional and structural changes in order to survive in the changed circumstances it faces.

◆ The resource allocator

Businesses consume resources. They do so in order to pursue the opportunities that present themselves. These resources are valuable and must be used in the best way possible if the business is to be successful. Few businesses face a simple yes or no answer when considering future possibilities. It is not the cost of investing in a project that matters so much as its opportunity cost: the returns that might have been gained if the resources invested in the project had been invested elsewhere.

Managers must decide which of the opportunities that offer themselves is the best one at a particular time. In practice this means that managers must decide how to allocate the resources they have to hand across a variety of different projects. This consideration resolves itself into a series of immediate and practical tasks. For example, should the business invest in that advertising campaign or would the money be better spent on a new sales representative? Should export efforts be directed at the Far East or are the developing economies of central Europe likely to offer a better return? Should investment be directed at a new product, or might it be more profitable to acquire that competitor? It is questions like these that managers must address every day. In doing so they are taking on the resource allocator role.

As with the entrepreneurial role, the resource allocator is dependent on the informational role in order to make good decisions about where resources are best placed.

◆ The negotiator

People come together and work in organisations because value can be created by differentiating and co-ordinating tasks. The extra value created must, however, be shared both within organisations and between the different organisations that come into contact with each other.

Individuals and organisations must be active in advocating their right to a particular share of resources available. This advocacy is reflected in the negotiator role. Sometimes this role is concerned with sharing resources with outside organisations. The sales manager will negotiate with customers. The purchasing manager will negotiate with suppliers. Finance managers will negotiate with investors and lenders. Sometimes it will be concerned with the internal allocation of resources. Personnel managers will negotiate remuneration packages with employees. Managers will negotiate with resource allocators in order to gain a budget for investment in the projects they wish to see happen.

Not all negotiations are so formal. Many negotiations take on an informal character. They may manifest themselves as unofficial 'understandings' between managers about how resources will be shared. Organisational politics is often both a consequence of, and limited by, unofficially negotiated outcomes. It should not be thought that all negotiations are a 'zero-sum' game; that if one party wins, the other must loose. Effective negotiators look for win-win solutions. Nor is effective negotiation about taking a stance and holding to it. It is more about identifying what is wanted out of a situation and then being flexible in finding ways to achieve what is wanted.

Any one management role will have a profile which combines each of these ten pure roles in a particular way. The way in which these roles define the profile of management responsibilities within the organisation will depend on a range of factors. The organisation's size will be a critical determinant. The bigger the business and the more managers it employs, the greater will be the latitude for managers to specialise. In a small business, a single entrepreneur may take on most, if not all, the roles at some time or other. In a large multinational corporation, managers may be in a position where their roles will be more narrowly defined.

The complexity of the organisation and its environment will also be important. Complexity refers to the amount of information managers must process before making a decision. If complexity is high, informational roles will be important and it may be necessary to have managers dedicated to these roles. A fast-growing organisation undergoing rapid change may present a special leadership challenge and demand that particular attention be paid to interpersonal roles. The profile of management roles will reflect the organisation, the stage in its evolution and its environmental situation.

6.2 The client–consultant managerial role interaction

The consultant *is* a manager. We must understand the nature of the consultant's tasks in terms of their being *management* tasks. Like any manager, the consultant will, at times, take on many if not all of the ten roles defined by Mintzberg. The consultant's role parallels and integrates with that of managers within the client organisation. It is through the interaction of these roles that the client–consultant relationship is built.

The managers who make up organisations work in a network of relationships. These relationships exist between managers working within a particular organisation and between the managers in different organisations who come into contact with each other. The consultant who moves into an organisation must define the relationship he or she wishes to create with the managers who already work in the client business, and, often, with some of those in other organisations with which the client comes into contact. Two considerations will determine what sort of relationship this will be. These are:

◆ the nature and structure of management roles in the client organisation; and

◆ the objectives of the consulting exercise.

Every organisation is different, and so is every manager. However it is possible to see consistent patterns in the way in which managerial roles take shape. Different organisations will require a different profile of management roles. But every organisation will demand that managers carry out the interpersonal, informational and decisional roles in a way which is right for the business. These roles must be carried out with the right degree of competence and in balance with each other.

The motivation to call in a consultant (a topic discussed fully in Chapter 7) arises because managers have identified a project which they think will benefit the organisation but they recognise that they are not in a position to deliver it themselves. The reason for their inability to deliver may be articulated in the form of resource or skill gaps. In entering to fill these gaps the consultant is offering to complement and develop the role profile within the organisation.

The managerial roles described by Henry Mintzberg provide a clue to the kind of interaction that will take place between the consultant and the client organisation's management team. We can use a visual metaphor to picture the ways in which a consultant can interact with and develop the business management role profile.

Think of the role profile as a triangle with each apex representing one of the groups of roles. This is illustrated in Figure 6.1.

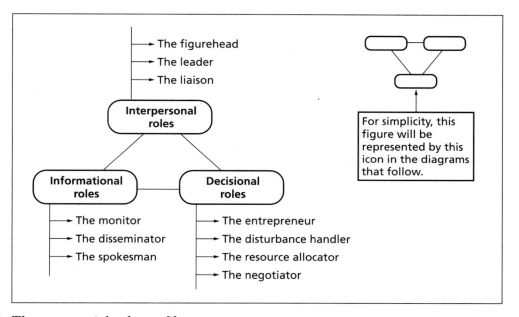

→ The figurehead
→ The leader
→ The liaison

Interpersonal roles

Informational roles

Decisional roles

→ The monitor
→ The disseminator
→ The spokesman

→ The entrepreneur
→ The disturbance handler
→ The resource allocator
→ The negotiator

For simplicity, this figure will be represented by this icon in the diagrams that follow.

Figure 6.1   The managerial role profile

Using this simple diagram we can create a visual depiction of the five primary types of consultant–management role interaction: supplementing, complementing, differentiating, integrating and enhancing.

◆ Supplementing

Supplementing involves the consultant adding to the existing skill profile to increase its capability but not alter its overall shape. The consultant is an additional resource who takes on a project that could well have been taken on by an existing manager had time been available. An example might be a business with a local sales base using a consultant with sales experience to test the possibility of expanding into a new area. Had a sales manager from within the company been available then he or she would have done the job in exactly the same way. In principle, the consultant could be recruited into the organisation and there would be little change in the way in which he or she operates with and interacts with the rest of the organisation.

This type of consulting role offers a way of enabling the business to manage demand fluctuations in a low-risk way. The consultant allows the business to add and subtract human resources in a flexible manner. The consultant is neutral in development terms and does not aim to make any fundamental changes in the organisation. We can picture the supplementing role as a simple addition to the existing role profile (*see* Figure 6.2).

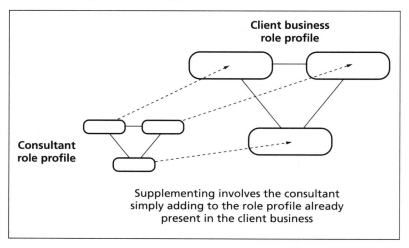

Client business role profile

Consultant role profile

Supplementing involves the consultant simply adding to the role profile already present in the client business

Figure 6.2   The consultant–manager role supplementing interaction

◆ Complementing

Complementing occurs when the organisation notices a gap in its profile of management roles and asks the consultant to fill that role. This may require the consultant to specialise in any one of the basic role types.

For example, a consultant may be required to complement the organisation's liaison role and develop the way it represents itself to the outside world. Projects which enhance the business's marketing approach or develop presentations to financial backers are important examples. Consultants can play an important role in supporting existing managers to improve leadership, through, say, the development of a unifying organisational mission.

A wide range of projects can involve the consultant complementing the informational role. Important examples might include marketing research and the setting up of management information systems. These projects will make demands on both the monitoring and disseminating aspects of the informational role. The consultant may also be active in supporting the spokesman role. Developing communications aimed at customers and investors is the task of the public relations expert. Lobbyists may be employed to communicate and influence decision makers in government.

The consultant can contribute to the decisional role in a variety of ways. Speculative business development projects which explore a range of possibilities for the business in the future complement the *entrepreneurial role*. A consultant may be called in as a *disturbance handler* to help the business's management deal with a crisis. The setting up of budgeting management control systems is an example of the consultant complementing the work of the *resource allocator*. Some consultants specialise in *negotiating* and can contribute to the way in which the business approaches important customers, suppliers or investors.

The complementing role can be pictured as the consultant filling in a gap in the management's existing role profile. Figure 6.3 shows how this may be illustrated.

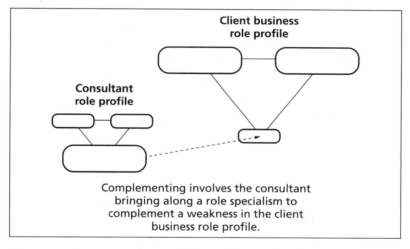

Figure 6.3   The consultant–manager role complementing interaction

◆ Differentiating

The overall profile of management roles will depend on a number of factors. The size of the organisation will be critical. The larger the business the greater the latitude for allowing managers to specialise their roles. One aspect of the process of organisational growth will be an increasing tendency towards role specialisation. For example, a small business will tend to have a leading entrepreneur (perhaps with a high level of ownership) undertaking the decisional and the spokesman roles. He or she may also have responsibility for the informational roles as well. As the business grows the entrepreneur can allow other managers to take on more responsibility. A sales and marketing function may emerge to take on the spokesman roles and promote the product to customers. A management information system can be set up to monitor financial data and so supplement the informational role. The entrepreneur can also delegate certain areas of decision making to subordinate managers.

This process of role differentiation is critical if the organisation is to grow successfully. It is only through such specialisation that the business can not only grow, but improve its performance as it grows. However, such differentiation is not always easy. Managers (not least successful entrepreneurs) often resist giving away areas of responsibility. They would rather use the organisation's growth to 'build their empire'. This can result in the manager having too large an area of responsibility, too much information to analyse and not enough time. Invariably, the quality of decision making suffers.

Consultants can help facilitate the process of role differentiation. At one level this involves designing appropriate organisation structures, defining managerial responsibilities and setting up communication systems. But this is just the 'hardware' of the organisation. Managers must feel comfortable with their new responsibilities, be motivated to work within them and interact positively with colleagues. Changing the software is a change management process calling upon a specialist type of consulting. This type of role differentiation can be illustrated as in Figure 6.4.

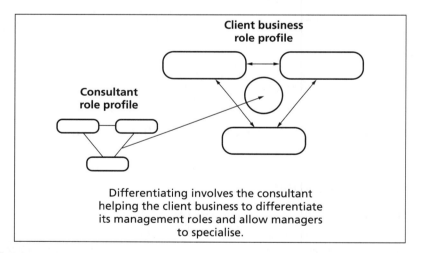

Figure 6.4 The consultant–manager role differentiating interaction

◆ Integrating

Mature organisations are characterised by well-defined organisation structure and role responsibilities. These become established and are subject to organisational inertia. They may persist even when they are no longer appropriate. If the business's environment and competitive situation change then an evolution in the way the business does things may be called for. If environmental change is particularly fast, the occasional revolution may be called for. Such changes demand that the old role profile be broken down and a new profile allowed to emerge. The new roles may combine or integrate a number of aspects of the old roles.

An important recent trend in organisational change has been the shift from vertically ordered functions to horizontally ordered teams. Traditional departments such as marketing, finance, operations and the like have been supplemented, or even replaced, by small multidisciplinary teams. The focus shifts to the team undertaking specific tasks, rather than the department fulfilling fixed roles. This allows a more flexible response to the shifting needs of the marketplace.

This process makes a number of demands on managers. Of course, team working must be made effective (a topic discussed in Chapter 23). But there are more subtle demands as well. The hierarchical department offers a traditional path for promotion in the organisation. If it goes, managers may see no clear way for advancing and may become demotivated. If the team structure is combined with traditional functions (a structure known as a matrix organisation) managers may become disorientated at having two bosses (the team leader and the departmental manager). Such 'challenges' to the departmental manager's authority may also be a recipe for political infighting.

As with differentiating, the consultant called in to integrate roles into a new, more flexible structure must address both hardware and software issues. A new structure must be invented and the change management issues needed to motivate managers to work within it must be addressed. Role integrating may be illustrated as in Figure 6.5.

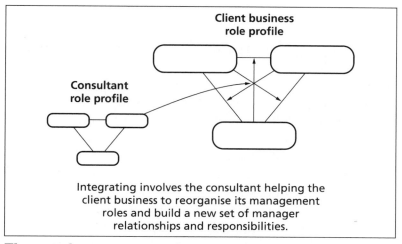

Integrating involves the consultant helping the client business to reorganise its management roles and build a new set of manager relationships and responsibilities.

Figure 6.5　The consultant–manager role integrating interaction

◆ Enhancing

Enhancing is the most general type of role development process. It demands not so much that the role profile of the organisation be changed, but that the manager's overall level of performance be improved. There are a variety of ways this might be achieved. Training of individual managers is usually an important part. This training may be directed towards improving technical and functional skills or may develop interpersonal skills such as motivation and leadership. Training may be supplemented through structural changes such as improved communication systems and attention to overall strategic understanding. The process of role enhancement is illustrated in Figure 6.6.

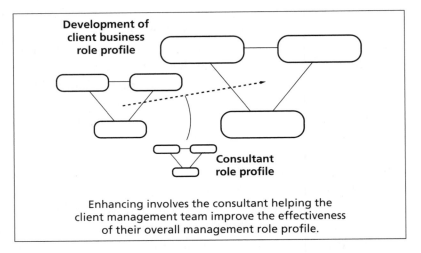

Development of client business role profile

Consultant role profile

Enhancing involves the consultant helping the client management team improve the effectiveness of their overall management role profile.

Figure 6.6   The consultant–manager role enhancing interaction

6.3 The responsibilities of the management consultant

All managers have responsibilities. They have responsibilities both to organisations and to the individuals who work in them. At one level, organisations are collections of individuals, so it is individual managers who must take on responsibilities on behalf of the organisations they work for. The consultant is in a special position. He or she must take on the responsibilities of being a manager, not just for the organisation they work for, but also for the organisation they work with.

It has been suggested (by Archie Carroll in an article in 1979) that managerial and organisational responsibilities operate at four levels. These may be referred to as the economic, the legal, the moral and the discretionary.

◆ Economic responsibilities

The fundamental economic responsibility of the manager is to act in a way which is consistent with the long-term health of their business and maximise its value for its investors. This is not to suggest that the manager, like the economist's perfect entrepreneur, simply tries to maximise short-term profits. Real-world managers do not have the information to behave like this. Short-term profits to investors may be diverted in order to fund reinvestment projects aimed to achieve growth and so deliver more profits in the future. Potential profits may be compromised if other responsibilities are given priority. An area of economics called *agency theory* suggests that the interests of managers and investors differ and that, under certain circumstances, managers will act in their own best interests.

Given these constraints, it may still be properly said that the consultant's economic responsibility is to advocate only projects which genuinely seem, in light of the information available, to be in the best interests of the business as a whole, given its stated strategic objectives and the concerns of the stakeholders who have an interest in it.

◆ Legal responsibilities

All businesses have a responsibility to operate within the rule of law. Laws provide the official 'rules of the game' through which businesses interact with each other. Legal systems around the world differ, but generally have two codes: the *criminal*, which the state takes responsibility for implementing and the *civil*, in which the responsibility for initiating proceedings lies with individuals. Business activity is subject to both codes.

Nowadays, most governments try to minimise the impact of legislation on business. In that legal restrictions impede business activity, they are seen as an evil, albeit a necessary one. Consideration of the impact of a new law on business is, these days, usually taken into account in the legislative process. This means that the laws that remain are usually there for a good reason.

The consultant has a legal responsibility to ensure that the activities of the organisation he or she is working for, and any activities he or she may advocate on its behalf, are legitimate in light of the criminal and civil laws to which the business is subject. The exact nature of this legal responsibility, and the extent to which the consultant may face recrimination if it is breached, will depend on the law involved, the consultant's contractual obligations and the degree of culpability for outcomes.

Ensuring that this condition is met, especially when the business is operating in a highly technical area, or a part of the world with a different legal system, can be quite challenging. In this case, taking legal advice from experts (not least about one's own responsibilities) may be an important part of the consulting exercise.

◆ Moral responsibilities

Moral responsibilities go one step beyond legal ones. The societies in which businesses operate function on the basis of a whole complex of rules, norms and expectations. Some of these rules are written down in the form of laws or contractual agreements (which are often subject to civil law). But many are unwritten. They may not even be spoken. They are merely an understanding about what is 'right' and what is 'wrong'. They are expectations about how people should behave towards each other. These rules may not even be noticed – until they are broken!

Though it is not always made explicit, every society, and to some extent every distinct grouping within a society has its own code of morality. These codes often relate to the way in which stakeholders will be treated, above and beyond simple contractual rights. For example, most managers feel a higher degree of responsibility to employees than their contracts of employment dictate. This can manifest itself in many ways. Losing people is painful: a business may retain people who are not absolutely necessary. Entrepreneurs who own their business may allow family members a greater performance latitude than non-family members.

Many cultures have their own distinct rule systems. In displaced ethnic groups networking may be supported by moral expectations about the responsibilities of members of the community towards each other. Edicts on the way in which debt is structured are common, as are rules about reciprocity of favours. Recognising such moral codes is an important aspect of the consultant's job.

The consultant must recognise that he or she is as subject to these moral responsibilities as to the legal ones. Moral responsibilities are not merely 'nice to have'. Ignoring them will limit the effectiveness of the consulting exercise. Outcomes which go against the moral expectations of the client will, at best, not be implemented. Outright rejection can often occur.

◆ Discretionary responsibilities

Discretionary responsibilities are those the consultant decides to take on as part of a personal moral order. They are not responsibilities the industry would normally be expected to observe.

Discretionary responsibilities usually relate to a refusal to work in certain project areas, or to work towards project outcomes of which the consultant does not approve. This may mean avoiding certain industry sectors or types of project. Typically, such discretionary responsibilities arise as a result of the consultant's personal concerns about a range of domestic political issues, the environment or business activity in the developing world.

Although this may mean that the consultant must occasionally turn down valuable projects, it can also be a means of differentiation from the values other (perhaps competing) consultants advocate. Discretionary values may make a consultant more attractive to certain individuals and organisations. There is nothing inconsistent in using discretionary responsibilities as a means of gaining an edge in the marketplace. Where discretionary values offer an edge they may eventually set the standard for consulting as a whole.

6.4 Modes of consulting

All managers have their own approach to the tasks they face and the way they deal with people. This is an important factor in determining the manager's style. A critical element here is the perception the manager has about his or her fundamental role in the organisation. Consulting is also characterised by different approaches which reflect fundamental assumptions about the role of the consultant. These are referred to as *modes*. In his 1987 book *Process Consultation*, Edgar Schein characterised three basic modes based on the relationship between the consultant and client. These are the expert, the doctor–patient and the process.

◆ The expert mode

In the expert mode the client identifies a particular problem with the business. The client then analyses the problem and articulates it to the consultant. The consultant then uses his or her expertise to identify a solution to the problem. This form of consulting is often found in areas where the consultant has a specialist knowledge which the client organisation recognises it lacks.

◆ The doctor–patient mode

The doctor–patient mode is also characterised by the consultant acting as an expert. In this mode, however, the consultant also takes responsibility for diagnosing the problem in the first place. The client may just express an opinion that the business 'could be better' in some way or that 'something is not quite right'. Again, the consultant is expected to contribute specialist knowledge and insights to the business.

◆ The process consulting mode

Both the expert mode and the doctor–patient mode demand that the consultant, an outsider, offer a solution – a prescription – to address the problems that the business faces. Process consulting takes a different stance. It is based on the premise that the only people who can, ultimately, help the business are the people who make it up. The consultant, as an outsider, cannot impose a solution on the organisation. What the consultant can do, however, is assist those who make up the organisation with the process of recognising problems and then discovering the solutions to them. The consultant is not so much an expert, more a facilitator of change.

Schein makes a strong case for the process mode. This is for good reasons. Consultants can recommend better ways of doing things but these will only become reality if the people who make up the organisation feel they have ownership of the new approach, that they have had a part in creating it and that it will work for them. A process approach to consulting helps ensure that the client organisation feels it is coming up with its own solutions to its own problems and so solutions which are right for its business. A note of caution is in order though. Consultants do bring along expertise and should not be frightened to recognise that they are doing so. Further, the client will often expect the consultant to show evidence of expertise and to 'take charge' of the issues the business faces. 'After all,' it is often heard said, 'that's what they are being paid for!' An over-reliance on a process approach can sometimes leave clients feeling that they have done all the work themselves. Indeed, by the very nature of the process mode, the more proficient the consultant is in using it, the greater the risk that the client will feel that the consultant has not made a 'real' contribution.

Rather than advocate one mode as right in all circumstances the effective consultant recognises the advantages of flexibility. He or she learns when, and under what circumstances, to adopt each mode.

6.5 Types of client

In a paper in 1997, Edgar Schein has suggested that process consulting can be enhanced by an appreciation of the different types of client involved. He suggests that the consultant interacts with a number of individuals within the client organisation and that the concept of the individual client may be problematic. Rather, the consultant interacts with a network of individuals who play subtly different roles. Schein suggests that there are six such client types.

◆ Contact clients

The contact client is the person, or persons, who first approach the consultant and propose the consultant addresses a problem or issue on behalf of the organisation.

◆ Intermediate clients

Intermediate clients are members of the organisation who become involved in the consulting project. They will work with the consultant and provide information. They will sit in on meetings and influence the way the project unfolds. Intermediate clients may be the actual recipients of the final report.

◆ Primary clients

The primary client is the person or persons who have identified the problem or issue the consultant has been called in to address and who are most immediately affected by it. It is they who will be willing to pay in order to have the issue resolved.

◆ Unwitting clients

Unwitting clients are members of the organisation who will be affected by the intervention of the consultant. However, they are not aware that they will be affected.

◆ Indirect clients

Indirect clients are members of the organisation who will be affected by the intervention of the consultant and who are aware that they will be affected. However the consultant is not aware that the project will have an impact on them. Indirect clients may feel either positive or negative about the consultant's intervention. They can be very influential behind the scenes and, unbeknown to the consultant, can facilitate or hinder the progress of the project.

◆ Ultimate clients

Ultimate clients are the total community which will be affected by the consultant's intervention. This will include members of the organisation and, possibly, members of the organisations who come into contact with the client organisation. The ultimate client group forms the universe of whose interests the consultant must take account when progressing the project.

1 Most consulting teams differentiate individual roles within the team. In this way they get the best out of a team effort. The exact profile of roles varies. Often the following roles make an appearance:

   – a team co-ordinator;

   – an information gatherer;

   – an information analyser;

   – a report writer;

   – a report presenter;

   – a client contactor;

   – a team councillor.

   These roles are discussed more fully in Section 12.2.

   Allocate each of these consulting roles to one of the ten types of management role defined by Mintzberg. Note that more than one may be involved.

2 In private, consider the types of project on which, as consultant, you would not wish to work. Think in terms of business sectors and project outcomes you feel would go against your personal moral code of discretionary responsibilities. Present your discretionary responsibilities, with a brief rationale, to the rest of the group.

**Summary
of key ideas**

◆ Consulting is a special type of management activity.

◆ The consultant can be understood to provide ten types of managerial role to the client business. These are placed in three groups:

   – the interpersonal (featuring the roles of the figurehead, the liaison and the leader);

   – the informational (featuring the roles of the monitor, the disseminator and the spokesman); and

   – the decisional (featuring the roles of the entrepreneur, the disturbance handler and the resource allocator).

◆ The consultant must integrate these roles with those already operating in the client business. This can happen in one of five ways:

   – supplementary (adding extra skills to those already present);

   – complementary (adding a missing role);

   – differentiating (helping managers distinguish roles among themselves);

   – integrating (helping managers build a new order of roles and individual responsibilities);

   – enhancing (helping managers make their existing roles more effective).

◆ The consultant must operate with four levels of managerial responsibility. These are:

– economic (a responsibility to ensure that the projects advocated are in the best interests of the client business);

– legal (a responsibility to ensure that projects operate within the law);

– moral (a responsibility to ensure that project outcomes meet with the moral and ethical expectations of the client); and

– discretionary (the right of the consultant to select or reject projects on the basis of personal ethical considerations).

7

How consulting adds value

Learning outcomes

The main learning outcomes from this chapter are:

◆ to understand what *motivates* a business manager to bring in a consultant;

◆ to recognise the ways in which a consultant can *add value* for a business;

◆ to understand the things a consultant can *offer* a business by way of valuable support.

7.1 The decision to use a consultant

Why should a business manager ask the advice of an independent consultant? The decision is a significant one for a number of reasons. There may be an immediate financial cost. Leading management consulting firms have daily rates which are well into four figures. Even if the consulting is 'free' because it is being undertaken through an undergraduate consulting team, or the cost is being borne by a small business support agency, there may still be significant indirect costs. The consultant team may need money from the client to undertake marketing research, for example.

There will also be a cost due to the need to dedicate management time to the consulting exercise. If a consulting project is to be successful, the consultant team must be supported in their activities. They will need briefing sessions and regular review meetings. The management time that must be dedicated to this is valuable, especially in a small business. Also, the activities of consultants can be upsetting to the business as a whole. Consultants will disrupt a manager's routines. If not managed effectively their involvement can raise suspicions and lead to political infighting between managers.

The decision to call in consultants is like the decision to buy anything else for the business. It happens after a consideration of the costs and benefits involved and a conclusion that the benefits outweigh the costs. This is not a one-off decision. It is something that the client business constantly assesses. Maintaining the client's confidence and the belief that the consultancy exercise has something of value to offer is a critical responsibility for the consultant.

This presents a particular challenge for *management* consultants. Consultants who work in highly technical areas such as computing and engineering clearly offer the business an expertise the business itself does not have. That they offer something different and valuable is evident. On the other hand, every business, without fail, will have *management* expertise. And the chances are (or at least the business will *feel*) that this expertise is greater than that offered by outsiders who have no knowledge of the business, its customers and its markets. In any case, even if the business recognises the need for additional management resources, why should consultants be used? Why not just employ more managers?

In short, the management consultant must constantly ask two very fundamental questions:

1 What can I offer the client business that will enhance its performance and help it achieve its objectives?

2 How can I communicate to the client business that what I offer is valuable?

As was discussed in Chapter 1, answering these two questions involves the application of analytical, project management and relationship-building skills. These will be considered fully in the following chapters. This chapter aims to set the scene for discussion of how these skills may be developed and applied by considering what a management consultant has to offer the client business.

The actual outputs of a consulting exercise centre on providing one or more of six things: information, specialist expertise, a new perspective on problems, support with internal arguments, support in gaining a critical resource and the creation of organisational change. Each of these will now be examined in depth.

7.2 Provision of information

Managers make decisions. If those decisions are to be good ones, they must be based on a full and proper understanding of the business and its situation. Information is needed if decision making is to be effective.

Some areas of information which are of critical importance to a business include:

◆ the business's customers: their needs and buying behaviour;

◆ the business's products: their design, technology and development;

◆ the markets in which the business operates: their size, growth and dynamics;

◆ outside organisations which can offer support: who they are, what they offer and how they can be contacted;

◆ the business's competitors: who they are, their strengths and the threat they pose.

Information is valuable to a business. As a result it has a cost. Information is a resource that must be managed. Much information has a direct cost, that bought from market researchers, for example. Even if there is no direct cost there may be a hidden cost in the management time and effort in gathering information. Even if managers are willing to face this cost they can only do so if they know what information is available, where it is stored and how it can be accessed. There is no guarantee they can do this.

The consultant can offer the small business manager a service in providing him or her with information which can help the business. However, this is only the start of the consultant's service. Decisions are not made on the basis of hard data alone. Those data must first be processed and interpreted. The consultant can add value by analysing and presenting information in a way that enables the business manager to make effective decisions from it. To do this requires the analysis skills that will be considered in Part 4 of this book.

7.3 Provision of specialist expertise

Some managers, especially those running small businesses, must be generalists. The demands of managing a small business are such that managers cannot afford to specialise in a narrow area of management such as marketing, operations or finance. They must do all these things at once. This means that at times they will seek the advice of people with specialist knowledge.

Some important areas of management which can benefit from the insights and ideas of a specialist are:

◆ business strategy: its development, evaluation and planning;

◆ marketing strategy development: defining a successful marketing mix;

◆ marketing research studies: utilising sophisticated research methodologies;

◆ promotional campaign development: how to ensure that promotional drives are well designed and cost effective;

◆ new product development programmes: converting customer needs into a successful product offering;

◆ developing proposals for financial support: identifying and approaching backers and making a good case for their support;

◆ information systems development: enabling managers to get the information they need to make decisions;

◆ planning exporting and international marketing: providing the business with a valuable route to growth.

Projects such as these benefit from the application of technical knowledge and an ability to use specialist analysis techniques. Rather than have to learn these themselves managers will often call upon the support of consultants.

The key to successful consulting in this area is not to make decisions on behalf of the manager but to *help* the manager in making their own. It is their business, they have a detailed knowledge of what it is about and know what it aims to achieve. This knowledge of the business is much greater than any the consultant can develop in the short time he or she will be working with the business. The consultant adds value by bringing along a 'tool-kit' of conceptual frameworks and idea-generating models which can be used to make sense of the information and knowledge the manager already has. This then enables the manager to make better decisions. This is the essence of the process approach to consulting discussed in Section 6.4.

The management of projects involving the provision of specialist expertise will be discussed further in Chapter 10.

7.4 Provision of a new perspective

Managers are not decision-making automata. They are human beings who must analyse complex environments, use well-developed, but necessarily limited cognitive skills and then make decisions in the face of uncertainty.

Managers use 'cognitive maps', 'mindsets' or 'dominant logics' through which they see their managerial world. These act to focus the manager's attention on certain aspects of their environment, select particular facts as relevant, link causes to effects and then suggest courses of action. Such cognitive schema are not rational decision-making devices. They manifest themselves as the manager's interests, priorities, prejudices and judgement. Cognitive schema become established and resist change. They determine the way managers see their organisations and competitors. They have a bearing on the way joint ventures are managed, for example. Interested students are referred to the articles by Caloris, Johnson and Sarnin (1994), Daniels, Johnson and de Chernatony (1994) and Prahalad and Bettis (1986) for illuminating discussions of these issues.

In simple terms, managers limit their problem-solving ability because they often get too close to an issue. They only see it in terms of their existing expectations, understanding and 'way of doing things'.

The consultant can add value by helping the manager step back from a problem, to see it in a different way and to see new means to its solution. Indeed, the consultant should ultimately aim to help managers see 'problems' really as opportunities to do things differently and perhaps better.

To do this the consultant may just offer a fresh mind to an issue. Better still, the consultant can contribute some conceptual frameworks which open up thinking and aid the development of the manager's cognitive schema. They can also offer support in helping individuals and groups become more innovative in their thinking by using the creativity techniques described in Chapter 15.

7.5 Provision of support for internal arguments

Managers do not always agree with each other. Disagreements arise over a wide range of issues. Conflicts of opinion take a variety of form. They range from open, honest exploration of different options to often quite nefarious political intriguing. They can be seen as a refreshing opening of possibilities or they may lead to smouldering resentment.

A manager may be tempted to use a consultant not so much to provide an impartial view but in order to back up their own position in a debate. A consultant's opinion is of clear value here. It can be presented as 'independent' and as coming from an 'expert'. How should a consultant react to being used in this way?

The first thing to note is that the existence of different perspectives and a tolerance of dissent which allows them to be expressed is a healthy thing. Managers should be paid to think and express themselves and must be free to do so. In a competitive environment (in which ideas compete for resources) they should also be free to marshal whatever resources they can to make their case. This may include external consultants.

A consultant must recognise that he or she is not employed by a company in the abstract, but rather by *individuals* within a company. The decision to use consultants is made by a group or 'decision-making unit' within the business. (This idea is covered in detail in Chapter 19.) The consultant is responsible for delivering findings and advice to individuals. The consultant must be sensitive to the interests of those individuals and what their objectives are. This may involve supporting them in internal debates. However, the consultant must be careful.

If the consultant is too obviously in the camp of a particular manager, his or her impartiality will be impaired. Other management groups may become suspicious and will find grounds on which to reject the consultant's advice. If the consultant is seen to be twisting facts to fit a particular position his or her credibility will be damaged. At a minimum the consultant will lose the support and goodwill of other managers. This can make the consultant's job difficult and uncomfortable. So being called upon to support a particular position, especially when it is contentious, demands sensitive management on the part of the consultant.

A few useful ground rules are:

◆ Understand the 'politics' of the consulting exercise.

◆ Be sensitive to who is supporting different positions in the organisation.

◆ Recognise who will benefit and who will lose from the different options under discussion.

◆ Make sure the objectives of the consulting exercise are clear and in the open.

◆ Make sure any information used can be legitimated and any analysis undertaken justified.

◆ Build rapport with the client (a skill discussed in Chapter 22) and be honest with the client about the strengths and weaknesses of his or her argument.

◆ Introduce and explore options which reconcile different positions in a win-win way.

◆ Provide the client manager with information and insights but allow him or her to make a particular case within the business – don't be tempted to advocate it on his or her behalf.

◆ If put in a position where credibility might be lost, remind the manager that a loss of impartiality and credibility will defeat the point of using independent consultants in the first place!

7.6 Provision of support in gaining a critical resource

An organisation must attract resources in order to survive. One of the manager's most critical functions is attracting resources on behalf of the firm. Some important resources for the business include:

◆ the goodwill of customers;

◆ capital from investors;

◆ capital from government support agencies;

◆ people with particular skills and knowledge;

◆ specialist materials, equipment and services.

The consultant can offer the client business valuable support in gaining these resources. Key tasks involve identifying who can supply the particular resources, how they might be contacted and the issues involved in working with them. The consultant can be particularly valuable by working with the client and developing a communication strategy which helps the business be successful in its approach to suppliers of critical resources.

Gaining the goodwill of customers is the function of marketing in its broadest sense. The consultant can assist in the developing of marketing plans, communication strategies and promotional campaigns. There are a number of support programmes provided by government and non-governmental organisations to businesses, especially small businesses. They take a variety of forms and change regularly. They often demand that a specific, well-organised proposal be made. The consultant can be of great value in structuring a proposal and advising on how it might be delivered.

People, especially people with special knowledge and skills, are a critical, if not *the* critical resource for businesses. Consultants can add much value by advising a business on its people requirements, developing an understanding of the market for such people and developing advertisements to attract them. The consultant may also advise on the interview and selection procedures.

A business may have identified suppliers of the materials and services it needs to undertake its activities. It is increasingly recognised that a business can improve its performance by actively *reverse marketing* itself to suppliers. This ensures that suppliers are aware of the business's needs and are responsive to them. It may, for example, encourage suppliers to innovate and make their offerings more suited to the buyer's requirements. This demands communication with both existing and potential suppliers, a process a consultant can assist greatly.

Many businesses will benefit from further cash injection by investors. Different stages of growth create different capital requirements. An important, and exciting, type of consulting activity is the assistance given in helping businesses gain the support of investors such as banks and venture capitalists. This involves developing a picture of the potential of the firm and why it might offer an exciting investment opportunity, identifying suitable investment organisations, preparing a business plan for them and perhaps even formally presenting it.

The different types of output consulting projects aim to acquire are not mutually exclusive. A consulting exercise may combine elements from a number of them. Each project should be considered on its own merit: how it adds value for the client and helps his or her business achieve its objectives.

7.7 Creation of organisational change

All organisations are undergoing change all the time. Sometimes this is a 'natural' response to the internal dynamics of organisational growth. At other times it may be in response to an external impetus or shock which forces the organisation to modify the way in which it does things. All of the types of project above may, if they are to be implemented successfully, demand some degree of change in the structures and operating practices of the business. They may also demand that managers change their roles and responsibilities.

Change usually meets resistance. Managers, like most human beings, tend to be conservative when it comes to altering the way things are done. This is only to be expected. Although change may offer new possibilities it also presents uncertainties. It is only natural that a manager tries to hold on to what he or she knows to be reliable and rewarding. How can he or she be certain that a different future will offer the satisfactions achieved at present? Are the changes in his or her best interest? Even if change *seems* to offer the possibility of greater satisfaction, what are the risks? What happens if the manager is dissatisfied with the outcomes? What 'insurance' can he or she call on? It is concerns such as these which can lead to distrust of consultants operating in a business.

The effective management of organisational change demands that these questions be addressed. Sometimes organisations call for change as the primary goal of the consulting exercise. In response to this, *change management* has developed as a specialist consulting area. More often, though, change management is required as a subsidiary area in order to effect the implementation of more specific organisational projects, such as business expansion or structural reorganisation. Whatever the motive and source of the change, the effective consultant must be aware of the human dimensions to the change he or she is advocating and be competent in addressing the issues it creates.

Team discussion point

Read the following short case study.

Natural Beauty Ltd is a business which manufactures and markets a range of premium-priced toiletries and beauty products with a 'no animal testing – natural ingredients' positioning. Distribution is direct to the customer via catalogue ordering. The business was started some eight years ago and after enjoying early success now employs 11 people. It recognises its success and is ambitious for growth.

Maggie, a member of the firm's 'commercial team' (the business is run on a co-operative basis and prefers not to define formal management roles) has approached an undergraduate consulting team to assist the business and help it formulate its expansion plans.

During an introductory meeting with the consulting team, Maggie explains that the business feels it has a worthwhile product with good potential in the marketplace. There is a general feeling, however, that the present approach of the business – direct marketing in the UK – is largely saturated. If the business is to grow further it must take a different approach. There is a lot of debate within the commercial team as to the best way forward. Two options are emerging from the discussions.

The first is a move from direct marketing into retailing in the UK, possibly on a franchise basis. The second option is to expand the direct marketing approach into continental and eastern Europe. Maggie admits to preferring this option. Despite the fact it will mean finding partners in Europe to act as agents she feels it is the lower-risk option.

She asks the consulting team to evaluate both options on behalf of the business and make a recommendation as to the best way forward.

With your team consider which of the outputs discussed in this chapter might be involved in the final consulting project which can add value for Maggie and Natural Beauty Ltd.

Summary of key ideas

◆ Consultants must be able to do something for a business that it is unable to do for itself.

◆ This must genuinely offer new value to the client business.

◆ Important areas of value addition include the provision of:
  – information;
  – specialist expertise;
  – a new and innovative perspective;
  – support with internal arguments;
  – support in gaining critical resources such as capital, people or productive factors;
  – driving organisational change.

◆ Many consulting projects involve a combination of a number of these elements.

◆ The consultant must constantly communicate to the client the new value he or she is creating through these outputs.

8

The consulting process

Learning outcomes

The learning outcomes from this chapter are:

- to recognise the sequence of activities which characterise the typical consulting project;

- to appreciate the management issues each of these stages presents to the consultant;

- to understand how the challenges of each stage may be approached to ensure the success of the consulting project.

8.1 Overview of the process

A *process* is a sequence of events directed towards achieving some overall outcome. When we recognise a process we recognise the interconnectedness and interrelatedness of independent actions. It is not just *what* we do that matters. It is the *order* in which we do things.

A consulting project will only be successful if the right actions are carried out in the right order. A client will not accept a solution to a problem he or she does not yet recognise exists. It is premature to decide on the best options for a business if no analysis of what that business is about has been carried out. It is no good presenting the customer with a bill if he or she has not received any advice yet!

Most consulting projects go through eight stages. The process starts with an initial contact between the consultant and the client. This is followed by a recognition that the consultant can help the business in some way and a project is initiated. In the third stage the consultant will suggest further investigation into and analysis of the issues facing the client's business before proposing a set of formal objectives that both should work towards. The consultant will then document those objectives in the form of a formal proposal. This constitutes the 'contract' between the consultant and client.

The sixth stage is the implementation of the project. This stage will demand further information gathering, evaluation of the business issues, analysis and evaluation of options and formulation of recommendations. When this is complete, those findings and recommendations will be communicated back to the client in some way. This communication will aim to encourage and facilitate implementation. In the final stage, the consultant may maintain contact with the client if this can in some way benefit one, or preferably both, parties. This process is illustrated in Figure 8.1.

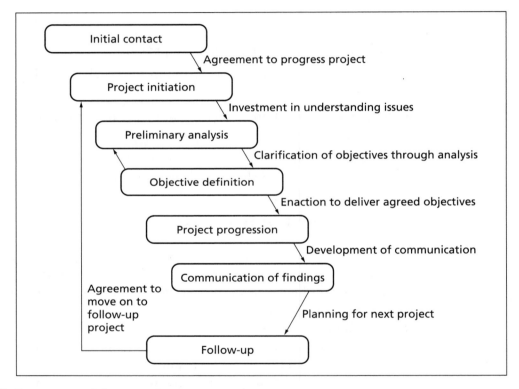

Figure 8.1 Dynamics of the consulting project

Every consulting project is different. The eight stages of different consulting exercises will vary in length and complexity. The consultant's approach to each stage will differ depending on the nature of the consulting project and the client with whom he or she is working. This said, every successful consulting project is successful because the consultant has managed each stage effectively. We will now examine each stage in detail.

8.2 Initial contact

Consultants meet with potential clients in a great number of forums. In principle, there are four mechanisms by which the consultant and client meet and decide they should work together.

◆ The consultant and client meet in an impromptu way.
◆ The consultant proposes his or her services to a client.
◆ The client seeks out the services of a particular consultant.
◆ The consultant and client are brought together by a third party.

Project initiation may occur with both consultant and client sharing a clear understanding of what the client wants. Quite often, though, the client is unclear as to specific objectives. He or she may just feel that things could be better with the business. In this case, the consultant must be adept at probing the client and getting him or her to reveal something about the business. Such probing must be undertaken with subtlety if it is not to be seen as obvious and invasive. This demands effective use of the questioning techniques detailed in Chapter 22.

Business networks bring many people together seeking ways to help each other. This is often an important forum for consultants to make contact and present what they have to offer. Business networks exist in and between business sectors. They may be stimulated by professional bodies which will set up conferences and seminars. An example is the *Marketing Network* associated with the Chartered Institute of Marketing.

Consultants, like any other business service providers, are responsible for promoting the service they offer to their customers. This may be through professional bodies which offer some endorsement for the service on offer and support its promotion. Consultants can also promote themselves via advertising, particularly in specialist industry publications. Direct marketing to potential clients may also be a useful tool.

Clients may sometimes approach a consultant in search of advice. This may be in response to the consultant's promotional activities or be a result of recommendations from another satisfied customer.

8.3 Initiating the project

The decision to work together is a significant one for both the client and the consultant. The client is making the decision to invest in his or her business through buying the insights and advice of an outside expert. The consultant is deciding to offer his or her expertise to the client. This demands a considerable commitment and means the consultant cannot pursue other projects. Taking on a particular project represents an *opportunity cost* to the consultant.

Both client and consultant must be clear on exactly what is being initiated. It could be the entire project. It is more likely, though, that it is actually an invitation by the client to the consultant to make a *formal proposal* for the project (stage 3 of the process). This will certainly be the case if the consultant is being invited to make a proposal or pitch in competition with other consultants. Even if no competition is involved and the client is inviting the consultant to move straight on to the full project an interim proposal is still a good idea. As discussed below, it is an effective means of managing the client's expectations about the project's outcomes.

The actual initiation of the project can take a variety of forms. The degree of formality that the initiation takes is particularly important. It may be a simple verbal agreement to go ahead. It may take the form of an informal note or letter. In other cases the project may be initiated by a formal and detailed contract.

The formality of the initiation will reflect the interests of both client and consultant. A number of factors will affect this. The most important are as follows.

◆ How well the consultant and client know each other

If the consultant and client know each other very well then the project can be initiated with a low degree of formality. If there is a good deal of trust between both parties to the exercise then both will rely on the fact that the details of the project can be adjusted through mutual agreement as understanding develops.

◆ Expectations from the project

The agreement to initiate the project will reflect the expectations of the client as to the outcomes of the project. If those expectations have been thoroughly thought through by the client and have been well defined, the client may use the initiation of the project as an opportunity to articulate those outcomes and communicate them to the consultant. In this case the initiation may take a more formal guise.

◆ Level of resources committed to the project by the client

The more the client is likely to invest in the consulting exercise (by way of money, people and time), the more likely it is that he or she will want to document the decision in some way and to formalise the initiation.

◆ Investment by the consultant in making the formal proposal

As noted below, preparing the formal proposal demands time, energy and possibly direct expenditure on the part of the consultant. How much commitment is made here will depend on the nature (and value) of the project, the need to collect information, the level of detail in the proposal and the mechanism of delivering it to the client. A great deal of preparation may be needed, especially if the pitch for the project is a competitive one. In this case, the consultant may require the client to offer a degree of commitment to undertaking the project and to make this commitment explicit in the terms of the proposal.

◆ The need to communicate within the client business

If the client business is quite large, the consulting exercise may be initiated by a manager in the middle of the organisational hierarchy. If so, such a person may want to record the decision to initiate a consulting exercise. He or she may need to do so in order to inform superiors and to comply with internal decision-control procedures.

◆ The need to inform third parties

The delivery of the exercise may be of interest to a number of people outside the client organisation. Often institutional investors such as banks and venture capitalists will demand the opinions of outside experts before committing capital. If the business is subject to a possible acquisition, the acquirer may require that the business be evaluated by a consultant. In these cases the initiation may be formalised so as to keep the third party informed.

8.4 Preliminary analysis of the issues

The consultant must make a decision about what can be achieved by the consulting exercise. It is this that will be offered to the client in the formal proposal. This decision must be based on an understanding of the business and its situation. Background research and an evaluation of the business will be called for. This stage calls on the analytical approaches discussed in Part 4 of this book.

There are three key questions to be answered by this preliminary analysis. These are:

1 What are the major opportunities and issues the business faces?
2 What prevents the business capitalising on the opportunity or dealing with the issues?

3 How can the consultant's service help the business overcome this block?

It is the answers to these questions around which the formal proposal will be made.

It should not be forgotten that this is a *preliminary* analysis. Any analysis demands an investment of time and effort (and possibly direct expenditure) in developing an understanding. This investment must be of the right order for the project. On the one hand it should be sufficient so that a proposal can be made which is relevant, meaningful and, critically, attractive to the client. If the consultant is in a competitive situation then investing in this understanding may offer good dividends. On the other hand, the investment should not be too high in relation to the final scope of the project. Clients rarely pay the consultant for making the initial proposal. The costing of this preliminary evaluation must, ultimately, be included in the overall bill for the exercise. If the pitch is competitive the consultant will not see any return on the investment if the proposal is not successful.

A simple test can be applied before a consultant dedicates resources to gaining new information at this stage. This is to ask how the information will be used. If it is needed to develop an understanding of how the client *potentially* may be helped it may be useful. If it will only be used for *delivering* that help, it can safely be left until a commitment has been made to the full project.

8.5 Defining objectives

A management project of any significance should be defined around its *objectives*; that is, what it aims to achieve. Objectives provide a means of communicating the reason the project exists, provide a common focal point for all involved and act as an indication of what level of investment is appropriate, given the options available for other projects.

Defining proper objectives is a very important part of the project. A critical element in the success of the consulting exercise is that its objectives are well defined and understood by all involved. It is the objectives of the project that the client is 'buying'. Defining objectives is a project management skill discussed fully in Chapter 11. At this stage it should be noted that objectives represent the link between where the business is now and where it might be with the consultant's help. It is also useful to note that objectives are different from *outcomes*. An objective is what the consulting project will achieve. An outcome is what the business will be able to do as a result of the consulting exercise.

8.6 Making a formal proposal

The formal proposal is a pivotal point in the consulting exercise. It represents the consultant's statement of what he or she can achieve on behalf of the client business. The proposal defines what the client will be paying for. Investing time and effort in the preparation and communication of a good proposal always pays dividends.

A full exploration of the details to be included in and the structuring and writing of a formal proposal is given in Chapter 9. An important point to be made at this stage is that the proposal operates at a number of levels.

The key functions of the proposal are as follows. The proposal:

◆ provides a concise and efficient means of communicating the objectives of the project to the client;

◆ guides analysis and ensures investment in information gathering is at an appropriate level;

◆ gives the consulting team a common focus when differentiating tasks and organising the project delivery;

◆ provides a fixed point of reference which can be referred back to if it is felt the project is drifting;

◆ can be used to manage the expectations of the client.

This last point is very important. If properly written and presented, the proposal maintains the realism of the client and prevents expectations of the outcomes becoming unrealistic. This can easily happen and if expectations get too high, even a good project will disappoint the client.

8.7 Project progression

Progression represents the actual undertaking of the project. At this stage the consultant applies his or her insights, expertise and knowledge to create a new understanding for the client. Every consulting project has its own character but also includes some essential activities which are common to most projects. The important ones are:

◆ Information gathering

An understanding of the business and its context must be developed. Information is needed to understand the opportunities and issues the business faces and its capabilities in relation to them. Information gathering is an ongoing activity which is assisted by the techniques discussed in Chapter 18. A crucial point that will be developed in this discussion is that the need for information must always be challenged in relation to its cost and the objectives of the project.

◆ Analysis and interpretation

Information on its own is of little use. It is the *sense* that the consultant can make of it that is valuable for the client. The consultant must interpret the information and create a new perspective from it. Developing this new perspective can be aided by the creative approaches described in Chapter 15 and the auditing techniques in Chapter 17. Analysis does not occur in isolation from information gathering: it is iterative with it. Information prompts analysis and analysis highlights information gaps.

◆ Interaction with the client business

The consultant team, or a representative of it, will usually maintain contact with a manager, or managers, in the client business. This may be driven by the need to keep the client informed of the progression of the project. It may also be a consequence of the need to obtain further information about the business. Contact can be through meetings, telephone calls, written and electronic communications. Whatever the motivation, or the means, interacting with the client is an opportunity not just to give and obtain information but also to build a relationship with the client which can lead to a more effective project. Approaches to building this relationship are discussed in Part 5 of this book.

◆ Project management and monitoring

The project proposal commits the consultant to three things. These are a set of *agreed objective*s which will be delivered at a *specified time* for a *given budget*. Slippage in any one of these aspects can lead to unsatisfactory outcomes for the client, the consultant or both. Monitoring is the activity dedicated to ensuring that the project is progressing in a satisfactory manner. It will involve ensuring that key events are happening on time and that expenditure is in line with that anticipated. Effective monitoring procedures ensure that if slippage does occur, remedial action can be taken to get the project back on track.

◆ Keeping records

Effective consultants invest time in keeping a good record of the progression of a project. As a minimum, this will be a file of important documents and notes on communications. This may be supplemented by a project log such as that discussed in Chapter 5. It may involve more formal records such as plans and budgets.

Keeping records is good practice for several reasons. It enables progression of the project to be monitored. Queries may be resolved quickly by reference back to communications. Most important, though, is the fact that a good set of records allow the consultant to reflect on the project, learn from the experience in an active way and so enhance performance in the future.

8.8 Communicating the findings

Consulting is an activity which can build value through interaction with the client. The benefits of the exercise are delivered over time, especially if a process consulting approach is taken. Even so, the client will see the final communication of the results of the consulting exercise as an important event. This is often seen as the delivery of the actual consulting 'product' – the tangible item the client has actually paid for.

8.9 Following up

There are a variety of reasons why the client and consultant might want to keep in touch after the formal outputs of the project have been delivered. Some of the more important are as follows.

◆ Advice on implementation

The final report will make a series of recommendations to the client. It is usually up to the client to put those recommendations into practice. However, the client may feel the need to call further upon the skills and insights of the consultant for clarification of points in the final report and for guidance on how implementation might be effected. An agreement to support the client in this way may be a feature of the project proposal.

◆ Prepare ground for new project

Even if the consultant has not made an explicit agreement to support the client after the final report has been delivered it may be judicious to do so. If the client is satisfied with the outputs of the project then there is the possibility that the client and consultant may both gain by working together on a future project.

◆ Seeking an endorsement

A consultant builds his or her career on reputation. If a project has been undertaken well then that is something the consultant might use in the future. The endorsement of a satisfied client, a statement that he or she has benefited from the advice of the consultant can be very valuable. This will be particularly so if the client represents a well-known business which is challenging in the demands it makes on its suppliers. Of course, confidentiality is important. Some circumspection may be needed in referring to a particular project. But this is an issue that can usually be resolved.

◆ Project review and evaluation

As noted in the point about record keeping, effective consultants engage in active learning. They are always alert to the possibility of improving their performance. This demands they learn from their experiences. Reviewing how the project went, in terms of both positives to be repeated and negatives to learn from, is an important part of this. The views of the client may be sought, either through informal discussion or by means of a more formal questionnaire.

◆ Networking

The consultant may seek to maintain a relationship with the client merely to build his or her presence in the business network. The benefits may not be immediately clear, but awareness of the consultant and what they can offer is built. There is always the possibility that new business will emerge if the client recommends the consultant to a contact.

Team discussion point	Most consulting teams differentiate individual roles within the team. In this way they get the best out of a team effort. The exact profile of roles varies. Often the following roles make an appearance:

– a team co-ordinator;

– an information gatherer;

– an information analyser;

– a report writer;

– a report presenter;

– a client contactor;

– a team councillor.

These roles are discussed more fully in Section 12.2.

Discuss, as a group, how each role might contribute to each stage of the consulting process.

Summary of key ideas

A consulting exercise is a project which moves through a number of distinct stages. The key stages are:

◆ Initiation: the consultant and client meet and decide to work together.

◆ Preliminary analysis: development of an understanding of what the consultant can do for the client.

◆ Formal proposal: a statement by the consultant to the client of what the project will achieve for the business.

◆ Progression of project: actual undertaking of the project.

◆ Delivery of results: communicating the findings to the client.

◆ Following up: post-delivery activities.

Different projects move through these stages in different ways but each represents a distinct management challenge that can be met by using analysis, project management and relationship-building skills.

9

Preparing the project proposal

Learning outcome

The learning outcome from this chapter is:

◆ to recognise the key elements of the project proposal and how they may be articulated in order to have an impact and to influence the recipient.

9.1 The function of the project proposal

The project proposal is a short, straightforward document. It has two simple aims. These are to state what the consulting exercise aims to achieve and to get the client to commit to it. Despite its brevity the project proposal is very important. It is the pivot about which the whole project revolves. A good proposal gets the project off to a good start. A weak one will hinder the project from the outset.

The proposal is a statement to the client of what the project is about and what it will do for the business. The proposal is what the client is *buying* from the consultant. It needs to present what the consultant has to offer in a positive light. It has to make the consultant's offering appear as an attractive investment given all the other things the business has an opportunity to invest in. If the consultant's pitch is a competitive one, the proposal has to present the consultant as the best available.

A further and equally important function of the proposal is to manage the client's *expectations*. An individual's satisfaction with a product or service is not usually based on the absolute utility of what he or she receives. More often it is based on outcomes relative to expectations. If expectations are met or exceeded, then satisfaction will occur. If expectations are not met then disappointment will inevitably result. If the client recognises the proposal as what he or she is buying then it is against this that the final project delivery will be compared.

Some managers have an unrealistic idea of what a consultant is capable of, or at least capable of given the resources the manager is able to invest in the consulting project, both in terms of the money the client is putting forward and the time and capabilities of the consultant. If this is so then the manager is likely to be unsatisfied with the results of a consulting exercise *even if, in absolute terms, that project is a good one.* On the other hand, a manager who has doubts about the ability of a consultant to offer anything of value may well be pleasantly satisfied with the results of a quite mediocre project. (Though of course, such a manager may resist using a consultant in the first place!)

The proposal must serve a twofold function. On the one hand, it must 'sell' what the consultant has to offer. On the other, it must manage the expectations of the client manager so that he or she does not make an unreasonable demand on the consultant given the resources that are available. The project proposal demands a balanced approach from the consultant. The temptation to 'get a sale' by offering a lot must be tempered by a care not to raise the client's expectations so high that they cannot be met. There are a few simple rules which will allow this balance to be struck.

First, understand what the client would *really* like for his or her business. Do not fall into the trap of assuming that he or she will want what the 'textbooks' suggest they *should* have, or that they must take what you think is best for them. Managers often reject the obvious answers for very good reasons. Second, enquire into, and gain a thorough understanding of, the extent to which the client expects the consulting exercise to contribute to the overall goal for the business. It is particularly important to ensure that the client makes the distinction between the consulting project offering a *means* to achieve the business's goals and its actually *implementing* them: between the consultant pointing out a *direction* for the business and actually *taking* it there. This is an issue about which the consultant and client can easily develop different expectations.

Developing this understanding of the client's needs and expectations must take place at the preliminary analysis stage of the project. It is best done through a personal meeting between the manager and the consulting team or a representative of it. At this stage the objective of the meeting should be to gather information about the business and what might be done for it. It is not a time to start negotiating on outcomes.

It is better to wait until the written proposal has been presented before starting negotiating on precisely what can and cannot be achieved. The proposal helps here. It provides something tangible around which discussions can centre. The initial proposal can always be modified in light of further discussion. How to approach these negotiations will be dealt with fully in Chapter 11. If the proposal is modified, however, do produce a finalised written version so that finalised aims, objectives and outcomes are clear to all and can be referred back to.

9.2 What to include in the proposal

The proposal needs to be succinct and must make an impact. It must speak for itself; you cannot rely on having an opportunity to explain it in person. Typically it will be one to two pages long. If it is longer than this it will risk losing its impact.

As with any business communication, the proposal should always be approached with a fresh mind. There are always new ways of doing things to be discovered. However, there are some key elements which, when included in the proposal, do add to its impact and help it communicate effectively within the constraints described above. These will now be described in detail.

◆ A title

All that is necessary is a short title for the project, perhaps the client company's name and a brief descriptive phrase. This provides a reference for the project in the future and helps locate it in the minds of all involved.

◆ Client's requirements

This should be a brief statement about the company, the opportunities or issues it faces and the scope of the project. The scope may be drawn from the types of consulting project described in Chapter 7. The background statement should aim to convey the fact that the consultant understands the key issue or issues and is committed to addressing them. It should not be a complete description of the business and its situation. This would be far too long and as the client possesses this information would not be interested.

◆ Overall aim

This is a statement of what the project aims to achieve, in broad terms. This might be thought of as the mission for the project from which definite objectives might be drawn.

◆ Objectives

This is a list of the detailed objectives for the project. Objectives should be active; they are statements of what the project will do. A good way of starting the list is to use the phrase:

> *This consulting exercise aims to: . . .*

◆ Outcomes

Outcomes are subtly different from objectives. They are a statement of what the business *will be able to do* as a result of receiving the consulting exercise and the delivery of its objectives. Again, they should be active. A good way of starting the list is to use the phrase:

> *As a result of this consulting exercise the business will be able to: . . .*

Both objectives and outcomes are best summarised in the form of a bullet-point list. Objectives and outcomes should be complete in themselves. Do not be tempted to expand on them or qualify them with subsidiary paragraphs. If the consulting exercise is long and complex it may be proper to develop interim objectives and outcomes for the intermediate stages of the project. The development and articulation of good objectives and outcomes is discussed in Chapter 11.

◆ Our approach

This section provides an opportunity for the consulting group to describe how it will address the exercise. It should highlight the approach in broad terms. It might detail activities such as market research, analysis and guidance with implementation. It should not give a detailed exposition of the methodologies which might be adopted. This section is an opportunity for the consulting team to indicate what it has to offer. The emphasis should be on why what the group can offer is different or special. It is a further opportunity to manage the client's expectations and in particular to emphasise the distinction between developing a plan for the business and actually implementing it.

◆ Time plan

The time plan is an indication of when the outcomes of the exercise will be delivered, and identifies important milestones *en route*. Milestones are key events along the way to the final delivery and might include things like meetings with the client and information providers, interim reports and presentations.

The amount of detail in the time plan will reflect the length and complexity of the project.

◆ Costings

Costings are statements of how much the project will cost the client. Important elements are the consultant's fees, the consultant's expenses (often just a *pro rata* cost on top of fees) and any direct expenditure needed. Direct expenditure might be needed for buying market research or undertaking surveys.

It is as important to know what *not* to include in the project proposal as to know what to put in. A lot of background on the business does not usually help. It 'pads out' the proposal making it longer than it need be. It tells the client things he or she already knows and runs the risk of losing his or her interest before the important aspects of the proposal are reached.

The temptation to discuss the methodology that will be adopted should also be avoided. The formal business analysis techniques used by the consultant in developing an understanding of the business and how it might be moved forward are the consultant's concern – not the client's! A simple analogy with the repairing of your car makes the point. If you take your car to the garage for repair, you are not particularly interested in what tools the mechanic will use. Management consulting is the same. The consultant is an expert who is brought in because he or she knows how to call upon a range of tools to deal with business issues. There is no reason to reveal those tools to the client before the project starts.

Team discussion point

Consulting teams work best when team members differentiate the tasks to be performed. Some common roles are as follows:

– a team co-ordinator;

– an information gatherer;

– an information analyser;

– a report writer;

– a report presenter;

– a client contactor;

– a team councillor.

These roles are discussed more fully in Section 12.2.

How do you see each of these roles contributing to the preparation of the project proposal? Discuss your ideas as a group.

Summary of key ideas

The project proposal is a critical part of the consulting project. It does two things:

◆ It sells what the consultant has to offer.

◆ It can be used to manage the client's expectations about the outcomes of the consulting exercise.

The proposal should be a short, impactful document. The key elements to include are:

1 a title;

2 a brief statement of the client's requirements;

3 an overall aim for the consulting project;

4 a list of specific objectives – what the project aims to do;

5 a list of specific outcomes – what the business will be able to do as a result of the project;

6 a statement about your approach to the project – how you intend to tackle the project and why this will be effective.

If appropriate, the following may be added:

7 a time plan detailing key events; and

8 a costing for the project, detailing fees and expenditure.

The project proposal should be prepared after an initial meeting to discuss the client's business and requirements. Initial proposals can always be modified after discussion with the client to produce a final proposal. An initial proposal can be used as a basis for detailed negotiations with the client.

9.3 An example of a project proposal

Exhibit 9.1 presents an example of a project proposal along the lines discussed in this chapter.

Exhibit 9.1 Consulting proposal

Greyline Printers: support for a business expansion programme

Your requirements

Greyline Printers is a small, but ambitious and fast-growing firm offering a range of printing and reprographic services. The consulting team has been invited to work with the senior management team and explore the opportunities for growth the business might successfully capitalise upon, given the business's current resources.

Overall aim

The main aim of the consulting project is to give Greyline Printers a clear sense of direction for the way in which the business might be expanded into new market sectors.

Objectives

The consulting project aims to:

1 evaluate the market context of Greyline Printers;

2 identify high-growth customer segments;

3 develop an understanding of what those customers require from a good print and reprographics supplier – in terms of both products and service support;

4 identify major competitors of the business;

5 evaluate what those competitors offer and identify how Greyline Printers might develop a competitive edge;

6 summarise the findings in the form of a brief for the business's sales team;

7 make recommendations on a PR campaign to increase awareness of the company and its products among target customers.

▶

Outcomes

As a result of this consulting exercise Greyline Printers will be able to:

1 develop an understanding of the market sectors that are most attractive for new business development;

2 dedicate valuable resources towards the exploitation of those market sectors;

3 position itself in a way which is competitive given the current profile of competitors.

In particular the business will be able to:

4 refine its product range and service offering to increase competitiveness;

5 initiate a sales campaign dedicated to gaining new customers in those sectors;

6 support sales activity with a well-focused PR campaign.

Our approach

Our approach will emphasise the importance of reliable information to the decision makers of Greyline Printers. Secondary marketing research will be used to establish a picture of the dynamics of the print and reprographics market and the competitive situation. Building on this, primary market research will be used to investigate customer needs and expectations. The findings will be used to give a clear direction for future new product development. Market intelligence will be summarised in a form that makes it accessible to the sales team. A review of publications which reach important customers will be undertaken. This will be used to develop for Greyline Printers an awareness-building communication plan.

Time plan

Key events in the project will be as follows:

October 1997:	Initial meeting with client to discuss requirements.
November 1997:	Initial proposal presented to client and reviewed.
November 1997:	Final proposal based on review: agreement to go ahead.
December 1997–May 1998:	Progression of project. Further meetings with client (three expected over period). Secondary marketing research.
June 1998:	Primary research with buyers.
June 1998:	Preparation of final report. Sales brief and PR plan appended.
July 1998:	Presentation of findings to client.

10

Types of management consulting project

Learning outcome

The learning outcome from this chapter is:

◆ to appreciate the types of project consultants are called upon to undertake.

10.1 Business planning and development

The discussion about the management role of consultants (Chapter 6) and the ways in which they add value (Chapter 7) makes it clear that the challenges consultants face is as wide as management itself. However, when consultants are called in to undertake work on behalf of a business it is with a specific project in mind.

One of the broadest project types is 'business planning' or 'business development'. This is a phrase often encountered in businesses which have ambitions to grow and develop. A project of this type is a great opportunity. It offers the consultant a broad remit to contribute to the development of the business. However some care is called for in interpretation.

Business development is a very broad term. It can mean different things to different people. The first task the consultant faces is to establish exactly what the client wants from a business development project. Sometimes the client has something very specific in mind. Common outcomes desired from business development include:

◆ growth of the business within its core markets by capitalising on market growth or market share increase;

◆ expansion of the business into new market sectors;

◆ development of new products;

◆ increasing profits through cost reduction programmes;

◆ internal structural reorganisations.

The client may simply state that he or she wants to 'grow the business'. If this is so then the consultant will need to step back, evaluate the possible options for growth and propose the best path to the client. At this stage many business development projects resolve themselves into one or more of the project types listed below. The effective consultant can use the project proposal to establish exactly what the client wants and to manage his or her expectations about what can realistically be achieved.

10.2 Marketing research

Marketing research is the process through which managers discover the nature of the competitive environment in which they are operating. The objective of marketing research is to obtain information which managers can use to support their decision making. Information reduces risk and enables managers to dedicate valuable resources in a more reliable way. Marketing research falls into four types, based on the type of questions it aims to answer and the source of the answers.

1 *Quantitative research* provides answers to questions when those answers need to be expressed in statistical or numerical form. It aims to answer the 'how much, how often and how many' questions that managers pose.

2 *Qualitative research* provides answers to questions which do not demand a quantified answer. It provides the insights that answer managers' 'who, what and why' questions.

3 *Primary research* is information collected and collated specifically for the project in hand.

4 *Secondary research* is based on information that has been collated earlier for reasons other than the project at hand. It takes the form of existing reports, articles and commentaries which just prove to be relevant to the project.

These approaches to answering managers' questions about business opportunities are reviewed more fully in Chapter 18.

Marketing research takes a number of forms. At one level it is market 'intelligence': an ongoing review of articles, reports and customer gossip about a market. At another level it might be a cognitive study aimed at consolidating the experience of a group of managers and insights into their working environment.

Ultimately, it can demand the use of complex statistical techniques or sophisticated psychometric methodologies to develop a complete picture of how customers see and buy a product category and the details of their expenditure. At this level marketing research demands a high degree of expertise on the part of the researcher.

Good consultants recognise their limitations. They know when it is time to call in the experts. This does not mean they cannot add value for the client. A consultant is in a better position to develop a brief for a professional marketing research exercise and can help the client understand what the results mean. For this reason, consultants often subcontract marketing research when necessary.

10.3 Marketing strategy development

Marketing research is a very powerful approach to identifying business opportunities. Exploiting them, though, requires a *marketing strategy*. A marketing strategy defines the approach the business will take in order to get the customers' attention and – critically – get them to spend their money on the business's products or services.

The key elements of a marketing strategy are dictated by the marketing mix. The marketing strategy will be built on the answers to the following questions:

◆ What products do customers want from a sector's producers?

◆ In what way are competitors failing to provide these products?

◆ What price are customers expecting or willing to pay?

◆ What channels are available for getting the product to the customer?

◆ Who might be the partners in the distribution process?

◆ How might they be approached?

◆ In what ways can customers be informed that the product is available?

◆ How can the customers' interest be stimulated through promotion?

In developing a marketing strategy the consultant is answering these questions. Often, getting the answers will demand the contribution of experts such as marketing researchers and advertising specialists. If this is the case the consultant can be involved in a number of ways. The consultant might simply be asked to highlight these needs so that the client can pick the project up. Alternatively the consultant may be invited in to support the client in working with such experts. In some cases, the client may give the consultant complete control and have him or her subcontract work with specialists as an integral part of the consulting project.

Implementing a marketing strategy involves a range of activities. The implementation can resolve itself into the product development, promotional and sales activity projects detailed below. Clearly, an effective, well-presented marketing strategy project creates follow-up opportunities for the consultant.

10.4 Developing promotional campaigns

A promotional campaign is any programme of activities dedicated to informing customers about a product, stimulating their interest and encouraging purchase. Examples include advertising and public relations campaigns, sales drives, direct mailings, exhibitions and in-store demonstrations.

Though each of these approaches is different the consultant faces a common profile of tasks when developing such campaigns. The key questions the client will be asking will be:

◆ What methods will prove to be cost effective?

◆ What will be the mechanics of running the campaign?

◆ How can it be monitored?

The consultant must develop an understanding of how much it will cost, using each technique available, to contact a potential customer, the impact each is likely to have on the potential customer, the likelihood that they will make a purchase, how much they will spend if they do and over what period. A comparison of the techniques can then be made which, in light of the client's promotional objectives and available budget, provides the basis for designing an effective promotional plan.

10.5 Planning sales force activity

For many businesses, especially small and medium-sized businesses, the sales team is the primary promotional tool. Expenditure on sales force activity is one of the most important investments the firm will make. Detailed and thoughtful planning of sales force activity is an activity which offers real returns. This is an area in which the consultant can offer valuable support. Some of the key issues that might be addressed include the following.

◆ Overall organisation of the team

How should the team be organised? For what should individual sales people have responsibility? Options include a geographic area, a group of customers or a product category. The answer will depend on the size of the team, the type and range of products sold and the nature and size of customers.

◆ Sales team training

What skills do the sales team need in order to be effective? How might they be encouraged to focus on customer service rather than 'short-term' sales? How might they become more active in obtaining market intelligence while out selling? Might the sales team use their knowledge of customers to contribute more directly to new product development?

◆ Sales team motivation

Most sales people are motivated by a combination of fixed salary and a performance-based bonus. This bonus element is a critical element in directing and motivating the sales team. Some important issues to be addressed when designing the bonus scheme include:

◆ What level of expenditure do managers wish to invest in the bonus scheme?

◆ How can the bonus be used to align the thrust of the sales with the firm's overall strategic objectives?

◆ Will the sales team find the scheme transparent and easy to understand?

◆ Will it be seen as 'fair'?

◆ Does it leave latitude for managers to deal with contingencies and conflicts?

◆ How will the bonus scheme fit with the organisation's broader motivational and development strategy?

◆ Planning sales campaigns

A sales campaign is a plan detailing how the sales team will be used. It may reflect ongoing activity or it may be a short-term period of special activity to support, say, a new product launch, the firm's entry into a new geographic area or a move into a new customer sector. The important decision elements of a sales campaign include:

◆ which members of the sales force will be involved;

◆ what products will be given priority;

◆ which customers will be targeted;

◆ in what geographic area;

◆ the sales literature that will be used;

◆ the special prices and deals that can be used to motivate purchase;

◆ bonuses and rewards for sales performance;

◆ other marketing and PR activity that will support the sales drive.

The decision about each of these elements will affect both the cost of the promotion and its overall success. Insights may be gained from both the qualitative management experience and quantitative management science methods. Clearly, there is an opportunity for the consultant to add considerable value here.

10.6 New product development

It is a business's products (which can include services as well as tangible products) that the customer ultimately buys. They are the basis on which a business is built. A well-designed product that addresses the customer's needs in an effective manner is only part of a business success story: but it is an *essential* part. New product development represents a complex project which draws in most, if not all, of the firm's functions. Research and development, marketing and sales, production, purchasing and human resources will all be called upon to make a contribution. New product development is often undertaken by interdisciplinary teams which cut across departmental boundaries.

The consultant can offer support to the new product development programme in a number of ways. The most important include:

◆ understanding the customer's needs through market research;

◆ technical advice on product development;

◆ identifying and contacting suppliers of critical components;

◆ development of marketing and PR campaigns to support the launch;

◆ developing promotion campaigns to get distributors on board;

◆ financial planning and evaluation of the return on new product investment.

In a broader sense, the consultant may be invited in to facilitate change management programmes designed to integrate the new product development team and enhance its performance.

10.7 Developing proposals for financial support

Businesses often need injections of capital. New start-ups and high-growth businesses, in particular, need funds – in addition to those provided by customers – in order to ensure they reach their potential. Investment capital can be obtained from a number of sources. Banks and venture capital companies are important to new and high-growth businesses. Government grants may be available to small businesses in some areas. More mature firms can obtain funds from stock market flotation. Consultants are often called in to offer advice in four critical areas:

◆ evaluation of the business's investment needs;

◆ identification of funding providers and how they might be contacted;

◆ developing an understanding of the criteria employed by funding providers and how these might be addressed;

◆ developing communications with funding providers, particularly in relation to proposals and business plans.

Though general in form, these project areas will vary in their details according to the business and the fund provider it is approaching.

10.8 Staff recruitment

People, it is often said, are a business's most important resource. Attracting the right sort of people to contribute to the business is certainly an important challenge managers must address, especially those in high-growth businesses.

A consultant can be of value in this area in several ways. Important contributions to recruitment projects might include:

◆ assessing the firm's human resource requirement and identifying skill and knowledge gaps, both currently and predicting for the future;

◆ creating advertisements (with insights into both message and medium) to attract the right people;

◆ developing assessment criteria, interview procedures and, possibly, psychometric testing of candidates;

◆ advice on the reimbursement packages new recruits will expect.

Successful recruitment often demands a degree of specialist knowledge. As a result it is often an area in which dedicated consultants operate.

10.9 Information systems development

Managers need information if they are to make good decisions. They need information on both the business's external situation – its competitive environment – and its internal state. Information is, as Paul Tom points out in his 1987 book, a corporate resource. Management information systems aim to collect and organise such information and present it to managers in a usable form. Nowadays management information systems are usually based on computer technology. They therefore require a good deal of technical expertise to implement. However, even the non-technical consultant can add value, particularly in developing an understanding of the information needs of the business, the way in which information flows around the organisation and the competitive advantage that might be gained through investment in information technology. Such a consulting exercise provides a sound basis on which to progress the technical implementation and helps ensure that it will be rewarding.

10.10 Exporting and international marketing

Most large firms have an international if not truly global dimension to their operations. Many high-growth firms soon recognise the opportunity the international stage offers them as a route for expansion. For most businesses, moving into the international arena is a step into the unknown. They lack experience of the competitive and regulatory environment. Their understanding of the customers will be limited. They must deal with distributors and partners they have not dealt with before. The most successful moves into international operations are those which are based on sound preliminary research and a thorough understanding of what to expect. The consultant can assist this process of discovery.

In particular the consultant can supply:

◆ an overall insight into regional social and macroeconomic development;

◆ an analysis of the growth and evolution of specific markets;

◆ an evaluation of consumer needs and requirements and how these are being satisfied currently;

◆ information on regulatory and legal issues;

◆ details of the existing supply structure and competitors present;

◆ an investigation into distribution channels and possible partners;

◆ information on advertising and promotional opportunities.

These insights can be used to develop an overall strategy of entry into international markets including decisions such as whether to rely on exporting or to set up permanent international operations.

A consultant may be called in to address any one of these projects in a 'pure' form. The boundaries between the projects are somewhat arbitrary, though. Many real projects combine aspects of these project types. International marketing will involve marketing research. A new product development or management information project may demand the recruitment of specialist staff. Business development may demand that financing be obtained from external investors. However, planning of such hybrid projects is usually helped by resolving them into their core aspects. This clarifies both the setting of objectives and the monitoring of their delivery.

Team discussion point	Chapter 7 discussed the mechanisms by which consultants can create value for their clients. In summary, these were:

◆ the provision of information;

◆ the provision of specialist expertise;

◆ the provision of a new perspective;

◆ the provision of support for internal arguments;

◆ the provision of support in gaining a critical resource;

◆ the creation of organisational change.

Each member of the team should select one of the project types listed in this chapter. Using the framework in Chapter 7, each team member should prepare and deliver a short (one-page) presentation detailing how each means of value creation can support the project type selected and ensure that its outcomes will be satisfactory for the client.

Summary of key ideas

Consultants take on a variety of projects on behalf of their clients. The most common include:

◆ business planning and development;

◆ marketing research;

◆ marketing strategy development;

◆ developing promotional campaigns;

◆ planning sales activity;

◆ new product development;

◆ developing proposals for financial support;

◆ staff recruitment;

◆ information systems development;

◆ exporting and international marketing.

Some projects may combine one or more of these pure types.

11

Defining objectives for the project

Learning outcomes

The key learning outcomes from this chapter are:

◆ to understand the distinction between the aim, objectives and outcomes of the consulting project;

◆ to be able to define an effective aim, objectives and outcomes for the project;

◆ to be able to articulate the aim, objectives and outcomes in a convincing and influential way.

11.1 Aims, objectives, outcomes and actions

When we engage in conscious action we do so with a view of what the future will be like. We anticipate future conditions when we make a decision and act on it. For example, an investor is not just interested in the current profitability of a company. He or she is also interested in what the company's profitability in the *future* will be.

Managers do not simply accept what the future conditions might be like. They try to control them. Good managers actively *shape* the future. Managers operate with a conscious picture of the state they wish to create: where they want their organisation to be, what they want the organisation to do, what they want it to be like. This desire colours management language. Managers talk in explicit terms about what they and their organisations wish to achieve. They use a variety of words to describe these ambitions. They will talk, for example, about their *goals*, *aims*, *objectives*, *missions* and *outcomes*.

Sometimes these words are taken to be synonymous with each other. At other times, users imply subtle distinctions between them. It is useful for the consultant to recognise differences in meaning between such terms. This aids thinking about the rationale for the consulting project and makes communication more efficient and likely to have an impact. Appropriate and well-defined aims, objectives and outcomes are the cornerstone of effective project management. They are worth investing in. They provide the solid platform on which a successful project can be built.

Aims, objectives and outcomes are developed by the consultant in the preliminary analysis phase of the consulting project. They are communicated to the client through the proposal. They function to keep the project on track and help the consulting team maintain focus during the process of delivery. They can then be used to assess what the project has actually achieved at delivery. The following discussion highlights the differences between aims, objectives and outcomes and how that difference might be used to aid the consultant in analysis and communication with the client at the different stages of the project.

◆ Aims

The aim of the project is its *overall goal*. It is the *broad* scope of what that project aspires to achieve. An aim is the starting-point of a project. It is first articulated as a desire: a sense that things might be different and better. Most businesses share a set of common desires. For example: to grow, to be more profitable, to be more secure, to compete more effectively and so on. It is from these general desires that the aim of a consulting project can be distilled. In defining an aim, a consultant is refining the desires of the firm's managers. The way in which this will be done will depend on a number of factors. Some of those the consultant needs to take into account include the following.

The extent to which managers have already articulated their desires for the business

Some managers have a very clear view of what they want to achieve. Others only harbour a vague sense of the direction they want to take their business. The consultant may obtain a well-specified project. Often, though, the consultant must help the client comprehend and articulate what he or she wants to achieve on behalf of the firm. This does not mean that the consultant imposes an aim and objectives on the client. Rather the consultant must *facilitate* the client's articulation of what he or she wishes to do.

The level of detail in that articulation

As a business moves forward to pursue its aims it changes. It modifies its internal processes. It must adjust the structures which give the business its form. It develops its relationships with external stakeholders. Sometimes managers have thought these things through in detail. At other times they will have given them little thought. Consideration must be given to the *detailed* implications of pursuing and achieving particular goals for the firm as a whole. If managers have not done this, then the consultant must encourage them to do so and support them to appreciate these changes.

How appropriate the aims are for the business

Not all aims are appropriate for a business. A detailed consideration of what will happen if the business actually achieves the aims that managers are specifying may indicate that the outcomes might not help, and could even damage, the business. The outcomes may, for example, move the business into an area where competitive pressures are unsustainable. They may expose the business to too high a level of risk. In short, they may reduce rather than increase its ability to reward its stakeholders.

In this case, the consultant is obliged to inform the client that, in his or her opinion, the aim is not appropriate for the business. This will usually result in a reconsideration of the aims.

The extent to which aims are realistic, given the firm and its situation

Even if the aims are *appropriate* for the business, consideration must be given to how *realistic* they are. Can the business *really* deliver them? Two factors are important to this consideration. First: can the aims realistically be achieved given the situation in the market in which the firm operates? Aims must reflect the reality of the demand of the firm's customers. It is pointless having an aim of achieving sales of £10 million with a product whose total market is worth only £5 million. Second: are the aims reasonable given the resources the firm has available to pursue them. It is not usually realistic for a small firm to aspire to market leadership using just its own cash flow. It might do so if sufficient new investment capital can be found. If this is the course decided upon, acquiring this additional capital will need to be incorporated in the project.

The way in which the desires are particular to the firm and are distinguished from the general desires all firms have

All firms have ambitions of some sort. 'Generic aims' include a desire to grow, to increase profits, to make cash flow more stable and so on. These are common to most, if not all, businesses. The consultant must be careful to distinguish between those aims the firm will share with all other firms in its sector and those that can properly be said to be exclusive to the business. The distinction is important because businesses pursuing shared aims tend to meet in head-to-head competition. Aims which are exclusive may be a way of differentiating the firm and so reducing competitive pressures.

The scope of the consulting project relative to the business as a whole

Some aims are general. They relate to what the business as a whole wishes to achieve. Other aims may be more localised. They will relate to a limited part of the firm only. There are three dimensions along which aims usually become specific to a part of the business. If the firm is large enough, then they may relate to one particular part of the business or business unit within the firm as a whole. In addition, they might refer to the development of a particular product range out of the firm's entire product scope. Finally, they may refer to a particular functional activity within the firm, such as marketing, production or human resource management. These three dimensions are illustrated in Figure 11.1.

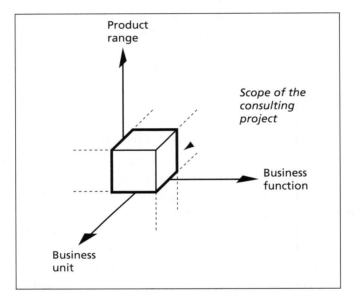

Figure 11.1 The scope of a consulting project

A project should be summarised by a *single* aim, not a list. The important thing is that the aim summarise the project in a succinct way so that all involved can recognise it. It might even be thought of as the *mission* for the project. It is not necessary that the aim quantify the project or give away all the details. That is the job of objectives and outcomes, discussed below.

The best way to start the aim is with a phrase like:

> *It is the aim of this project to . . .*

or:

> *This project aims to . . .*

For example:

> *This consulting project aims to give* New Firm Ltd *an analysis of its main competitors to aid decision making about competitive positioning.*

Or:

> *It is the aim of this consulting project to develop a promotional plan for the effective launch of the* Ideal *product range.*

◆ Mission

In many ways, a business may be thought of as a permanent and ongoing project. Certainly, an entrepreneur will see the development of his or her venture as a project of great importance. In the case of the whole business as a project the overall aim of the business may be defined in terms of the business's *mission*. A mission is the reason for the firm's existence. It is a statement of *what* it will achieve and *how*. A mission can include a statement of what the firm offers, to whom it is offering it, the source of its advantages in the marketplace, its aspirations and the ethical values it will uphold. (*See* Wickham (1997) for a review of business missions.) If a business has a stated mission it is a good idea to test the aims of a particular consulting project against it. They should resonate. The consulting project should help the firm achieve its mission. If it is recognised that it does, it can be a positive selling point for the project.

◆ Objectives

An aim is a *broad* statement. It is a *wish*. Objectives provide the details of how this wish will be made into reality. A single aim may be split into a number of objectives. These may be listed. A good way to start the objective list is with the phrase:

> *The objectives of the consulting project are to: . . .*

The specific objectives may be put into a bullet-point list after this statement.

A number of tests should be applied to an objective list to ensure that the objectives provide the basis for a good project. Good objectives must meet the following criteria.

Consistency

Consistency is the first and most fundamental test. Are the objectives consistent with the agreed aim? Will they deliver it? If not, they must be revised.

Definition

An objective must be well defined: it should not be ambiguous. A great number of problems can arise if the consultant and the client (or different members of the consulting team) read objectives in different ways. Avoid words that mean different things to different people. For example the word 'profitability' often appears in objectives. Improving it would certainly seem to be a good thing to do. Yet what does the word refer to? Is it profit margin? Or return on capital employed? Or cash flow? The simple rule is: If in doubt – spell it out!

Desirability

The test of desirability relates to the point about the appropriateness of aims discussed above. Will achieving the objectives actually be good for the firm? If the aim is appropriate and the objectives are consistent then logically they should also be desirable. This allows a double check that what the consultant is doing for the firm is worth while.

Feasibility

Feasibility asks whether the objectives are likely to be achieved given the environmental conditions the firm faces. For example: can sales be achieved given the size of markets, product advantages and competitive pressures? Always ask challenging questions. For example, if the business is to grow, can margins be sustained given the strengths of suppliers and buyers? Can new business be delivered in the face of competitor responses and so on?

Achievability

If an objective is feasible, it can be achieved in *principle*. For an objective to be achievable in *practice*, the firm must dedicate resources to pursuing it. Does the firm have the necessary resources? If it has, is this project the best available use for them? Account must be taken of productive resources and people as well as money. If the firm does not have the resources to hand can it obtain them? Is obtaining these additional resources part of the consulting project or is it a separate project? Care needs to be taken to clarify and agree whether the project is just about identifying and recommending a direction for the business or actually implementing the project and taking the business there.

Quantified

Ideally, objectives should be quantified. To 'grow the business' does not mean very much. To 'grow the business by 20 per cent' does. Whenever possible, objectives should be quantified by numbers. It is not just *what* will be achieved, but *when* it will be achieved and, critically, *what it will be worth when it is*.

Not all objectives can easily be quantified. Objectives such as 'to make our human resource management more effective' or 'to make employees' working time happier' do not offer easy numerical targets. Some would argue that they can, ultimately, be quantified. A starting-point might be the actual costs of the human resource management function and staff turnover. Others might argue for the inherently qualitative nature of such objectives. Quantitative information may be difficult (that is, expensive) to obtain. In any case, they may argue, forcing artificial numerical targets on such objectives robs them of their essence.

If objectives are left unquantified it is particularly important that the client's expectations are carefully managed and not allowed to become unrealistic. Some understanding of what these objectives mean for the firm must be found. It is important that what the project can achieve be communicated in an unambiguous way.

Signposted

An objective is *signposted* if it will be clear when it has been achieved. As the word implies, a signpost indicates that the project is going, or has gone, in the right direction. Signposts take a number of forms. They may be a physical output (a report presented, for example) or be indicated by a numerical measure (say, an increase in sales). Occasionally they may be revealed through qualitative information, for example a survey of employee satisfaction. Quantified objectives have inherent signposts. Qualitative objectives need signposts to be assigned to them. Good signposts are definite, are easily recognised and are agreed by all who have an interest in the consulting project. Do not assume that benchmarks are recognised and accepted by all involved. If in doubt, highlight the signpost and make sure it is agreed to.

Clearly, aims and objectives are involved in describing the same thing: the direction the business wishes to move in. They say this in different ways, though. In a 1977 article, James Brian Quinn makes a powerful case as to why broad goals and specific objectives should be separately articulated. Three reasons are important.

First, goals can be used to give a sense of direction without over-centralising decision making. Individuals contributing to the project can set their own objectives or sub-objectives and check them against the goal rather than have them set by the project leadership. For example, a goal might be set to generate sales from a new product. If so, decisions must be made about what the product will be like, its features, its price and so on. But the goal does not set these as specified objectives. The managers launching the product are free to use their experiences and local knowledge to set these themselves. An aim offers direction without dictating individual contribution.

Second, goals, being broad and unquantified, do not allow conflict over detail. It is details people often object to. For example, an objective to increase sales by 15 per cent might easily start an argument. Should it be 10 per cent or 20 per cent? Such a debate obscures the fact that there is unanimity on the central point: that growth is wanted. Recognising this as a general aim is a starting-point for agreement on the detail.

Third, goals define broad 'spaces' for achievement whereas objectives are narrow. Objectives are rigid, especially when they have agreed signposts attached to them. The point about objectives is that they be strived for. An objective is of little use if it can be changed easily. However, there are circumstances in which it might be legitimate to change objectives. The client may alter the requirements of the project. There may be a change in the resources available for the project. New information may become available which indicates a change in direction is judicious. Situations in which objectives might be changed are discussed in Chapter 14. In such cases the best move is to go back to the original aim and use it to devise new objectives in light of the new situation. This is much easier, and prone to less disagreement than starting from scratch and establishing entirely new objectives in the absence of an overall goal.

◆ Actions

Good objectives inspire managers to follow them through. They are a *call to action*. Actions are what managers actually do in order to achieve objectives. A collection of co-ordinated actions is a *plan*. It is implementing a plan of actions that actually consumes resources.

Plans organise actions in two dimensions. The first is linearly, as a *sequence in time*. Actions follow one another. Some actions can only be undertaken after others have been completed. Actions must be properly sequenced. The stages of the consulting project reviewed in Chapter 8 are an example. The second dimension is *co-ordination*, the ordering of actions between individuals. The advantage of team working is that it allows individuals to distinguish and differentiate the contribution they make. If the value this potentially offers is to be realised then individual contributions must be properly integrated. Planning will be dealt with in more detail in Chapter 12.

◆ Outcomes

Outcomes are what will be *made possible* if the objectives are achieved. Outcomes are the difference that is made by achieving the objectives. An outcome is something which takes the business along the road to achieving its organisational mission. It is the outcomes of a project that really sell it to the client. The outcomes define the value of the project to the client.

A good way to start an outcome statement is:

As a result of this project the business will be able to . . .

Defining outcomes gives the consultant a chance to check the value of what is being offered to the client. Three important aspects to question are as follows.

Are outcomes consistent with aims?

Are the outcomes of the project in line with the aims agreed for the project? Is the outcome the fulfilment of an aim? Will the outcomes take the business along the road that it wants to go? Critically, will the outcomes help the business deliver its mission?

Are outcomes attractive?

Will the client business and the decision-making unit involved in bringing in the consultant recognise the outcomes as ones which are right for the business and which they desire to see happen? Don't forget, managers are not always rational. They don't always do what the consultant might see as being in the best interests of the firm. Consultants drive change and change is usually political. Different managers see the benefits of change in different ways. If there is an issue, question how different individuals and groups might see the project outcomes. One approach is to consider the different types of client involved in the project (*see* Section 6.5).

Will the client recognise the value created by the consultant?

If managers find the outcomes attractive, do they recognise the contribution the consultant is making to their delivery? Do they feel that they can achieve them unaided? If not, why not? The process consulting mode (*see* Section 6.4) can be particularly prone to leaving managers feeling that the consultant has not made a contribution, especially when process consulting is at its most effective!

11.2 Understanding your own objectives

People work together because this allows greater value to be created. In working together, they agree to the aims and objectives of a project. However, individuals will have their own personal objectives which are distinct from those of others involved in the project. Managers pursue their own interests as well as the interests of the organisations they work for and with. The consulting project is no different. The consultant will have objectives which are distinct from those of the client. This does not detract from the potential for working together. Far from it.

It is the fact that the client and consultant have distinct objectives that allows them to work together and create value for each other.

◆ Gaining a valuable managerial experience

A consulting project is an opportunity to engage in a high-profile, senior-level managerial experience. If it is to be a valuable part of an overall management education then it needs to be an experience of a particular sort. It should involve contact with senior managers. It should demand that a strategic perspective be taken. It should require that initiative and innovation be brought to bear. Formal managerial skills should be used and developed. If any of these things are missing then the value of the consulting experience will be reduced. Ensuring that the project will have these elements should be an objective for any student undertaking a consulting project.

◆ Practising particular skills

The consulting project provides an opportunity to apply in a real business situation the ideas and skills developed throughout a formal business education. It calls in equal measure on all of the skill areas that mark the effective manager: *analysis skills* which enable opportunities to be spotted, *project management* which can be used to exploit those opportunities and the *relationship-building skills* which enable the value of those opportunities to be communicated and used to motivate others. The consulting project is a chance to see that these skills are of value and to refine their use. It is a proper personal objective that the project be pursued in such a way that those skills are called on in a meaningful and balanced way.

◆ Gaining evidence of achievement

The consulting experience also provides an opportunity to demonstrate managerial ability. The skills used in consulting are transferable to a variety of managerial roles. Successfully completed, the consulting project is something which can be used to enhance the curriculum vitae when applying for positions in the future. It is something that can be related at interviews. It is a very reasonable objective to view the consulting exercise as a way of gaining real and visible evidence of managerial competence. How this can be done is discussed fully in Chapter 27.

11.3 Understanding the client's objectives

Clearly, the main objective of the client is to develop the business in a particular direction. However, this is not the client's only objective. The client may also have a number of subsidiary objectives which will colour the way he or she approaches the project. Whereas the formal objectives of the project will be explicit, discussed and documented, the client's subsidiary objectives will usually be implicit. It is worth while to develop an understanding of them. Recognising the client's subsidiary objectives gives the consultant an insight into how a good working relationship can be developed.

Some important subsidiary objectives for the client might be as follows.

◆ An opportunity to develop general understanding

Consultants are experts. Experts have interesting things to say. The manager may regard working with consultants as an opportunity to explore and develop his or her understanding of management in general and the specific management tasks he or she faces. This general understanding will develop in areas which go well beyond the bounds of the particular project.

◆ An opportunity to explore the business in general terms

Managers must be close to their businesses. Their success depends on an intimate knowledge of and a sensitivity to the details of the business they are managing and the specific features of the sector in which it is operating. However, by being so close the manager may not find it easy to stand back and view the business as a whole. It is, as the saying goes, easy to lose sight of the wood for the trees. Working with a consultant is an opportunity to redress this situation.

◆ An opportunity to talk about the business

Managers are usually proud of the businesses they work for. An entrepreneur will be very pleased with what he or she has achieved. The interest the consultant shows is flattering. The consulting project gives the manager a chance to talk about the business in which he or she is involved. This is something most will relish. It is something the consultant can use. Asking the manager to talk about the business will be the first step in building a positive relationship and engendering rapport. It will give the manager the confidence to be open and provide the consultant with the information needed to do the project well. As will be discussed in Section 22.3, rapport can be built and openness encouraged through an effective questioning technique.

11.4 Reconciling your own objectives with those of the client

In a good consulting exercise, the client and the consulting group work together as part of a team. This does not mean that the client and consultant share every objective, however. As discussed above, the client and consultant bring along their own, distinct objectives to the project. Usually these will be compatible: the client and the consultant team can agree on a set of co-ordinated actions and common outcomes which will deliver the objectives desired by both parties. Occasionally, however, there will be a misalignment and the consultant and client must negotiate the objectives of the project so that they are reconciled. This process is illustrated in Figure 11.2.

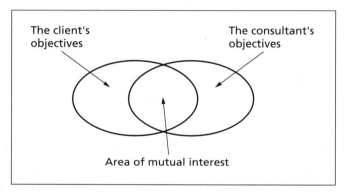

| Figure 11.2 | Negotiating objectives |

Misalignments occur for a number of reasons. Some of the most common are as follows.

◆ The client expects too much of the consulting team

The client may harbour unrealistic expectations about what the consulting team can achieve. The kind of problem which is highlighted may be of a highly technical nature. The project may require very specific industry knowledge to be applied. Often, the client will expect the consulting team to build relationships with outside agencies (particularly customers and investors) in a way which the team simply does not have the experience, or time, to manage properly.

Projects which demand that the consulting team go out and act as a sales force selling products to customers (rather than just develop and advise on a marketing or selling strategy) are examples of this kind of demand.

◆ The client expects too much of the project

The outcomes expected may be unrealistic given the resources the client is willing to put into the project. Unfortunately, whereas most managers recognise their own resource limitations, some think that consultants either have access to an unlimited supply, or are superhumanly efficient with those they have!

Typical here are market research projects. The client may be quite clear about the market information wanted but may not recognise the cost involved in gaining that information. It is not unknown for a market research company to be approached and, after its quotation has been found to be too expensive, for a consulting team to be offered the same project without resources made available. The cost of promotional campaigns may also be underestimated.

◆ The project does not have sufficient scope

It is easy for the client manager to look upon the consulting team as an additional, low-cost resource rather than as partners in the development of the business. It is tempting for client managers to hand over jobs that are important, but of low level. Such jobs may involve repetitive tasks. They will not demand that interpretive skills be brought to bear on information obtained. They will not challenge at a sufficient intellectual level. Such jobs are of such limited scope that they do not demand the full range of skills and insights that would be expected of a consulting challenge. Such jobs should really be undertaken by the business itself.

An example would be a project which involves simply creating a list of potential customers rather than developing an understanding of a new customer segment.

◆ The client is not willing to define specific outcomes

Not everybody works to objectives. Some managers simply don't bother. Others make a policy of not setting them. They prefer to deal with things on a contingency basis as they arise. They may present this as 'flexibility'. Problems will arise if the client resists setting objectives for the project. Without clear objectives, the consulting team has no idea of what to aim for. Expectations cannot be managed properly. It will be tempting for the client to simply see the consultant team as extra resource, to be called upon to do jobs that should be done by the business itself. If objectives are not set, the quality of the consulting exercise as a learning experience must be in doubt.

With a little thought, it is quite easy to deal with these situations. Some useful rules of thumb are as follows.

◆ Agree on aims before discussing objectives

As noted above, aims, because they are broad in scope tend to be less contentious than detailed objectives. It is better to agree on the overall aim of the project before moving on to specifics. If there is any debate about objectives, either within the consulting team or with the client, then the agreed aim can be used as a reference point.

◆ Break down projects into sub-projects

If the client is too ambitious about the project, or expects too much from it then expectations must be managed. Don't reject the idea for the project out of hand. Rather, get the manager to explore the project he or she is proposing. Break the project down into relevant sub-projects. It may be that one of these will present a more realistic project.

◆ Get the client to prioritise outcomes

Having broken the project down, assign objectives to each sub-project. Get the client to prioritise. If they must choose, which is most important to them? The argument to use is that it will be better for a realistic project to be done well, rather than risk disappointment at the outcomes of one which is too ambitious.

◆ Use the proposal

The proposal documents the project's aims, objectives and outcomes (*see* Section 9.2). If these are written and communicated, the client must recognise them. The aims and objectives of the project must reflect the interests of the manager. However, it is the consultancy team which will actually articulate and document them. This is an advantage which might be used positively. In the preliminary discussions with the manager it is likely that a lot of ideas will come out. In distilling these into the proposal, the consultant has an opportunity to emphasise and prioritise. Avoid the temptation to impose ideas on the client though. The latitude available here should not be used simply as an opportunity for the team to present the project they believe to be appropriate. The best projects are those to which the client has a genuine commitment.

◆ Understand the client's desired outcomes

Ultimately, it is the project's *outcomes* – the things that the business will be able to do as a result of the project – which are important. This is the difference that the project will make to the business. It is these that the client ultimately 'buys'. Emphasise the importance of this. Understand what it is that the client wants the business to do. Once this understanding is in place the project can be designed to achieve the outcomes. If the client has unrealistic ambitions then break the outcomes down and get the client to prioritise. Again, a good small project is better than a large mediocre one.

◆ Focus on win-win outcomes

Ultimately, the client and consulting team must work together. The manager will be getting insights of value to his or her business. The consulting team will be gaining a valuable learning experience. There is mutual benefit, not conflict. The consulting team should not hesitate to explain that they are seeking a project which will add to their experience in a meaningful way. The team should make it plain that the manager's knowledge and experience will be an important part of this. Most managers will be flattered that their insights are valuable in this way. It will certainly encourage them to shape the project so that it will provide a good learning experience. A general point: focusing on win-win scenarios like this is the essence of good negotiating practice.

Negotiating objectives is about aligning the project so that the outcomes desired by the client and those desired by the consulting team are achieved.

| *Team discussion point* | Read the following short case study. |

Flow Inform is a company which supplies computer models of process flow systems to the petrochemicals industry. The firm was founded in Sweden some 15 years ago as a consultancy by four academics. From the start, its products were very successful. An ability to accurately model the flow of chemicals in complex processes means managers are able to improve safety and reduce costs. The firm has grown rapidly. Turnover is now in the order of £35 million. The business has a head office in Stockholm and branch offices in the UK, Europe and America. Of the firm's 85 staff, 65 have technical expertise in chemical engineering or computer programming. The remainder are non-technical support staff. Technical staff are expected to be responsible for developing new products and marketing them to customers.

The firm is now the largest independent business in its sector. Competition is increasing, though. Some large chemical companies have set up in-house departments to develop computer models. These occasionally seek business outside the parent business. Two new independent firms have started up based at science parks with university links. Flow Inform believes it has a good competitive edge in its reputation and its ability to build new models quickly by plugging together pre-existing software modules. Flow Inform is well ahead of its competitors in the pre-written modules it has to hand.

Recently, the firm's growth has slowed. Senior managers believe the petrochemicals market is now saturated. Little growth is now expected from this core sector.

David Soames heads the UK operation for Flow Inform. Because of the North Sea oil industry, the UK is one of the business's key markets. In addition to his responsibilities for developing and marketing products for the petrochemicals industry, David has been given responsibility for identifying and evaluating new areas where Flow Inform can promote its products.

David has called in a consultancy team to help with the project. At the initial meeting he explains that he believes there are opportunities for Flow Inform's products outside its core markets and that growth will only be obtained from such new areas. He has not had a chance to explore any business sector in detail but has always felt that the water industry might be a good area to approach. He is also interested in the possibility of moving into some of the world's newly emerging petrochemical sectors, central Asia for example. At this stage, he is not sure if new business sectors or new geographic areas are the better option. He is interested in what the team have to propose and suggests a follow up meeting at which the details of the project can be agreed.

As a team, develop an aim, and a series of objectives and outcomes for the consulting project that can be used as the basis of a subsequent discussion with David Soames. The objective of these should be to stimulate a focused debate, rather than that they be a finalised programme for the project.

Summary of key ideas

◆ A consulting project is defined in terms of its *aim*, *objectives* and *outcomes*.

◆ The aim of the project is a single statement of the project's broad goal, what it aims to achieve. The aim need not be quantified or have a lot of detail. It is important that all involved in the project recognise the aim and agree to it.

◆ A statement of an aim might start: '*It is the aim of this project to . . .*'.

◆ The objectives of the project are a detailed list of the things the project aims to achieve.

◆ Good objectives are:
  – consistent: they will lead to the aim being fulfilled;
  – well-defined: they are unambiguous; they can only be read one way;
  – desirable: they will lead to outcomes all involved want;
  – feasible: they are realistic given the firm's environment;
  – achievable: they can be delivered given the firm's resources;
  – quantified: it is agreed when they will be delivered and what it will be worth when they are delivered;
  – signposted: it will be recognised when the objective has been achieved.

◆ The list of objectives can be started with the statement: '*The objectives of this project are to : . . .*'.

◆ Objectives are a call to action and to initiate a plan.

◆ The outcomes of a project are what the business will be able to do if the objectives are delivered. Outcomes are the *difference* the project will make to the client business.

◆ The statement of outcomes can be started with the phrase: '*As a result of this project the business will be able to . . .*'.

12

Project planning

The learning outcomes of this chapter are:

- to recognise the *key tasks* which contribute to the consulting project;
- to recognise how tasks might be *allocated* between team members;
- to develop a *plan* for the project with an allocated budget;
- to understand how *meetings* with the client can be made effective;
- to be able to *monitor* the project and its progression.

12.1 Defining key tasks

The objectives of a project are a call to action. They demand that a plan be put in place to make them reality. Different projects call upon a different mix of tasks. The profile of activity will depend on the nature of the project and the way in which it is creating value for the client. All consulting projects involve the same core tasks. It is around these that the project plan is constructed. These core tasks are as follows.

◆ Collecting information

Uninformed decisions are usually bad ones. One of the fundamental tasks of the consultant is collecting information so that it can be used to make decision making more effective, whether it be the decision making of the consultant or that of the client. Collecting information involves identifying its sources and then obtaining it. As noted in Section 10.2, information can be obtained from two sources. Secondary data are those which have been collected for another purpose and just happen to be useful to the project; primary data are obtained specifically for the task in hand. Secondary information can be obtained from newspaper and magazine articles, reports and company handouts. Business libraries have masses of such information. A good consultant knows his or her way around a business library and is imaginative in using it.

Primary data must be collected from source. Interviews and surveys must be carried out with key informant groups. This involves formal market research techniques. Effective consultants may or may not be competent in these techniques themselves. They will know how to brief a professional market research agency.

◆ Undertaking analysis

Information is of no use unless sense is made of it. This is the task of analysis. The term analysis covers a wide range of approaches and techniques. In essence, though, it is manipulating data so that patterns, interconnections and relationships become evident. Such manipulation may only involve intuitive insight and experience. At the other end of the scale, it can demand the application of complex numerical or sophisticated statistical techniques. Consultants may use the analysis to make decisions themselves or to present the information in such a way that the client finds it easier to make the decisions. Whatever the approach, analysis is an expert skill and one of the critical value-adding activities which the consultant can offer.

◆ Communicating with the client

Contact with the client managers needs to be sustained for two reasons. First, they are an important source of information. Second, it is crucial that a relationship be maintained with them. After all, it is they who are paying for the exercise. Communication takes a variety of forms. It may be verbal or written. It may be delivered in person or through some other medium. It is the consultant's communications that the client see. The quality of communication will dictate the client's perception of the project as a whole.

◆ Co-ordinating the project

Even a simple consulting exercise will demand that a number of people must integrate a wide range of tasks. A co-ordinating function will be needed if this is to be done effectively. At a functional level, co-ordinating involves planning and budgeting the project as a whole. At a human level it involves the leadership and motivation of team members. These four tasks are integrated. This integration is illustrated in Figure 12.1. It is from these four task areas that specific team roles are defined.

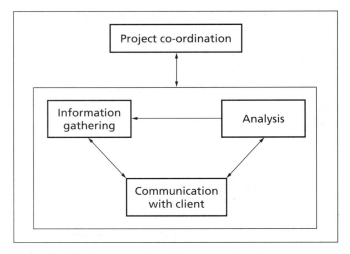

Figure 12.1   The core tasks of a consulting exercise

12.2   Individual roles for team members

The advantage of working in a team is that it allows individuals to specialise their contributions. Differentiating and co-ordinating activities is a way to make the team more effective. It also allows individuals to specialise in the way in which they want, and to develop the skills they prefer to use.

Some of the types of role the consulting project will demand are as follows.

◆ A team co-ordinator

The team co-ordinator is the individual who organises the team as a whole, who allocates tasks and ensures that deadlines and targets are met. In short, this person is the project leader. The leadership role will also demand assessment and motivation of other team members.

◆ A client contactor

As the project progresses it will be important to keep in contact with the client. This requirement will be driven by a need to get information from the client. It will also act to keep the client informed and reassured that the project is progressing. It is better if the client gets to know a particular member of the team and knows that it is he or she who they can contact. This enables a definite one-to-one relationship to be built. This relationship is the one around which the project rotates. It will be particularly valuable if there is a crisis in the project and objectives need to be renegotiated.

◆ An information gatherer

The information gatherer is the person who identifies what information is needed for the project, or who receives information requests from other team members and then finds sources of that information. When secondary research cannot provide answers the information gatherer may undertake or initiate primary research.

◆ An information analyser

The information analyser is the member of the team who takes information from the information gatherer and makes sense of it so that it can be used to support decision making. The analysis may call upon formal techniques which demand numerical manipulation (for example financial ratio analysis). The analyser can require the use of industry analysis methods (for example, those described by Professor Michael Porter in his 1985 book *Competitive Advantage*). At other times, more intuitive techniques will be used such as mind mapping and brainstorming (discussed in Chapter 15). In these cases the information analyser may facilitate the analytical creativity of the consulting team as a whole.

◆ A report writer

The final report is the physical manifestation of the project as a whole. It is the tangible thing the client is getting from the consulting team. The final report is important. It is not only a communication; it is a representation of the team as a whole. Modern word processing technology allows the report to evolve. It is not necessary to write and rewrite drafts. A framework can be laid down early in the project and the details can be filled in as the project progresses. It is useful to assign responsibility for this to a particular team member. This person will have responsibility not only for producing the report but for circulating interim drafts at intervals to get the opinion of other team members. This approach to developing the final report is expanded upon in Section 13.2.

◆ A report presenter

The final report must be delivered to the client. A good report speaks for itself. However, it can be useful for a member of the team to talk the client through it and be available to answer any questions the client may have. The report may be supported with a formal presentation. If so, a member of the team will have to prepare a presentation and lead its delivery.

◆ A team councillor

Teams are made up of individuals. And individuals occasionally come into conflict with each other. Disagreements can arise over a wide variety of issues. They may relate to the definition of objects or the management of the project. Often a conflict can arise if more than one person sees him or herself as the leader of the project. Personal issues outside the bounds of the project may complicate matters. Such conflicts are a normal part of team dynamics (and are discussed further in Section 23.4). However, such disputes need rapid resolution if the team is to work effectively. The team councillor is the person who acts as an arbiter and helps reconcile conflicts between members. In a more general sense, the team councillor will keep the whole team motivated and interested in the project, especially when the project is going through a difficult patch. Often, but not inevitably, the team councillor will be the person who has taken on the leader's role.

There is a great degree of latitude in the way in which these tasks are distinguished, formalised and allocated. Some teams will be quite homogeneous, with all members engaging in all tasks and perhaps only occasionally dedicating specific types of task. Others will operate with a high degree of formality, even to the point of having individual job descriptions within the team. A number of factors drive specialisation. Some of the more important are: the size of the team, the nature of the task the team is taking on, the expertise of team members, the longevity of the team, the team leader's style and external influences. These factors are explored in more depth in Section 23.2.

12.3 Setting a timetable

Objectives have little meaning unless it is known when they can be delivered. Setting a timetable for the project lets the client know when he or she can expect the outcomes to become available. It is also a way to set signposts so that it can be seen that the project is on track and to highlight when slippage is occurring. A timetable is the basis of effective time management (*see* Chapter 13). A good timetable also ensures that resources are used in an optimal way.

The level of detail in the timetable will reflect the complexity of the project. A simple project may only need a list of a few key events. An extensive project will require a detailed list of activities and their interconnections. At its simplest a timetable will be a list of important events and when they will be achieved. It is important to include things like an initial meeting with the client, the preparation of a formal proposal, a period for information gathering, analysis sessions with individuals and perhaps the team as a whole, regular contacts with the client and a period for preparing the final report.

12.4 Critical path analysis

Critical path analysis is a technique which has been developed to aid the management of complex projects. In essence, the technique involves identifying the critical path, the sequence of tasks that will define the schedule for the project as a whole. These tasks must be undertaken in order, and the time needed for undertaking them determines the rate at which the project progresses. Other tasks can be fitted around the critical path.

The method was developed by two American industrialists, J. E. Kelly and M. R. Walker, to aid plant maintenance in the chemicals industry. Critical path analysis has found particular favour in the management of very complex, new product development programmes, designing a new aircraft for example. In such projects, a very large number of tasks must be integrated if the project is to be achieved on time and on budget.

The method is quite straightforward. The individual tasks that make up the project are listed. The time needed to undertake the task (and if appropriate, its cost) is then assigned. The way tasks connect to each other is analysed. Particularly important is recognising when one task cannot be undertaken until another has been completed. Many tasks will not have a unique time period/cost relationship. One can be played off against another. Many tasks can be done more quickly – the term is 'crashed' – if more is spent. The relationship between cost and time is called the time–cost curve. Computer software is available to help with critical path planning.

Most consulting projects will not have the level of complexity which demands use of sophisticated planning techniques. However, a simplified version of critical path analysis can help organise the project. Figure 12.2 shows how the stages of the consulting project described in Chapter 8 are organised into a critical path. The times shown are typical.

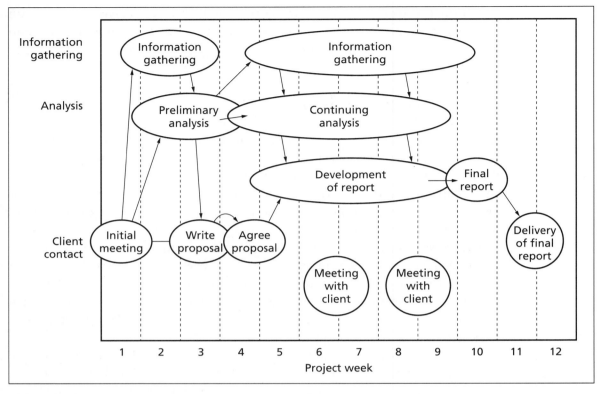

Figure 12.2 A simplified critical path analysis for a consulting project

12.5 Project budgeting

Most student consulting projects are undertaken for the experience they offer rather than as a way of generating funds. However, there will still be expenses. The client manager may make some money available to support the project, to pay for market research, perhaps.

Being able to cost and budget the project is a useful skill. Even if not used on the student project, it is a transferable skill that will be useful in the future. Broadly, budgeting means assigning expenditure in two dimensions: *over time* and by *type of expenditure*. The timescale will depend on the length of the project. Typically, weeks or months are used as the basis. The type of expenditure will depend on the nature of the project. Some of the most common categories of expenditure on consulting projects are detailed in Table 12.1. The budget has two parts. Expected expenditure is a forecast of what will be spent. This is money that must be reserved for the project. This is replaced by actual expenditure as the project progresses. Comparison can then be made. Actual expenditure is often different from what was budgeted. However, both under- and over-expenditure should be avoided. Over-expenditure means additional funds must be found. Under-expenditure means money that could have been used elsewhere is tied up.

Table 12.1 **A typical budget sheet for a consulting project**

Expenditure category	Period 1	Period 2	....	Period N	Category total
Travel expenses					
Periodical and reports					
Market research					
Telephones and postage					
Reprographics					
Period total					**Grand total**

12.6 Organising meetings and reviews

Meetings are among the most common of business communication forums. The formality of a meeting with the client will depend on the situation, the relationship with the client, the objectives and significance of the meeting and those present.

Meetings are so pervasive as a form of organisational communication that the advantages of actively managing them can be overlooked. Meetings are resource intensive. They are time consuming and can be a distraction. Dividends are available if thought and preparation are put into setting up and running meetings properly. Some key considerations are as follows.

◆ The meeting's objectives

Consider the objective of the meeting. What is it setting out to do? What will be achieved as a result of holding it? How do the objectives of the meeting fit with the objectives of the project as a whole? Are all present aware of the objectives? The project log is a good place to review these issues.

◆ Is the meeting *really* necessary?

This is an obvious question but one which is well worth asking. Might a less disruptive and time-consuming form of communication be better? The client will not be impressed by being called to a meeting he or she does not feel to be necessary.

◆ Consider who needs to be present at the meeting

Clearly, the members of the consulting team should usually be present at an important meeting. In principle, the client is free to invite who in their organisation should be present. In practice, however, they will often ask the advice of the consultant.

A balance needs to be struck. People are easily offended if they are not invited to meetings to which they feel they should have been invited. On the other hand, being asked to attend a meeting which is not relevant makes people feel that their time has been wasted. The solution is to advise the client to inform people about the meeting and explain its objectives. They can then ask those informed if they would like to attend. There will be more commitment to making the meeting successful if everybody attending has requested to be present.

◆ Plan ahead

Recognise that people are busy and diaries fill quickly. Try to give as much notice of the meeting as possible to give people a chance to plan their schedules.

◆ Consider what information will be needed at the meeting

Inform people of the information they are expected to bring to the meeting. If information is to be shared and discussed at the meeting then prepare and copy it in advance. Consider the way the information might be presented to make it easier to understand and more likely to have an impact.

◆ Prepare an agenda for the meeting

An agenda should detail the points that the meeting needs to discuss. It should be distributed in advance, along with the objectives of the meeting and indications of special information that will be required.

Make sure that the keys roles have been allocated for the meeting. These include:

1 A *chairman* who has overall responsibility for co-ordinating and guiding the meeting. This may or may not be the project leader.

2 An *opener* who has responsibility for opening the meeting and giving a short verbal presentation (which may be supported with visual stimuli) on what the objective of the meeting is and what the background issues are. This person is more often than not the chairman but having the same person take both roles is certainly not compulsory.

3 Someone to take the *minutes* of the meeting. Formal minutes detailing everything that has been said are rarely necessary unless the meeting is particularly formal. However, a short statement of the objectives of the meeting and details of the key action points decided upon (and who it has been agreed will follow them up) is useful. The minutes should be distributed to all who attend (plus other interested parties) as soon as possible after the meeting. Even if formal minutes are not required, the project log is a good place to keep personal notes on the meeting.

◆ Plan the venue

Planning the venue is the responsibility of the consulting team if they are calling the meeting at their own venue. Make sure the room is adequate for all who wish to attend. Consider seating arrangements. Get into the habit of allocating places rather than just letting people sit where they want. If you know that two people are particularly likely to come into conflict then sit them next to one another rather than opposite one another. (It is much harder to argue with someone who is sitting next to you!)

Before the meeting starts ensure that any communication tools (overhead projectors, flip charts, etc.) are available, set up and working. Are people seated so they can see them properly? A nice touch is to provide pens or pencils and paper for those attending.

◆ Maintain focus on the key issues

Meetings are a great chance for people to get together and discuss the host of issues that they have on their mind. It is easy for the original objective of the meeting to be lost and the conversation to be diverted into discussion of a variety of unrelated issues. It is the job of the chairman to maintain the focus of the meeting and ensure that it keeps to its objectives. Learn to recognise when productive discussion on one agenda point has come to an end. When this happens close discussion on it with a summary of the key points raised and move on to the next point. It is useful to have an idea of the time available for each agenda point to keep the meeting on schedule. If the discussion has drifted on to an issue unrelated to the core business of the meeting, a good way to redirect the discussion is to summarise the point being discussed and offer to take it to a separate forum. Get those involved in the discussion to agree to this. This simple device can prevent people feeling they have not been allowed to have their say.

Pre-agreement on particular contributions may also help keep the meeting on track. For example: 'Right, that brings us to the marketing issues. A, I think you had a number of points to make on that.'

◆ Involve everybody

People vary greatly in their confidence. Some people are open and extrovert. They will contribute easily and with little prompting. Other people are more introvert. They will not feel comfortable about pushing in to make their contribution. This doesn't mean to say that they have nothing to say. Far from it! The quietest people often have the best ideas. Another important role for the chairman is to ensure that space is created for everybody to contribute. Doing this involves two things. First, controlling the contribution of extroverts; second, encouraging the contribution of introverts.

These two things go hand in hand. If someone is dominating the debate, you cannot just tell that person to be quiet, not without creating a lot of ill-feeling anyway! There are a number of useful devices for handling this, such as interrupting with, for example, 'That's actually a very interesting point – how does everybody else feel about this?' or 'Thanks for raising that, A. How will it affect you, B?' The point of these interventions is to move the conversation on while leaving the dominating speaker with the feeling that he or she has made a useful contribution.

Encouraging quiet people to speak is often just a case of redirecting the conversation towards them; for example: 'What's your opinion, A?' or 'How will that affect your approach, B?' If someone is particularly nervous about contributing in meetings it may help to discuss their contribution with them before the meeting and set aside a slot within the meeting for them to make it.

It is useful here to recognise how people have differentiated their tasks within the team. If an issue comes up which will benefit from the comments of one who has taken a particular role, then use this to draw that person into the discussion.

12.7 Monitoring achievement

Good objectives have signposts attached. It is evident when they are achieved. The progression of the project towards its objectives should be monitored. Keep track of signposts and recognise when they are passed. It will be motivating to see the project progress in this way. If a signpost is missed, this should be a warning to get things moving.

A variety of time management techniques to help with monitoring the project are discussed in Chapter 13. A good place to review the achievement of objectives is in the project log. If the log is planned ahead, the points at which various stages of achievement are reached can be noted in advance.

Team discussion point	Read the following short case study.

The Manor House Restaurant is a small, but well-regarded, restaurant in the south-east of England. It has seating for 30 people and four bedrooms. The restaurant's manager, Linda Morgan, has invited in a consulting team.

The main issue, she explains, is that the restaurant is very busy at the weekend, but that it is empty during the week. Profits and cash flow would be much better if people used the restaurant outside of weekends.

Linda has a 'database' of customers (a collection of visitors' books going back five years). She has asked the consulting team if they will go through the book to analyse how often people are using the restaurant. She wants regular customers to be identified. She plans to offer them a special rate if they will use the restaurant during the week.

After the meeting, the team agree that the project is not particularly exciting. (They were expecting something more challenging than just going through old visitors' books!)

How would you approach this situation? As a team develop a strategy to negotiate with Linda and open up the project. You might consider the following:

◆ What are Linda's desired outcomes?

◆ How do these relate to the details of the project she has suggested?

◆ Can the project be broadened in a way which will work for Linda and make it a more rewarding educational and managerial experience?

Summary of key ideas	◆ A few simple planning rules can make the consulting project more rewarding and more successful.

◆ The consulting project will be managed around the key tasks of collecting information, performing analysis, communicating with the client and the overall co-ordination of the team.

◆ The team can take on individual roles based on these key tasks.

13

Time management

Learning outcomes

The key learning outcomes from this chapter are:

◆ to recognise the value of effective time management;

◆ to understand the simple rules which make time management effective;

◆ to be able to use simple systems to support time management.

13.1 The importance of time management

Time is one of the most valuable commodities a manager has. Most managers are not limited by knowledge, inspiration or even energy. They are limited by the time they have available to do things. Effectively managing time is rewarding and it is not difficult. It is largely a matter of common sense and practice. It is a good investment. Freeing up time frees up the manager to achieve more.

Effective time management is not just about doing more. It is also about *enjoying* doing things more. Managers who manage their time well are in control. It shows. They approach their jobs in a more relaxed way. They avoid panics. Indeed, they are in a good position to deal with panics created by others. Appearing relaxed and in control is an important part of demonstrating leadership.

13.2 Effective time management

Time management is more a matter of good management practice than complex systems. Effective time managers follow a series of simple rules so that they make best use of their time. With a little practice these rules can become second nature. The most important rules are as follows.

◆ Be aware of time

Don't let time catch you out! Deadlines loom up. Recognise that time is passing by. A task may seem a long way off. However, it can quite suddenly become current, especially if the project is a busy one and you are distracted. Be aware of the tasks that are coming up. If you don't have the kind of memory that is good at keeping track of what needs to be done when, a time management system that reminds you (discussed below) can be of great help.

◆ Prioritise tasks

The consulting project will demand that some tasks are undertaken before others. Some tasks will be 'bottlenecks'. If they are not done, many other things will be held up. A critical time management skill is to recognise which tasks are more important at a particular time. Importance is not an absolute. The priority of a task will change as the project progresses. A task which is of low priority can suddenly become high priority, especially if it is delaying the rest of the project.

◆ Anticipate tasks

In short: do tasks when you *can* – not when they *need* to be done. No manager can fill every moment of his or her working life. There are always periods when no job is demanding immediate attention. This is the way it should be. Having periods of low activity is part of the reward for good time management. Such periods are an opportunity. They offer a chance to anticipate and tackle jobs for the future. Assess what jobs can be undertaken now even if they are not an immediate priority. Because they are not being tackled under pressure you will do them better. You will find you enjoy doing them more.

Anticipating tasks is an investment. A task which is completed early cannot suddenly present itself as a priority. More low-activity periods are created for the future. More tasks can be anticipated. The process builds itself in a virtuous cycle.

◆ Avoid putting jobs off

We all enjoy doing some things more than others. Team working allows people to undertake a specialised role. Even so, there will still be some jobs we don't feel like doing. It is very tempting to concentrate on those jobs we like and put off those we are not so fond of. This temptation should be resisted. A job which is not enjoyable, when undertaken at ease in one's own time, will be even less enjoyable if it is done under pressure because it is a priority and can't be put off any further. The job certainly will not be done well under these circumstances.

In fact, the best tasks to anticipate are the ones you find least enjoyable. This gets them out of the way and leaves you free to take on those tasks you do enjoy doing. It will also give you time to reflect on the task. Ask why you don't like doing it. What is it about the task that you don't enjoy? Can the task be undertaken in a different way so that it is less onerous?

◆ Break tasks down

Many tasks on a consulting project can be broken down into a series of subsidiary tasks. The final report, for example, involves a series of activities. A structure must be decided for the report. This will be reflected in the contents. A management summary must be written. Diagrams must be prepared. Each of these tasks is to some extent independent of the others. If a complex task is broken down into smaller parts then it may be possible to approach that task in stages.

There might not even be a need to write the final report in one go. Modern word processing technology will allow it to evolve as the project progresses. A structure can be laid down. The body of the report can be filled in as ideas emerge. Sections can be written, and then rewritten. This will ensure that the report communicates the project findings in a professional manner.

◆ Ensure deadlines are understood

Make sure that all involved in the project are clear on deadlines. If in doubt, raise the issue. If you think others are not aware of a deadline, communicate it. Be ready to plan, discuss and negotiate deadlines, especially for non-critical tasks. Make sure that agreement is finally reached and that all are aware of that agreement.

◆ Preparation

Time when members of the project team meet with each other, or with the client, is particularly valuable. You and other team members will have other projects in progress. The client will be busy with his or her role in the organisation. In fact, the time needed to support the consulting team may be one of the factors leading to the client's resistance to using consultants in the first place. In many cases, this will be a more important factor than the consultant's direct cost.

Preparation for meetings not only means contact time is used effectively; it will also project an overall professionalism that will reassure the client. As advocated in Section 12.6, manage meetings effectively. Before a meeting, decide on the objectives of the meeting. What outcomes are desired from it? Define an agenda for the discussion and stick to it. If information is needed, ask if the client should be given notice so that it can be collated. If the client will need information, make sure it is taken to the meeting. If a detailed response is needed, send the information in advance.

◆ Support others with time management

A consulting project demands that people work together. Someone whose time management is not good can let the whole team down. Effective time managers do not just manage their own time: they help others manage theirs as well. Supporting others in this way is an important leadership responsibility.

Always make sure others are aware of deadlines. If someone is having problems with time management, advise them on how they can improve. Set objectives for learning on time management. Don't make the project hostage to poor time managers. Build in interim deadlines so that outputs can be checked before they become critical.

13.3 Time management systems

A time management system has two essential parts. First, a guide to breaking down projects into their component tasks. Second, a means of reminding when the task is due to be completed. A third part, a guide to reviewing the task, may also be included.

A time management system is easy to set up. A number of systems are commercially available. However, all that is really needed is a few ordinary items of stationery.

◆ One-page plans

A one-page plan is a flow chart which illustrates the stages of the project. Time is usually depicted along the horizontal axis. Different types of activity are defined on the vertical. For a small project an A4 or A5 sheet will suffice. For a complex project a larger sheet may be needed. This may take the form of the critical path analysis discussed in Section 12.4.

The progression of the project can be monitored as it progresses along the horizontal axis. The jobs coming up, and how they connect to other jobs, can easily be reviewed. The consequences of pushing a task back can also be seen.

◆ Tasks-to-do list

A list of tasks to do is a system which divides the project into intervals (usually weeks or days). Each interval is given a page of its own and on this page the tasks that need to be done can be listed. Some prefer to list only the major task headings. Other like to put in a great deal of detail. It is a matter of how much reminding you need. A bound diary or a loose-leaf folder can be used.

◆ Job cards

A job-card system splits the project into task types rather than time intervals. Each task is given its own card with a note as to when it should be completed. The cards can then be sorted into completed, current and to-be-done files. Blank postcards with a file box make a good job-card system.

◆ Using the project log

The project log (*see* Chapter 5) can be used as the basis of or to support effective time management. A task-to-do list can easily be added to the log. A one-page plan can be added at the front. Loose job-to-do cards can be stored in insertable plastic sleeves.

The project log not only allows you to keep track of tasks and make time management more effective. It also provides a forum for their review, thus making time management part of the active learning programme.

Team discussion point	Modern word processing technology means that the final report need not be written at one sitting. It can be evolved as the project progresses. An outline contents can be laid down and the details can be filled in as information is gathered and ideas develop. Using the team roles discussed in Section 12.2, discuss how each role can contribute to the overall development of the report. How might the logistics of this be managed? What will be the time management responsibilities of each role?

Summary of key ideas	◆ Time is one of the manager's most precious assets.
	◆ An ability to manage time makes the manager more effective, in terms of both productivity and, potentially, leadership.
	◆ A number of simple systems can be used to support time management.
	◆ The project log provides the basis for a good time management system.

14

Managing project shocks

The learning outcomes from this chapter are:

◆ to recognise the types of *problem* which might challenge the progression of the project;

◆ to appreciate the most effective *response* to make in the face of such challenges.

14.1 Types of project shock

Things go wrong! No matter how good the planning, there will always be things outside the consultant's control. No matter how good the anticipation, some events will be unpredicted. Planning is not just about defining a course of action. It is about building in the flexibility to respond to the unexpected. Some of the more common reasons why the project is knocked off course are as follows.

◆ Changes in client interests

One of the most common challenges to the project is that the client's interests suddenly change. This may be because he or she suddenly sees a new project more positively, or as having higher priority, than the one initially discussed. This can easily happen with a small, fast-growing business which faces constantly changing priorities.

◆ Changes in the client business situation

A consulting project is relevant only in that it helps the business achieve its goals. The project's aim must resonate with that of the business as a whole. If a major change in the business's situation takes place and causes it to change its overall goals, the relevance of the consulting project will change as well. The project may suddenly not be relevant at all! If the business faces particular difficulties, the priority of the managers may be to address immediate concerns. Short-term interests will come to the fore. Interest in longer-term goals and the consulting project's contribution to them may seem to evaporate.

◆ Cuts in expenditure

Even if the consulting exercise is offered on a no-fee basis, resources may have to be dedicated to supporting activities such as market research. Budget cuts are a fact of managerial life. If resources are tight the project may be targeted as having low priority. Clearly, a cut in the money available will limit the activities for which it was planned.

◆ Loss of key people

If the people contributing to the project differentiate their tasks, they ensure the value of their contribution. If they leave the project their loss will be noticed. People can move on for a variety of reasons. Within the client business individuals can be promoted or leave to join another organisation. Members of the project team can leave to join other organisations (or, if students, to take other courses). The impact of such a loss on the project will depend on the role played by the individual and the ability of the remaining members to undertake that role.

◆ Misinterpretation of information

The course plotted by the consulting project, the direction in which it aims to take the business and the tasks needed to get it there are built on the interpretation of information about the business and its environment. If this information is misinterpreted the project may lead the business in the wrong direction. Recognition of misinterpretation will then call for the direction of the project to be changed. Typical areas of misinterpretation are overestimating the resource capabilities of the business, underestimating, or missing altogether, a competitor in the marketplace and over-optimism about the potential of a market or a product within it.

Clearly, the impact of a misinterpretation on the project will depend on the information concerned and the nature of the misinterpretation. Its impact will depend on the initial assumptions made about the information misinterpreted. The potential consequences of misinterpretation can be minimised by recognising the limitations of the information available, modelling the scenarios that result from changing that information and building appropriate flexibility into the plan adopted. In short, develop a positive cynicism. Always ask: what will happen if this information is wrong? If the consequences are significant, the first step is to check the information. Second, be aware of contingency plans that can be implemented if it is incorrect.

14.2 Responding to project shocks

An effective response to a project shock is the sign of a good manager. Making an effective response to a crisis is evidence of true leadership. By their very nature, shocks are unpredictable. To manage them, consultants must call upon their experiences, insights and reserves of energy. Each shock must be tackled on its own terms. However there are a series of ground rules which make the management of a crisis effective.

◆ Preparation

Although the details of a crisis may come as a surprise, crises themselves should not. They are a fact of managerial life. A good consultant expects the unexpected. He or she is prepared to move into action when a shock hits the project. What might go wrong will have been thought through. Scenarios will have been considered. Contingency plans will have been sketched. Critically, the effective consultant is prepared to do what is necessary in order to get the project back on track.

◆ Avoid panic

Consultants have their own objectives in relation to a project. As discussed in Section 11.4, these are sympathetic to those of the client organisation, but they are different from them. The consulting team will have made an investment in the consulting exercise in order both to make it a good learning experience and to produce evidence (the proposal, the report, the log) that learning has taken place. If this is threatened, panic is a natural response. Team relationships are stretched. Recriminations take place; blame is apportioned. Such a response should be avoided. Panic achieves nothing. If the learning experience is to be salvaged, a cool, measured response is needed. Better than just avoiding panic in oneself is an attempt to control panic in others. An ability to do so is a key leadership trait.

Once the nature of the shock has been appreciated, effective crisis management demands that the following steps be taken.

◆ Refer back to aims and objectives

The first response to a project shock should be to refer back to the aims and objectives of the project. Many events will affect the tasks of the project. They only matter if they have an impact on the achievement of *aims*. Check that they will do so. Ask if the task profile of the project can be modified so that the original aims and objectives can still be achieved. If resources are cut, can a lower-resource approach offer the same, or at least satisfactory results? If the objectives are affected can they be renegotiated within the framework of the original aims? If resources are limited, can some objectives be given priority over others?

As highlighted in Chapter 11, these questions should be asked about both the client's aims and your own. If either must be modified, it will be necessary to ensure that the modification retains its compatibility to the other.

◆ Evaluation of resource implication

If the shock affects the resources available for the project, the impact of this change needs to be considered. If the resource concerned is financial, the project budget must be reviewed. This is much easier to do if a budget has been prepared (*see* Section 12.5). Activities must be modified or dropped in a way which either least affects the original aims or fits best with new ones. If the resource is a person's skills within the team, the possibility of using other people to cover must be considered. If time and resources allow, an attempt may be made to replace that person. If the person is part of the client organisation, the loss of that relationship must be considered. Ask how that person fitted into the overall profile of relationships with the client. What information was he or she providing? Can new relationships be built with others in the client organisation to replace the person?

◆ Modification of plans

After consideration has been given to the impact of the shock on the project's aims and objectives and if necessary these have been modified and resource implications have been evaluated, the next stage is to consider the implications for the project plans. Ask what tasks will be affected. How will their undertaking be affected? What about the timescale of their delivery? What knock-on effects will there be on tasks further downstream? If the aims and/or objectives are altered will new tasks be needed? Will planned tasks have to be dropped? These questions will be easier to answer if a formal plan has been developed.

◆ Communication

Ultimately, the management of a crisis depends on the effective management of communication. Don't be tempted to hide problems. Rather, draw people in and make them party to resolution of the problem. Consider who will be affected and how. Ask what ideas they might bring to bear on the problem and resources they can offer towards its solution. Be prepared to brief affected parties. Take a measured approach. Avoid both understating and overstating problems. Ensure that others are informed of all the issues. But avoid panicking them.

Above all, if there is one rule to effective crisis management, it is this: when communicating a problem try to communicate its solution as well. Or at least, open up the possibility of a solution to which others might contribute.

Team discussion point

Read the following short case study.

Argyll Chemistry is a small chemical analysis laboratory providing mineral chemical analysis to the local mining industry. It has a staff of 19. The senior management team consists of three people: Dr John Argyll, the MD, Joan Argyll, his wife, who is the finance director and Dr Paul Ohmes who heads chemical services. The fourth member of the management team, Carl Allen, has a more junior role, is relatively new and is responsible for marketing and business development. Three staff deal with administrative and office support. The remaining 12 employees are technical staff. They are grouped into three teams. Each team is headed by a development chemist who has three analytical technicians reporting to him or her.

Joan has called in a consulting team to look at the firm's business base. She is concerned about the decline in the local mining industry and believes the firm should broaden its customer base. She has put Paul Ohmes in charge of co-ordinating the project with the team.

A proposal has been developed and agreed with Paul. The main thrust of the project is an investigation of the possibility of the firm offering its services to the textile, food and paints industries who operate in the area. A small sum of money has been put aside for telephone and postal surveys. The team intend to deliver its report to Paul.

The project has gone well. Paul has taken an interest in the project and has supported the consulting team. He has introduced the team to other members of the management team. All seem to be keen on the project. The team has noted, however, that Carl is not particularly helpful. He has missed a meeting and has been slow in providing information. This has not hindered the progression of the project too much, though.

Three months after the start of the project, however, the team discover that Paul is leaving to join another firm. They contact Joan, who informs them that Carl will be assuming management of the project. The team try to contact Carl but find that he will not be available for some time.

Consider this project shock. What are its implications? What actions should the team take in order to make sure that the project progresses to its conclusion? How might different team roles (*see* Section 12.2) contribute to the resolution of the shock? You may find it helpful to consider the different types of client involved (refer back to Section 6.5).

Summary of key ideas	◆ Consulting projects can be knocked off course for a variety of reasons. Usually shocks result from changes in client interest, external events or changes in resource availability.

◆ An ability to respond effectively to a project shock is the sign of a good consultant. Key elements in a response strategy are preparedness for what might happen, a focus on the implications for the aims of the project, analysis of the resource implications and how this affects plans and communication of the issues.

◆ Good leadership in a crisis situation is characterised by a measured response, control of panic in others and an emphasis on solutions rather than problems.

Understanding the business and its potential

Developing analytical skills

15

Creative approaches to analysis

Learning outcomes

The key learning outcomes from this chapter are:

◆ to recognise importance of a *creative approach* by the consultant;

◆ to understand the basis of different *analysis strategies*;

◆ to appreciate how information may be *visualised*;

◆ to understand the different *cognitive styles* managers use to make sense of the world and the cognitive strategies they bring to bear on problems;

◆ to be able to use a variety of *creativity-enhancing techniques*.

15.1 The importance of creativity and innovation

One of the most fundamental changes in the way managers approach their tasks over the last twenty years has been the growth in the information available to them. At the touch of a button a manager can call up an amount of information it would have taken a manager just one generation ago weeks, if not months, to collect. This information can take a variety of forms: it may be numerical information, facts, opinions or items in a list.

Despite the growth in the availability of information, managers' jobs do not seem any easier. If anything they are harder. Managers must learn not only to make decisions, but also to collect, manipulate and store ever more data upon which effective decision making must be based.

Ultimately, most managers have access to the same information about the competitive world they work in. 'Secrets' are less important in business than many think. Information technology makes data on the business and its environment readily available. Numerous commercial and government organisations offer information and analysis on business sectors. Modern market research techniques can quickly identify new potential business opportunities. The Internet provides a stream of information on customers, suppliers and competitors.

Competitiveness is not so much built on *access* to data but on ability to *use it effectively*. Underpinning this is the ability to identify and adopt an appropriate analysis strategy so that data become information and information becomes the knowledge that leads to effective decision making. Analysis may call upon straightforward and familiar techniques. The simplest may be so trivial that they may not be recognised as analysis at all – the addition of sales from different product lines to produce an overall sales figure, for example. At the other end of the scale there are techniques which are extremely sophisticated and demand an intimate knowledge of their operation if they are to be used properly. Many statistical methodologies used in market research fall into this category.

Whatever the analysis technique adopted, analysis is an area where the consultant can add value. The consultant creates value by identifying the client's decision-making requirements, directing the client towards the right technique, assisting him or her in using it and helping to identify the insights it offers.

15.2 Analysis strategies

Fundamentally, analysis is about identifying the patterns and relationships that exist in data. An analysis strategy is a specific way of manipulating data so that such patterns and relationships can be revealed. Data in their raw form are not very informative. We and our minds are the product of evolutionary pressure. Our evolution has not equipped us to make sense out of rows and tables of figures. What it has done is make us good at making decisions when faced with clear verbal or visual codes. A good analysis strategy orders and organises data so that they are converted into verbal or visual codes that can inform decision making.

Most of the analysis strategies used by management consultants make use of one or a combination of the following basic approaches.

◆ Categorisation

Categorisation is a process whereby data, facts or items are sorted into different groups by virtue of their features. This allows the significance of the information to be identified. Important examples of categorisation used in management include the strengths-weaknesses-opportunities-threats ('SWOT') model and the political-economic-sociological-technological ('PEST') model used to analyse a business and its situation. Here factors which make an impact on the business are sorted on the basis of their type, making their implications clearer.

◆ Classification

Classification is also a process whereby items are sorted into different groups. This time, however, the groups are defined by external criteria rather than by arbitrary features. An example of the use of classification is Porter's generic strategy model (1980). Here, a business's strategy is defined as cost leadership, differentiation or focus. These strategies do not have simply an arbitrary relationship to each other (as do the categorisation examples). Rather, they are defined by the external criteria of competitive approach and business scope.

Porter's generic strategies are a specific example of *strategic group analysis*. This is a powerful technique which can provide an insight into the structure of an industry and the competitive environment of an individual firm. The method involves identifying the factors which characterise players in an industry and determine how they compete. These factors are then used to classify the players into different strategic groups. This technique has been used extensively to help managers understand their competitive environments and position their firms within them. A good review of the technique is that of Peteraf and Shanley (1997). Strategic groups are explored from a cognitive perspective by Reger and Huff (1993).

◆ Numerical analysis

Numerical analysis is any technique where numbers are combined in order to understand how they relate to each other. An *equation* or *function* is a 'recipe' which describes in definite terms how the numbers should be combined. Generalised instances of data are represented by symbols – called *variables* – in these equations.

The simplest form of equation is the *ratio*. In a ratio one number is divided by another so that the relative magnitudes of the numbers, rather than their absolute magnitudes, are revealed. Financial analysis uses a variety of profitability and liquidity ratios to assess the performance and stability of a firm. This is discussed further in Section 17.4. Statistical analysis uses more complex numerical relationships. It is used in a wide variety of business situations, including market research. Management science is a technical discipline which offers a highly sophisticated mathematical approach to support managerial decision making. For the student who would like to explore this avenue of decision making a good introductory text on management science is the 1994 book by Donald Plane.

◆ Association

Association is the recognition that two things are connected in some way. If two things are associated this suggests that the consideration of one thing might be made easier, or more revealing, if the other thing is considered at the same time. An example of association might be the fact that managers usually notice competitors within their own strategic group more than those in other strategic groups. Here the association is made between an organisation's presence in a strategic group and the cognitive picture of competition held by a manager from that organisation.

Association might be noticed as a result of using the analysis techniques described. It may be emphasised and enhanced by the use of the visualisation techniques described in Section 15.3.

◆ Correlation

Correlation is more precise than association. It is the recognition that the *variation* in one variable occurs in step with that of another. A correlation may be identified statistically by the measure of a correlation coefficient. A correlation of +1 indicates that the two variables follow each other perfectly and in the same direction. A correlation coefficient of 0 indicates that the two variables are totally independent. A correlation coefficient of –1 indicates that the two variables follow each other perfectly, but in opposite directions. An example of correlation might be the fact that in many industry sectors costs are seen to be positively correlated to market share. This suggests that increasing market share might in turn increase profitability. This suggests that a strategy to increase market share will increase not only sales but also underlying profitability. (*See* the review by Bourantis and Mandes (1987) for discussion of this issue.)

Correlation suggests that there *might* be a causal link between the two variables but it does not *prove* it. A good correlation is suggestive, though. It is an invitation to explore further for possible causal relationships.

◆ Causation

Causation *explains* correlation. Causation suggests that two variables are correlated because there is a cause and effect link between them. Causation provides an important insight for management, because, if a causal link exists, control of the cause will automatically lead to control of the effect.

Care should be taken in assuming the order of causation, though. Suppose that factor A is found to be correlated to factor B. It is true that A might cause B. But it is also true that B could be causing A. It might also be true that both A and B might be caused by a third factor, C. C may or may not be known. If necessary, another concept may have to be introduced in addition to the two known correlates to provide a full picture of what is going on.

The relationship between 'planning' and 'performance' provides a very good example of the problem of assigning cause and effect in management. This is particularly pertinent to us as so many consultancy exercises advocate and involve planning activity. It is a theme discussed critically by Henry Mintzberg in his book, *The Rise and Fall of Strategic Planning* (1994).

In some sectors it has been observed that there is a link between planning activity and financial performance. This is an *association*. Further, if planning is quantified as the investment of time and effort in creating, documenting and communicating long-range strategies and plans, and performance is measured as return on capital employed, then planning activity and performance vary together in a positive way. This is a *correlation*. From this it is tempting to assume that *planning* results in *performance*. This would certainly be a justification for engaging in it.

However this is only one possible interpretation of the correlation (which is of the 'A leads to B' type). It is also possible that good performance leads managers to plan (the 'B leads to A' type); or that planning and performance are the result of a third factor (the 'C leads to both A and B' type). Thus we must postulate further variables to understand the full causal picture. We can develop plausible arguments for all three scenarios.

◆ *Causal link A leads to B*. An example is: 'planning is an aid to decision making'. The argument might run as follows. Performance is improved if resource-allocation decisions are made better. Planning guides decisions about the allocation of scarce and valuable resources. Because these decisions are more effective when planned the business's performance is enhanced. On this basis planning should be encouraged.

◆ *Causal link B leads to A*. An example is: 'planning activity is a way of using "spare" resources'. The argument might run as follows. A good performance by the firm brings in resources. Managers want to use those resources. They may see planning as a way of doing so. Planning adds nothing to performance. In fact, it may be positively wasteful; it may, for example, be just a way for managers to show their ability and importance to colleagues. Planning is, in effect, an *agency cost* expended when the firm's managers can afford it. On this basis planning should be discouraged. Reducing planning may even enhance performance further.

◆ *Causal link C leads to A and B*. An example is: 'planning and performance are both the result of information being available'. The argument might run as follows: If managers have access to a great deal of information their decision making will be better, so the firm's performance will be enhanced; they may also feel that, because the information is obviously valuable, they should make maximum use of it. A good way to use it is in planning. Planning not only demands that the information be used; it is a very visible way of using it. Both performance and planning result from the availability of information.

In this case care should be taken about advocating planning activity. Planning itself does not enhance performance (information does). But this is only a 'first order' interpretation of cause and effect. A deeper analysis might reveal that planning activity does in fact influence the type of information managers seek. It might also influence the way information is used to support decision making. The caveat really shows that simple causal links are difficult to isolate in systems as complex as business organisations.

15.3 Visualising information

We often respond better to pictures than to numbers. Whereas we may not see the relationships present in a table of figures, we will immediately recognise the patterns in a visual depiction of those data. Visualisation offers an immediate representation of a field of data and the interrelationships within it. Visualisation can be used as a strategy on its own or as a supplement to the methods described above: the data may be 'raw' or they may have been generated by an analysis technique. Some of the more important means of visualisation include the following.

◆ Diagrams

A diagram is a representation which has a one-to-one correspondence with the thing being represented. In a diagram, the individual *elements* of the thing represented are depicted. They also retain a depiction of their *relationship* to each other. An important type of diagram is a *map* depicting a geographic area, or a *plan* of a site. Another type of diagram is a *technical figure*, for example that of a machine such as a car engine.

◆ Flow charts

A flow chart is a symbolic representation of a *process*. The stages in the process are represented by stages in the flow chart. The relationships between different stages can then be illustrated. Examples are the flow charts depicted in this book to represent the active learning cycle (Figure 3.2) and the consulting process (Figure 8.1).

◆ Graphs

A graph is a visual representation of the relationship between two or more variables. Graphs are very good for demonstrating trends and relationships. There are many types of graph. Most personal computer packages offer bar charts, line graphs, pie charts, scatter graphs and three-dimensional surfaces. The selection of the correct graph demands a consideration of the data, the information that is to be communicated, the demands of the audience and the impact desired.

◆ Matrices

A matrix is a visualisation which uses a compartmentalised grid to depict relationships. The grid is defined by two axes. Typically, each axis is divided into two intervals (giving four compartments) or three intervals (giving nine compartments). Such grids are commonplace in management. Important examples include the *generic strategy model* of Michael Porter, the *business expansion matrix* of Igor Ansoff, the Boston Consulting Group's (BCG) *cash-flow matrix* (*see* Hedley, 1977) and the *directional policy matrix* (DPM) developed by Robinson, Hichens and Wade (1978), three strategic planners with the oil company Shell. Another example is the *strategy process matrix* of Idenburg described in Section 20.4 of this book.

A grid is a very efficient means of presenting information in visual form. Up to four dimensions of data can be shown at once. The two axes define the first two dimensions. If a circle is used to depict an item on the matrix then the diameter (or area) of the circle can be used to depict a third. If the circle is replaced by a pie chart a fourth dimension can be included. Tony McCann (1995) has discussed why matrices are such a powerful means of information display.

Figure 15.1 gives an example of a matrix. Here a matrix is used to present important economic statistics of some Central European Countries. Three dimensions are shown. The horizontal axis represents 'wealth' (per capita GDP); the vertical axis represents foreign investment capital inflow; the size of the circle represents the country's population. The relatively large population of Poland, the high level of investment in Latvia and the relatively high wealth of Slovenia become immediately evident.

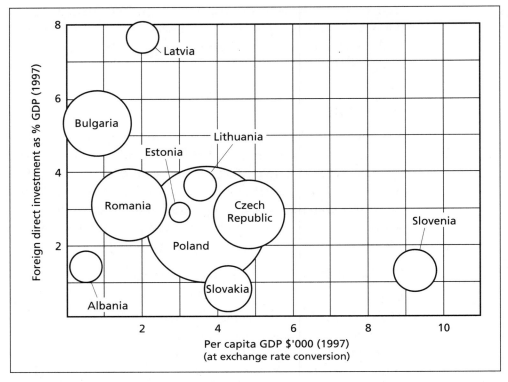

Figure 15.1 An example of information visualisation
Source: Based on data from *The Economist.*

15.4 Supporting analysis with *ad hoc* visuals

Verbal communication can be enhanced by the ability to create visual images on an *ad hoc* basis. Access to the means to create such images can enliven small group discussions. A formal presentation may be supplemented by visual images, perhaps created in response to later questions, or to expand on points already made. The means for creating *ad hoc* visuals can be a simple paper and pen, black or white boards, flip charts or blank acetates and an overhead projector.

The visual information generated has a number of functions:

◆ to act as a record of what is being discussed;

◆ to explain and explore particular points and issues;

◆ to provide a focus for and a guide to the group discussion;

◆ to summarise ideas and points of agreement.

The information in the visual image can be built up in stages and can take account of feedback from the audience. Therefore, the creation of *ad hoc* pictures is a powerful means of explaining complex issues. Some guidelines for making *ad hoc* visual communication effective are as follows:

1 Plan the image before starting.

2 Start small and in the centre of the available area, so that the image can be freely extended.

3 Build it in stages, checking the audience's understanding at each stage.

4 Invite the audience to contribute to the image.

5 If possible ensure that someone makes copies of the images and information gathered for later distribution.

Examples of the kind of visual devices that are particularly effective when created in this way are flow diagrams, mind maps, spider diagrams and position maps (discussed below).

15.5 Cognitive style and strategy

We all have our own approach to problem solving. The way in which we see the world and manipulate, process and store data about it is called our cognitive style. A manager's cognitive style will be a critical factor in how that manager works. A cognitive *style* is different from a cognitive *strategy*. Cognitive style is the fixed set of preferences an individual has for organising information about the world. A cognitive strategy is an approach selected at a particular time to deal with a specific problem. Cognitive style and strategy are important in relation to many practical considerations when dealing with and influencing other people.

Studies of cognitive style provide rigorous insights into the commonsense questions we ask when we wish to communicate with another person. For example, is that person a 'big picture' or a 'small picture' person? Would he or she want to stick to the broad view or would he or she be interested in the details? Should only the 'core' facts be presented or are the facts better located in a wider context? Should the facts to be used in an argument be grouped to reinforce one another or should they be left distinct? How might the manager be positively influenced? By a detailed logical argument or by an emotional plea? Can the manager's existing experience be called upon or should a new way of seeing things be advocated? How will he or she perceive risk? As something to be relished or something to be avoided? Will the manager make a decision now, or will he or she want to think about things for a while?

John Hayes and Christopher Allinson (1994) of the University of Leeds have written an excellent review of the work into cognitive style and its importance for management practice. These researchers identified 26 dimensions of cognitive style which have been described in the literature. The following tabulations are indebted to their review. Necessarily, this summary must be limited. The interested student is referred to the Suggestions for further reading (at the end of this book) for a full reference to this work.

I have organised the cognitive dimensions described in their study into three categories: the way in which the world is perceived, approaches to problem solving and approaches to tasks. I have done so for reasons of clarity. It must be recognised that, in practice, perception, problem analysis and task approach interrelate so such a distinction is to an extent arbitrary.

◆ The way in which the world is perceived

Table 15.1 summarises the dimensions of perception.

Table 15.1 Perception

Dimension	Description
Cognitive complexity/simplicity	Cognitive complexity refers to the number of dimensions used to categorise the world. A complex cognitive style uses a large number of dimensions to make sense of the world. A simple cognitive style uses few or even just one dimension.
Analytical/non-analytical conceptualising	Conceptualising refers to the approach taken to distinguishing items from each other. An analytical style uses distinct attributes as the basis for differentiating items. A non-analytical style uses broader relationships as the basis for differentiating them.
Levelling/sharpening	This dimension relates to the way new facts are incorporated into the cognitive scheme. A leveller tends to use existing cognitive categories to make sense of and store new experiences. A sharpener tends to set up new categories.
Incongruence tolerance/intolerance	Incongruence tolerance is a willingness to accept unusual events. Intolerance means incongruent events are not accepted. More data and confirmation may be sought in order to make sense of the incongruous.
Verbaliser/visualiser	The use of linear 'verbal' strategies for processing information as opposed to open 'visual' strategies.
Perceptive/receptive	A perceptive approach represents the tendency to process new data by adding to previously held concept categories. A receptive approach indicates a readiness to store the data in an unprocessed form.
Sensing/intuition	This dimension represents the priority given to 'actual' experience rather than feelings or intuition about it.
Thinking/feeling	This dimension has resonance with the one above. It reflects the priority given to the formal evaluation of data over emotional insights into it.
Active/reflective	This dimension reflects the preference for direct engagement in an experience rather than detached observation of it.

Dimension	Description
Splitters/lumpers	Splitters break down their experience of reality into its component parts. Lumpers group different aspects of their experience into an integrated picture.
Concrete/abstract	This is the preference for tangible objects over abstract concepts when thinking about the world.
Field dependent/ independent	This categorisation deals with the way in which background information is taken in with pertinent information. Field dependent thinkers tend to take background information into account. Field independent people focus on the essential stimuli and do not take account of background information.

◆ Approaches to solving problems

Table 15.2 summarises the dimensions of approaches to problem solving.

Table 15.2 Problem solving

Dimension	Description
Scanning/ focusing	This is the way in which information is selected as relevant to a particular problem. Scanners bring in a wide range of information. Focusers tend to concentrate on only the most immediately pertinent facts.
Converging/ diverging	This refers to the approach to a problem. Converging thinking seeks a single, correct solution using formal search criteria. Diverging thinking is broad, open and comfortable in using several solution strategies at once.
Systematic/intuitive	A systematic approach represents the tendency to work through each part of the data in turn in a sequential way. An intuitive approach 'stands back' to get the whole picture from the data.
Serialist/holist	Similar to the above. A serialist approaches problems in a sequential way, working through them one stage at a time. A holist ignores the details and tries to get a global 'fix' on the problem.
Adaptors/innovators	When faced with a problem an adaptor utilises a conventional solution, modifying it if necessary. An innovator attempts to come up with a new type of solution.
Literal-analytic/ poetic-synthetic	This is a cognitive style which relates to the use of analogies in problem solving. The literal-analytic prefer 'hard' analogies based on one-to-one correspondence. The poetic-synthetic are more comfortable with 'soft' analogies which draw on deeper and more metaphorical correspondences.
Logical/reference point reasoning	Logical reasoning demands a good survey of all available cases before conclusions are drawn. Reference point reasoning draws wider conclusions from limited experience or test cases.
Reasoning/intuitive	The preference for developing conclusions based on logical reasoning versus the preference for developing conclusions using insight and intuition.

◆ Approaches to tasks

Table 15.3 summarises the dimension of approaches to tasks.

Table 15.3 Approaches to tasks

Dimension	Description
Automatisation/ restructuring	This dimension refers to task preference. Automatisation implies a preference for repetitive tasks, restructuring a preference for new and different tasks.
Constricted/flexible control	This refers to the ease with which a manager can be distracted from dealing with a particular problem. Constricted control represents a susceptibility to distraction, flexible control a resistance.
Impulsiveness/ reflectiveness	Impulsive decision makers make quick responses. Reflective decision makers take longer to come to a decision. In general, the impulsive are quicker, but the reflective tend to make fewer errors.
Active/ contemplative	This refers to the preference for gaining insight into a problem by active involvement rather than detached contemplation and mental imaging.
Risk taking/cautious	Risk takers favour options which offer a good reward, even when they have a low chance of success. The cautious avoid any options except those with a good chance of success.

Cognitive style and strategy are important. They determine the way in which particular issues will come in and out of focus in the manager's attention and surface in the list of priorities. They underlie the way in which the manager might be convinced about a particular course of action. Effective communicators, negotiators and influencers develop an instinct for the cognitive styles used by others. They take them into account when developing relationships. Recognising another's cognitive style and resonating with it is inherent in building rapport (an idea developed in Chapter 22). Although this might look challenging, it is like any management skill, an ability which can readily be developed with practice.

15.6 Mind mapping

The first and most important person the consultant must communicate with is him/herself. The idea of communicating with oneself may seem a rather strange one. After all, we might argue, we know what's inside our own heads. In fact the contents of our minds are not just transparently available. We do not have instant access to our subconscious. In order to access our thoughts, memories and ideas we must constantly communicate with ourselves. We mentally (or even actually) talk to ourselves. We are engaged in a constant personal dialogue.

Analysis can be improved by recognising this personal dialogue and making use of it. We become more effective when we learn to actively bring up ideas from our subconscious and communicate with ourselves about them. One of the most powerful techniques for doing this is *mind mapping*.

If we write down ideas in an essay form we are constrained to a linear format. Because of the nature of writing (like speaking) one idea must follow another. Ideas are, at best, connected to two others: the one in front and the one behind. At a fundamental level, our minds do not work like this. Mentally, one idea is connected to a host of others in the form of a *semantic network*. Mind mapping is a technique which explores this network. It does not constrain concepts to be arranged linearly. Mind mapping is very well described, along with other creative techniques, by Tony Buzan in his book *Use Your Head*.

Mind mapping is a very straightforward technique to use. An initial concept is written down in the middle of a blank sheet. This sheet can be as large as is practical. Using lines and/or arrows the concept is then connected to the next one that comes to mind. The process is repeated. As the map builds, webs and branches of ideas form. Different colours or line styles may be used to relate ideas in different ways. The only rule is that there are no rules! Let your mind run away with itself. Connect ideas even if the connection does not, at first, seem sensible. Innovation comes from creating new relationships. If no new insight is obtained it does not matter. Don't forget, a mind map is a *personal* communication. There is no need to show it to anyone else if you do not want to. Once a map has been created, further mind maps can be used to rationalise and organise the ideas that develop.

By way of an example of the technique, Figure 15.2 illustrates the mind map I used to lay the foundations for this book.

15.7 Brainstorming

Though it might be undertaken as a group effort, mind mapping is first and foremost a personal creativity technique. Brainstorming is a technique which facilitates group creativity. The creativity of a group is, potentially, more than the sum total of the creativity of the individuals who make it up. By acting in concert to enhance each other's creativity a group can achieve more than individuals working alone.

To be effective, brainstorming must be organised properly. The brainstorming session should be led by a facilitator. (Perhaps, but not essentially, the facilitator will be the group leader. The person in the group who has responsibility for analysis also makes a good facilitator.) Find a room where the session can be held. There should be no disturbances. The room should have presentation facilities such as an overhead projector and acetates or a flip chart. Seating should be comfortable and informal. Everyone should be able to see the overhead or flip chart. Ideally, five to seven people will be involved. Larger groups may be used. More people means more ideas – but beware! The returns can diminish. The task of the facilitator becomes more difficult as the group becomes larger. If a large number of people can be involved it may be better to split the group into a series of sub-groups who can address particular aspects of the issue under study. Ideas may be brought together at the end using a plenary session.

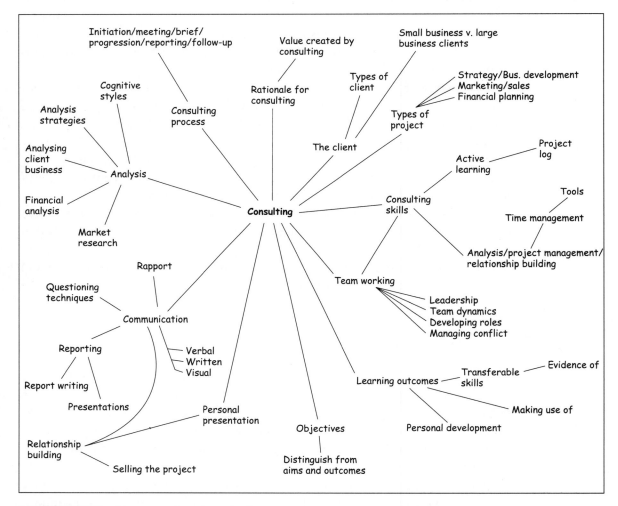

Figure 15.2 **An example of a mind map**

The facilitator should then announce the objectives of the session. This might be a statement of the concept, idea or product that is to be explored and what the session aims to achieve. Stimulus material, such as illustrations and examples of products, can be introduced at this stage.

The facilitator then invites comments, making it clear that only *positive* comments are allowed. Criticism of others' ideas is not accepted. *All* ideas are transferred to the overhead or flip chart. (The facilitator must resist the temptation to select ideas at this stage.) It is up to the facilitator to control debate, ensure that comments are positive and that the debate is relevant to the objectives. The facilitator should encourage all present to make a contribution.

When the ideas begin to dry up (usually after 20–30 minutes) the facilitator should start to draw the debate together. Key ideas are summarised. At this point criticism can be invited. Even at this stage it should be positive. Simple 'rubbishing' of ideas must be discouraged. When this criticism has been completed (again it takes some 15–30 minutes) the facilitator can draw the session to a close with a summary of what has been achieved.

It is always good practice to produce a written summary of what has been found at the session. This can be distributed to those present at the session. It is a record of the session and may encourage the submission of further ideas.

15.8 Features analysis

Features analysis is a method for encouraging innovation specifically about products and services. It can be built on both mind mapping and brainstorming methods.

The first stage is to identify a product or service or a product or service category. The product or service is then stripped down into a list of features which define it in the eyes of its users. The next stage is to manipulate this list so that insights can be gained. Some ways of manipulating features include the following.

◆ Prioritising

Ask the following questions:

◆ Which features are most important to the user?

◆ What are users willing to pay for?

◆ How does this differ between different user groups?

◆ To what extent are users willing to play off one feature against another?

◆ # Modifying

Ask what happens when features are removed, made larger, made smaller, made more obvious or less obvious, are made variable and so on.

◆ # Blending

Ask what happens if features of one product are combined with those of another. How attractive would the hybrid product look to a potential buyer?

Figure 15.3 provides an example of features analysis in the form of a mind map.

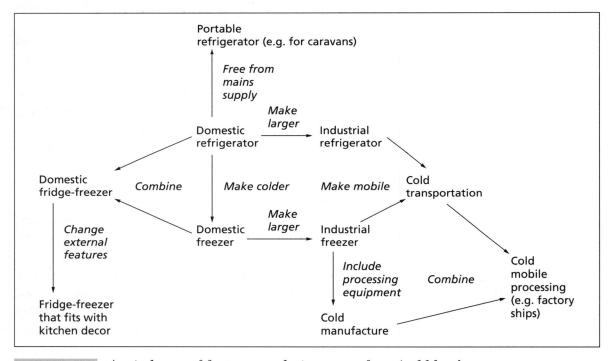

Figure 15.3   A mind map of features analysis on uses for a 'cold box'

15.9 Delphi auditing

Delphi auditing is a technique for gauging the opinion of experts on the development of some issue. It is named after the Oracle of Delphi, a famous classical Greek soothsayer to whom questions about the future could be put. The methodology was developed by O. Helmer of the Rand Corporation in 1966. Typically the technique is used to explore a development which will have an impact on the way the client business operates but about which there is little consensus. It works well with highly speculative issues. At the time of writing, the development of the Internet as a means of advertising or the impact of a single European currency on business would be good examples.

The first stage is to identify the issue to be explored. This should be thought through in detail. Ensure that the issue is relevant for the client and that it is well defined. Delphi auditing is a form of market research and has the expenses associated with market research. Recognise resource limitations: avoid being too broad in scope and ambitious in detail. A good small study is usually better than a poor broad one.

The next stage is to identify a list of people who have expertise in the relevant area. This can be easily obtained by consulting appropriate articles, papers and books. The experts selected may be academics, consultants or industrialists.

The third stage is to produce a questionnaire for the experts. The usual rules of postal questionnaire surveys apply. Make sure the questions are definite and unambiguous and will provide answers to the issues you wish to address. Be careful to distinguish between questions which demand a specific response (which can be quantified later) and those that invite general comment. General comments may need to be coded later.

For example, look at Exhibit 15.1 which presents two very different approaches to asking a question about the same issue.

Exhibit 15.1 **General and specific questions compared**

General question

> Some people have suggested that the Internet will be an important medium for advertising in the future. What are your views? Make your notes in the space provided. Please append a further sheet if necessary.

Specific question

How important do you think the Internet will be as an advertising medium, compared with other advertising media, in the future? Please indicate your views in the table below.

	Not important at all								Extremely important	
	1	2	3	4	5	6	7	8	9	10
Years from now 1										
5										
10										
20										

Don't make the survey too long. Your experts are likely to be busy people. While they will answer a short survey they may be put off by a long one. Encourage them with a covering letter explaining the project and its objectives and an offer of a copy of the survey analysis. Include a post-paid reply envelope.

Once the first survey is complete and has been analysed a follow-up survey can be used. This will present the findings of the first survey and ask the experts to comment on it (*see* Exhibit 15.2).

Exhibit 15.2	An example of a follow-up survey question

> We recently surveyed a number of experts on the impact of the European single currency on small business. It was suggested that three factors would benefit small businesses. These are:
>
> 1 reduced transaction costs;
>
> 2 predictable interest rates;
>
> 3 elimination of exchange rate fluctuations.
>
> How important do you think each of these will be? How do you think their impact on (a) manufacturing and service firms and (b) domestic sales and export sales will differ in importance?

If the issues are still unclear, then a third cycle may be included. Don't forget that a Delphi audit does not give definite answers. It is merely the best consensus of the experts selected for their views. Don't assume that the 'average' response is the one which will occur. Look at the range of responses and evaluate the different scenarios that will result.

*Team
discussion
point*

The information in Table 15.4 relates to businesses in the chemicals sector. It has been collected using the Internet.

Your team has been called in by a manager from Danay. She has asked how strategy in the sector affects performance. Develop a visual representation to make the relationship apparent.

Table 15.4 Businesses in the chemicals sector

Firm	Annual sales (£m)	Growth (5 yr av.).	Profitability (ROCE %)	Product types	Sales base
Gigachem	5000	5	12	Wide range	International
Foodprod	30	10	10	Food additives	UK
Allchem	3500	6	7	Wide range	International
Bioadd	2	32	15	Specialist	Europe
Pharmchem	50	13	11	Pharmaceuticals	UK
Engomat	35	10	10	Engineering products	Europe
Specmat	5	30	20	High purity	Europe
Vorchem	1025	−4	5	Wide range/low cost	International
Marlube	507	−5	11	Lubricants	Europe
Monolay	54	3	21	Surface coatings	UK
Everon	5	10	16	Biotechnology	Europe
Danay	10	8	18	Biotechnology	UK
Emaprod	1502	6	5	Wide range/low cost	International
Vormadol	42	10	14	Lubricants	Europe
Gusta	15	−2	12	Food products	Europe
Drugserv	25	10	14	Pharmaceuticals	Europe
Coatex	150	7	12	Surface coatings	Europe
Megachem	4502	6	6	Wide range	International

*Summary
of key ideas*

◆ Business success is not dependent only on having access to information. It is also based on using it to create new insights and spot new opportunities.

◆ An analysis strategy is a means of manipulating data so that patterns and relationships can be revealed. Important elements of an analysis strategy include using categorisation, classification and numerical analysis followed by identifying associations, correlations and causal linkages.

◆ A good way to reveal patterns and relationships in data is to visualise it. Important visualisation techniques include diagrams, flow charts, graphs and matrices (grids).

◆ All managers have their own cognitive style, which influences the way they see the world, and their own cognitive strategy, which influences the way they identify with information, process it and use it to tackle problems and tasks. An understanding of cognitive style and strategy can help with the development of communication and can influence strategies.

◆ A number of techniques can facilitate individual and group creativity. Particularly useful to the consultant are mind mapping, brainstorming, features analysis and Delphi auditing. These may be supported by *ad hoc* visuals.

16

Problem definition

Learning outcomes

The learning outcomes from this chapter are:

◆ to recognise the *rational*, *cognitive* and *political* dimensions of a business problem;

◆ to understand how a problem may be *defined* to make it amenable to resolution.

16.1 Evaluating the problem

Consultants are usually called in to the client business in order to address some 'problem' the business has, or at least that its managers perceive it to have. The problem will be defined as a limitation on the business, as something that stops the business reaching the potential that it 'naturally' has. The word problem has a negative connotation. To a consultant and the client business a problem may actually be *positive*. A problem might well be an *opportunity* the business could potentially exploit as much as an issue which restricts the business.

Problems do not present themselves. They are identified by the firm's managers. Managers interpret problems and decide to address them. A problem has three facets which determine the way in which it will be understood and acted upon by managers (*see* Figure 16.1). We may label these the *rational*, the *cognitive* and the *political*.

The *rational* facet refers to the way in which the problem is seen in a logical manner. It reflects a formal or semi-formal evaluation of the way in which resolution of the problem might affect the business. It will be based on a dispassionate consideration of the economic 'value' or cost of the problem and the business's capability to deal with it or, if it is an opportunity, to exploit it.

The *cognitive* facet refers to the way in which individual managers see a problem. It reflects the way in which the problem is processed by a manager's mental faculties. Cognitive style and strategy (considered in detail in Section 15.5) determine the way in which managers see the world, process information about it and deal with challenges. The manager's cognitive style and strategy will influence the way in which the problem appears in the manager's mental landscape and determine the priority the manager will give it.

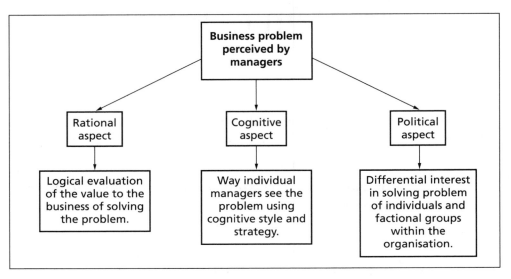

| Figure 16.1 | The facets of a business problem

Ultimately, the problems that a firm faces must be dealt with by the business as a whole. The *political* facet reflects the way in which a problem is received and processed by the individuals who make up the organisation. Not all managers have the same objectives. Different individuals and groups have different interests. A particular problem will affect different managers in different ways, and some more than others. Some issues may be problems for some managers and opportunities for others. These differences will affect the way in which the managers work together as a team to address the problem. Ultimately, if the organisation's politics become pernicious managers may actually work against each other.

The sensitive consultant recognises each of these facets. The rational is important because it determines the value the consultant can create by resolving the problem. The cognitive is relevant because it affects the way in which the consultant communicates with the client and can positively influence him or her. The political is significant because the success or otherwise of a project will depend on getting the whole organisation to see the benefits of a particular course of action and to unite behind it.

Four dimensions of a problem will be relevant to its definition. These are the *current situation* of the business, the *goals* of the business, that is the state it aspires to achieve, the *assistors*, things which help the business achieve its goals and *inhibitors*, those things which limit the firm and stop it achieving its goals (*see* Figure 16.2).

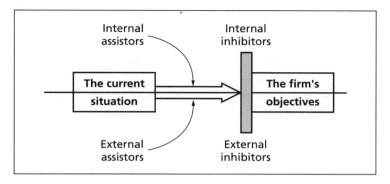

Figure 16.2 Framework for analysing business problems

Assistors and inhibitors may be both internal to the firm (that is, under the direct control of the firm's managers) or external to it (that is *not* directly under the control of the firm's managers). Some important assistors and inhibitors are listed in Table 16.1.

Table 16.1 Assistors and inhibitors

	Internal	*External*
Assistors	Cost advantages (scale/experience) Unique resources Innovative products Knowledge of products Knowledge of markets Business location (especially for distributors)	Relationships with customers Investor's goodwill Location in business network Expanding market potential High profit margins
Inhibitors	Lack of management experience Lack of capital Lack of knowledge about products Limited knowledge about the environment	Limited market potential (market decline) Competitor activity Changes in customer interest (particularly for fashion-sensitive products) High entry costs

The challenge for the consultant is to define the business problem in the following terms.

◆ How can assistors be used and developed to achieve the set objectives?

The key issues in relation to assistors are how the business can capitalise on internal assistors and how the firm's managers can take advantage of external assistors. It is important to ask whether the problem can be so defined as to enable managers to take control of external assistors and bring them in, in effect, to turn external assistors into internal assistors. An example is taking control of customer demand through an effective marketing campaign. Here the external assistor of customer goodwill is converted into an internal assistor of marketing capability.

◆ How can inhibitors be overcome or avoided so that the business can move forward?

Inhibitors limit the business. An internal inhibitor is the responsibility of the firm's managers. It is they who must take the initiative and address the problem. The priority given to this will depend on the business's plans and the significance of the inhibitor. An external inhibitor is a given. It is outside the control of the firm's managers. The firm must develop strategies which take account of the external inhibitors in the environment and avoid their impact. For example, a lack of knowledge must be addressed through organisational learning. Sectors in which competitors (especially stronger competitors) are active should be given lower priority than those in which absence of competitors creates an opportunity.

A problem is best defined in relation to these four facets. They can be used to guide investigation of the problem and to specify the information that is required in order to define it. This framework works well as the basis of a brainstorming session. This is best undertaken with members of the consulting team and with key information providers from the client business.

16.2 Reinterpreting problems as opportunities

Problems, by their very nature, are negative. They demand to be solved, but they do not inspire. Opportunities, on the other hand, are positive. They call to be exploited. Problems, especially when their resolution is difficult, tend to be divisive. Managers may work at devising solutions. However, energy will also be diverted into avoiding recrimination. After all, a problem is 'internal' to the business. It must have been caused by someone, somewhere. A problem is someone's *fault*. Rather than solve the problem, a manager may think it a better strategy to ensure that someone else gets the blame for it. This is a self-defence mechanism. Problems get caught up in the internal politics of the organisation and can exacerbate them.

An opportunity, on the other hand, is external to the firm. It comes from 'outside'. It is there to be exploited. It is not anyone's fault. Managers will resist identification of problems. They will minimise them or even deny their existence. On the other hand, they will queue up to take credit for identifying an opportunity. Managers can rally round and work together to take advantage of an opportunity. In general, people are constrained to deal with problems; they are motivated to capitalise on opportunities. For these reasons it is better, whenever possible, to talk about taking advantage of opportunities rather than addressing problems.

In many respects problems and opportunities are the two sides of one coin. It depends on whether one looks towards what has been achieved from the perspective of what might have been achieved or from the starting-point. Translating one to the other is often a matter of rhetorical approach. The old adage of the half-filled glass applies: is it half-full or half-empty?

For example, a new product launch has not gone as well as expected. This is a problem – the return on the investment is not as good as expected; on the other hand, it represents an opportunity to understand customer demand better and come up with an improved product. A competitor moves into a market. This is a problem – it will increase competition – but it confirms that the sector is an attractive one for the player who can get it right.

A word of caution is in order here. Although it is better, for the reasons given, to talk about opportunities rather than problems it is important to be realistic. Too much emphasis on the positives can make someone seem glib and unable to come to terms with the real world. People may begin to doubt the decision-making ability of the person. If the person cannot see the problem then how can his or her decisions address it? If the person does not allow him or herself to talk about problems then this limits the call to action he or she can make to others. Further, individuals who tend to see problems rather than opportunities (and this is to some extent a part of the cognitive perspective discussed in Section 15.5) may feel that their concerns are being ignored by those who emphasise the positive.

Turning problems into opportunities – negatives into positives – should not be a mantra; it should be a tool used as part of an overall communication strategy. It should not be used to deny problems, but to put them into context. Revealing the opportunity makes the problem seem tractable and tackling it even enjoyable.

It also takes the sting out of responsibility (real or imagined) for the problem in the first place.

Read the following short case study.

Exconom is a company specialising in cable and small bore pipe laying technology. The company started life as a technical division of a major utility. It gained its independence as the result of a venture capital backed management buyout (MBO) three years ago. The company now has 21 employees and a turnover of just over £4 million. The company's competitive edge comes from its technological capabilities with 'mole' excavating tools. This is equipment that can lay cables and pipes underground without the need to dig a trench first. This reduces cost and disruption. Exconom contracts its services to companies which need to lay cables. Electrical and gas utilities provide the core of business. This business is largely based on historical relationships with these customers. Marketing activities are limited. An as yet small, but high-growth sector which is expected to be important in the future is cable television though the company has not won any contracts here yet.

The company is run by four managers who led the management buyout. Three had long careers with the company and held senior positions before it was bought out. They undertake the personnel, finance and engineering functions. The fourth manager, Alan Romer, undertakes the marketing tasks. Alan joined the management team at the time of the buyout and made a capital investment in the venture. He has extensive experience in marketing engineering products. He was invited into the MBO team after the venture capitalists supporting the buyout suggested that they should enhance its marketing expertise.

Alan has called in a consulting team to help him with a project. He says that he wants the team to identify, and quantify, the value of opportunities for the business in a number of new areas. The team question him about the business and its abilities.

Alan explains that the business is sound and has a lot of potential for the future. However, the rest of the management team are limited in their ambitions. While they talk about the business moving into new areas, in practice they resist practical moves. They prefer to stick to the business applications they know and understand. The attitude tends to be one of not taking unnecessary risks while the company is under the 'control' of venture capitalists. In fact, Alan explains, although the venture capitalists will see a reasonable return on their investment (they have a five-year exit plan) they are a little disappointed that the company has not grown as much as initially suggested by the original business plan.

So far, Alan has argued for diversification of the customer base on an ad hoc basis in meetings. This has not really worked. Now he wants to put forward a proposal in the form of a cohesive plan. He wants the team to undertake the research necessary to develop this plan. His brief includes the comment that the management team tend to focus on details. They will only make a move if all implications have been considered. If he is to get his plan implemented he will need a lot of reliable information which makes the opportunities clear and unambiguous. Also, the emphasis should be on why the company's technology will work in the new application and will be attractive to customers.

Alan also mentions in passing the fact that he has heard of a couple of new companies in the sector using the same technology as Exconom. He would be interested in anything the team can pick up on these competitors.

As a team analyse the problem presented by the client. Can Alan's problem(s) be presented as opportunities?

Summary of key ideas

◆ The problem a consultant has been called in to address has three facets:

- the *rational*: the value the resolution of the problem will create for the business;

- the *cognitive*: the way the problem is perceived by individual managers;

- the *political*: the way the organisation as a whole reacts to the problem and the impact it (and its resolution) will have on different individuals.

◆ The consultant must be aware of each of these facets.

◆ When defining the problem it is useful to consider four dimensions:

- the *current state* of the business;

- the *desired goals* of the business;

- *assistors*: those things which will help the business achieve its goals;

- *inhibitors*: those things which will restrict the business and stop it achieving its goals.

◆ Assistors and inhibitors may both be further divided into internal and external dimensions. Those that are *internal* are part of the firm and are under the control of managers. Those that are *external* are given by the environment and must be accepted by managers.

17

Auditing the client business's capabilities

Learning outcomes

The learning outcomes from this chapter are:

◆ to recognise the basis on which businesses build their success;

◆ to be able to use a range of analysis techniques to audit the business and its environment;

◆ to use these techniques in order to recognise strategic options for the business.

17.1 The strategic capabilities of businesses

There are a number of ways in which business strategy can be defined. At one level, a strategy is simply the consistency of the actions the business takes, the fact that it sells a particular range of products to a definite customer group. Henry Mintzberg describes this as the 'pattern in the stream of actions' (Mintzberg, 1972). In this respect *all* businesses have a strategy of sorts. At another level, a strategy is the way in which the business will compete and beat its competitors. It is the way in which it develops an edge in the marketplace. Ultimately a strategy must dictate the way the business behaves, it must become a plan – a 'recipe for action' to succeed in the marketplace.

A firm's competitive advantage is the basis on which the performance of the business is built. A competitive advantage is something:

◆ which the firm *possesses*;

◆ which creates *value* for its customers;

◆ in a way which is *unique*; and

◆ which customers find it difficult (or at least expensive) *to imitate*.

Professor John Kay in his 1993 book, *The Foundations of Corporate Success* has developed a framework in which the competitive advantages of business are classified into four basic approaches. These are *strategic assets* (including lower *costs*), *reputation, innovation* and *architecture*.

◆ Strategic assets

Strategic assets may be defined as things which the firm possesses which give it an advantage in the marketplace. Kay identifies three main types of strategic asset. The first is a *natural monopoly*, that is, being present in a market which, by its very nature, will only accommodate a single player. The second is the support of *government* through legislation or other restrictions. These should be picked up on with the PEST analysis discussed in Section 17.3. The third type of strategic asset is *cost advantages* which have been accrued by having a presence in a market. These represent entry costs which deter new entrants. Cost advantages are particularly important and will now be examined in more detail.

◆ Costs

Customers look for *value*. This is not the same as *price*. Value is the benefits a product or service offers in relation to its price. All businesses must keep control of their costs. Only in this way can they keep their prices competitive and their profit margins sufficient to reward stakeholders and continue investment. Not all firms compete on price. Many, if not most, actually distinguish their offerings from those of their competitors to make them more attractive to a particular customer group. Because they do this the customers look for value rather than price.

Some businesses find it hard to differentiate their products. Such products are called *commodities*. In buying these the customer will look for lowest price. The most competitive business will be the one which has the lowest costs. Costs are related to output. Costs tend to fall as output increases through two mechanisms. *Economies of scale* arise as fixed costs – overheads – are diluted over greater output volumes. *Experience curve effects* drive down costs as practice – experience – in producing the output is gained. This experience allows the product to be produced more efficiently. Economies of scale are related to output in a particular period. Experience cost reductions are related to the total output accumulated over the firm's history.

Because of these effects the firm with the lowest costs is usually the one with the greatest market share. If it is not the largest player, then it must have access to a significantly different production technology. Commodity markets are usually characterised by a small number of large firms. Because they cannot drive down costs small firms find the going tough.

It has been argued that there is no such thing as a commodity: that any product can be differentiated from its competitors if a sufficiently imaginative approach is taken. This differentiation can be in the product itself or in the service aspects of its delivery. One thing consultants will often recognise when analysing a problem presented to them is that the business can enhance its performance by distinguishing its offerings from those of competitors. One means of differentiation is through market positioning, an idea discussed in Section 17.6.

◆ Reputation

Organisations are made up of individuals who form relationships with each other. Relationships can be used to build up *trust* and trust can be a source of competitive advantage. Trust is valuable because it lowers costs. If two people, or businesses, working together expect that the other party will renege on the deal, they must invest in monitoring each other. Expensive contracts must be set up. These must be policed. If the two trust each other these expenses can be avoided. One of the best ways of building trust is for two parties to work with each other over a long period. This may be through a partnership or, ultimately, as part of the same organisation. If firms are willing to invest in a relationship then any move to another firm at a later stage may result in an expense – a *switching cost*. The presence of this switching cost stabilises the relationship.

An important aspect of relationship building is *reputation*. A good reputation is an invaluable business asset. It attracts customers. A good reputation takes time to build up. It can be lost easily. Reputation may be encapsulated in a *corporate image* or *brand name*. These things need to be managed professionally. Consultants are often called upon to offer advice on the creation and maintenance of this reputation.

◆ Innovation

One of the sure ways to business success is to offer the customer a product that is both attractive and unique. The way to such products is through *innovation*. Innovation is a process. It has three essential stages. First, the *needs of customers* have to be understood at a deep level. Second, those needs must be translated into a product or service *concept* that can address them. Third, that concept must be made into an *actual* product or service and marketed and delivered to the customer. In some cases it may be possible to protect an innovation with a legal device such a patent, copyright or registration. If this can be done, the business will gain a localised 'competitive' monopoly.

The consultant can add value at each of the three innovation stages. An understanding of the customer's needs is something that can be gained through market research. Using that information to come up with new product ideas demands individual and group creativity. This creativity can be facilitated by experts. Designing and producing the product (or the service delivery process) needs technical expertise which may require to be supplemented. Many businesses, especially young, high-tech ones, are very effective at innovating. They may not be so sound in their marketing, that is, in informing customers about the product and positively influencing their buying behaviour. In such a case the consultant can fulfil an important *complementing* role, as described in Section 6.2, by providing that marketing expertise.

In sum, innovation is an organisational process. Effective innovation demands that the whole organisation works together to understand the customer, create ideas and turn them into reality. Making the business an innovational organisation demands organisational development and change. Again, this is a process that can be enhanced with the inputs of an effective consultant.

◆ Architecture

Kay defines architecture as the network of distinctive internal and external relationships which define the organisation. These relationships give the business a capability through the way in which it does things. Architecture can be used to lock in suppliers and customers and so reduce competitive pressures. It can encourage customers and suppliers to work together, so facilitating innovation and greater value creation along the whole value chain. Architecture is manifest through both organisational *structure* and organisational *processes*. Structure is the fixed set of relationships that define the organisation, process the way in which people interact through those relationships.

One aspect of architecture that is of particular interest currently is *organisational learning*. Clearly, a business that learns from both its successes and failures is one which is going to be more effective. Yet such learning is not automatic. A business must actually *learn* to learn. It must understand the knowledge it has, how that knowledge is stored, processed and used. This is an organisational development challenge that can often be better met with the insights and help of an outsider. Practical means to encourage continuous learning about markets, for example, is discussed by George Day (1994).

17.2 SWOT analysis

The *SWOT audit* is perhaps the most fundamental of strategic analysis techniques. SWOT is an acronym standing for 'strengths, weaknesses, opportunities and threats'. The SWOT analysis provides the consultant with a concise and comprehensive summary of a business. It offers an immediate and accessible insight into the capabilities of the business and ways in which it might use them. The terms refer to the features of the business set out in Figure 17.1.

Strengths	Weaknesses
Things under the control of managers which will help the business achieve its goals.	Things outside the control of managers which will hinder the business and prevent it from achieving its goals.
Opportunities	**Threats**
Things under the control of managers which will offer it a means of achieving its goals.	Things outside the control of managers which will hinder the business and prevent it achieving its goals.

Figure 17.1 SWOT features

Typically, a SWOT analysis will identify 10–15 each of strengths and weaknesses and 5–10 each of opportunities and threats. If fewer are identified, it is likely that things are being missed. If more are identified it is likely that there is some repetition. The SWOT analysis can be generated through a brainstorming session. It can also be used to keep a summary of features identified by other analysis techniques.

17.3 PEST analysis

The *PEST audit* is a framework for evaluating the environment in which the business operates. PEST, like SWOT, is an acronym. It stands for 'political, environmental, sociological and technological'. The audit is sometimes referred to as the *STEP* (in which the same terms are used, but in a different order). The PEST factors are as follows.

◆ Political factors

Political factors are those that relate to governance and the attitudes of government agencies. Look for political favour and disfavour, influence with government, lobbying and potential new laws which may give or take away legislative monopolies or change the conditions under which trading will take place.

◆ Economic factors

Economic factors are those that relate to the overall economy. Look for growth in economic wealth (GDP) and its distribution in relation to customer groups. Consider the effects of economic booms and recessions. (These are not always negative, as discounters tend to do well when overall wealth is falling.) Other important factors include the impact of interest rates (which make borrowing more expensive) and exchange rates. A strengthening of a currency makes imports cheaper and exports more expensive. Exporters are hit when a currency strengthens, importers benefit. A weakening of the currency has the reverse effect.

◆ Sociological factors

Sociological factors are those that relate to the societal development of buying groups. Look for changes in social trends and attitudes which will affect consumption. Broad trends include population changes, increasing overall wealth and the fragmentation of tastes. Long-term processes such as globalisation and the integration of the world's economies should also be considered. Medium-term processes such as demographic changes will also affect markets. Short-term trends such as fashions and fads can be very important to some categories of product.

◆ Technological factors

Technological factors are those that relate to the knowledge used in the design, production and delivery of outputs. Technology is continually changing. New products are constantly being developed and existing ones are redesigned. Computers have revolutionised design, as robotics have manufacturing. Telecommunications are creating new opportunities for the way in which services are delivered. These are broad technological trends which will have an impact on every business in some way or other. Each industry and sector has its own 'proprietary' technological base where the effects of technological developments are localised. Look for things which might affect production, especially in the way it allows more value to be offered to the customer or costs to be lowered.

Developing an understanding of PEST factors can involve a degree of specialist expertise, particularly in understanding the technological factors. Effective consultants do not always aspire to gain such expertise. It is impossible for them to do so if the consultant wishes to offer his or her services across a range of different sectors. Rather, the good consultant develops a way of communicating and working with experts and tapping into their expertise. One way of doing this is to use a Delphi audit, as discussed in Section 15.9.

17.4 Financial analysis

The financial situation of a firm is fundamental. The health of a firm's finances is not just an indication of how successful its competitive approach has been in the past. It is also an indication of the resources it has available to reward its stakeholders and to invest in new projects. In making an evaluation of a business, its performance and its potential for the future the consultant must be cognisant of its financial situation.

Finance and accounting are disciplines in their own right. They have some highly technical aspects. They are areas which have their own experts. A lengthy review of accounting, auditing and financial analysis is out of place in this book. These issues are covered extremely well elsewhere. All that is necessary here is to outline the principles of financial analysis and give a flavour of the approach to analysis which is important to the consultant.

Businesses are required by law to keep accurate records of their income and expenditure and to produce accounts. The complexity of the accounts needed will depend on the business and its legal status. They are quite straightforward for a small sole trader. They are extensive and complex for a publicly quoted multinational. Accounting practice varies to some extent between different countries. However, the principles behind all company accounts are the same.

There are two fundamental financial documents: the *balance sheet* and the *profit and loss account*.

◆ The balance sheet

The balance sheet is a statement of what the firm owns (its *assets*) and what it owes (its *liabilities*). The balance sheet represents a snapshot in time. It is a statement of what is owned and owed at the time the balance sheet is produced. Accounts usually have two balance sheets (or the balance sheet quotes two columns of figures), an *opening set* and a *closing set*. The closing set is for the date of the balance sheet, the opening set for an earlier point in time (usually one year earlier). Comparison between the two gives an indication of the changes in the firm's assets and liabilities over the period.

There are various sorts of assets. They are usually classified in terms of *liquidity*: that is, how easy it is to convert them to cash should the need arise. *Tangible assets* are things which have a physical form. They include things like buildings and machinery. These are normally considered to be less liquid than any *stock* stored by the business. Stock is those things which the firm normally exists to trade in, or materials which can be converted into stock. The most liquid assets are cash and investments held by the business, as well as any debts owed to the business. (Care needs to be taken in respect of 'bad debt' which cannot be called in.) Assets that could, in principle, be turned into cash within one year are called *current assets*. Current assets are normally taken to be cash, liquidisable investments, stock and outstanding debts owed to the company.

Intangible assets are things which do not have a physical form but which may, potentially, be sold. Important examples are brand names, copyrights and patents.

Liabilities are things to which the firm has access but which (technically at least) it owes to outside parties. Liabilities are of two sorts. *Short-term liabilities* are due for settlement within the normal accounting period, usually one year. *Long-term liabilities* are due for settlement after that. The key liabilities are *debts* owed to creditors (suppliers, including employees), *interest* owed to those who have lent to the company, outstanding *tax* owed to the government and *dividends* due to shareholders.

As it is the shareholders who actually own a company, they own the difference between its assets and its liabilities. This difference is included in the balance sheet as *shareholders' funds*. It is included as a liability so that the two halves of the balance sheet are equal – so that they actually balance.

◆ The profit and loss account

The *profit and loss account* is a statement of the trading activity of the business over a period, again usually one year. It relates to the income and outgoings of the business. *Income* is the revenue gained from normal trading activity, that is, sales. Exceptional income from sources which do not represent normal trading activity (for example, investments) will also be included but will be indicated separately in the accounts. *Outgoings* are the expenditures on those things that are needed to keep the business running. Immediate costs are for raw materials, productive equipment and services and salaries. Together these immediate costs are known as the *cost of sales*. Other expenditure is on paying the *interest* on loans, *tax* to governments and *dividends* to shareholders.

The difference between income and expenditure is the *profit* generated by the business. Different types of profit are quoted after the deduction of different types of outgoings. These are described in Table 17.1.

Table 17.1 Outgoings and profit

Total income minus	Equals
Cost of sales (raw materials + production salaries + production services + depreciation)	Trading profit
Distribution costs (distribution materials + distribution salaries + depreciation on distribution equipment) plus *Administrative costs* (overheads + all other costs not disclosed elsewhere)	Operating profit
Interest on loans	Profit before tax (PBT)
Tax to government (national and local)	Profit after tax (PAT)
Dividends to shareholders	Retained profits

The different levels of expenditure included in the profit and loss account give an indication of the *cost structure* of the business.

◆ Financial ratios

The figures in the balance sheet and profit and loss account do not, in themselves, offer a full picture of the firm in relation to its competitors and its sector. What is important is how they relate to each other. The figures are related to each other through *financial ratios*.

Financial ratios fall into three types. *Performance* (or *operating*) *ratios* measure how well the firm is using the resources it has to hand. *Financial status ratios* measure the stability of the business and indicate how well it could weather a financial storm affecting income or expenditure. If the business is quoted and trades shares in a market, then *stock market ratios* give an indication of its performance as an investment vehicle.

The key performance ratios are those which relate to profitability. This may be measured in two ways. The first is the profit margin, the ratio between profit and total sales.

Profit margin = Profit/Sales

Different profit margins use different profit lines (such as operating, PBT, PAT, as outlined in Table 17.1).

The most fundamental measure of performance is *return on capital*. This is not just profits but the profits generated in return for the money being used. Two capital return ratios are used.

The *return on capital employed* (ROCE) gives an indication to managers of the profits they are generating for the money they are using. It is defined as:

ROCE = Operating profit/Capital employed

where capital employed is usually defined as total assets minus short-term liabilities.

The second capital return ratio is *return on equity* (ROE), which is of interest to investors. It indicates the way in which an investment in the firm is generating a yield. It is defined as:

ROE = PAT/Shareholder funds

Two financial stability ratios are particularly important. The *debt ratio* measures the balance between equity capital provided by investors and loan capital provided by lenders. This is defined as:

Debt ratio = (Long-term + Short-term debt)/Capital employed

This ratio is important because interest on debt must be paid, whatever the business's performance whereas a dividend payment is based on performance. If the company has a high debt ratio then it may face cash flow problems if profits are squeezed.

Interest cover is a measure of how much 'room' the profits give to pay off interest on loans. It is defined as:

Interest cover = Operating profit/Interest owed

Two ratios are used to measure the *liquidity* of the firm. Liquidity is the ability of the firm to pay off its debts at short notice were it to be asked to (say if it were to go out of business and be broken up).

The *current ratio* measures the extent to which short-term or current assets can be used to pay off short-term liabilities. It is defined as:

Current ratio = Current assets/Current liabilities

The *quick ratio* (also known as the *acid test*) is a much tougher test. It is a measure of a company's ability to pay off its liabilities *immediately*. It does not allow stock to be included as a liquidisable asset as it may take some time for stock to be sold. The remaining *liquid assets* are cash, liquidisable investments and debt owed to the company (after allowing for bad debts that might not be called in). It is defined as:

Quick ratio = Liquid assets/Current liabilities

Stock market ratios are of interest to investors. They give an indication of how well a firm's stock (its shares) are performing as an investment opportunity. They can be used to help with the decision to buy or hold or sell that investors must make.

If a firm has issued shares then those shares will be traded in a market which gives them a price. The *earning per share* (EPS) indicates how much of the firm's profits (after tax has been paid) can be allocated to each share:

EPS = PAT/Number of shares issued

In effect, this is how much of the firm's profits are 'owned' for each share held.

The *price/earnings* (P/E) *ratio* is a measure of the value that the market places on a share in relation to its current earnings:

P/E = Market price of share/EPS

A firm's *market capitalisation* is its total value as the market sees it. It is defined as:

Market capitalisation = Market value of shares × Number of shares

From this it can be seen that the P/E ratio can also be written as:

P/E = Market capitalisation/PAT

A P/E ratio is a kind of market rating. A high P/E ratio suggests that the market places a high value on a firm even though its current earnings are relatively low. There are two reasons why this might be so. First, the firm may have quite low risks. 'Safe' money will be worth more than 'risky' money. The second reason is that the market may expect the firm's earnings to grow in the future. The market feels that the firm has good *prospects*.

Shareholders are rewarded in two ways. The first is by means of *capital growth*, the increase in the underlying value of the company's share which enables a profit to be made when the shares are sold. The second is through *income*. This is the flow of *dividends* paid out of company profits. Each share entitles its owner to a particular cash dividend. One form of reward can be played off against the other. If the firm's managers hold back profits (so do not pay dividends) they can use the money to invest in the firm's growth (so increasing share capital value). The *dividend cover* is a measure of how much of profits are held back as against being given to shareholders as dividends. It is defined as the number of times the actual dividend could, potentially, have been paid out:

Dividend cover = EPS/Dividend per share

The final key ratio of interest to investors is *dividend yield*. This measures the value of the income flow as investment, that is, in relation to the underlying value of the share. It is defined as:

Dividend yield = Dividend per share/Market price per share

Care should be taken when using ratios. They give absolute indications of a business's performance. They can be revealing. Yet they only provide a full picture when they are compared with other ratios. This comparison may be *historical*, as a trend in the ratios of a particular firm over time, or *cross-sectional*, as a comparison at a particular time of the ratios of a number of firms in the same or related sectors.

17.5 Evaluating the product portfolio

Most firms sell a range of products. A business which sells a single product is rare. It is certainly risky. A firm which dedicates its resources to one product is metaphorically speaking 'putting all its eggs in one basket'. Its fortunes will fluctuate with the performance of that one product. It is very vulnerable if a competitor launches a similar product. Firms which sell only one product are usually very young. Inevitably, they are keen to diversify their product offerings. If a firm sells more than one product, each product makes a different revenue contribution and a different demand on available investment resources. Portfolio analysis is a means of evaluating this relationship.

The first stage of any portfolio analysis is to break the company's product range into a series of sub-ranges and lines. This is a hierarchical process. The number of levels in the hierarchy depends on the number of products in the company's portfolio and its complexity. The key consideration is that the products be classed in a way which is *strategically* meaningful, that is, not just in terms of product type or technology. It is also necessary to bear in mind that different products appeal to different customer groups and are subject to similar demand and competitive constraints.

Portfolio methods are well covered by books on strategic analysis. The following summary is only intended to highlight the more important methods. Interested students are referred to the original references.

◆ The Boston Consulting Group matrix

The Boston Consulting Group (BCG) matrix was first described by Hedley in 1977. It aims to give an indication of cash flow stability in a firm by illustrating how cash-generating and cash-absorbing parts of the product portfolio are in balance. The key dimensions of the matrix are the growth rate of the sector in which the product range lies (plotted vertically) and the competitive index – the ratio between the market share of the range in its sector divided by that of the most important competitor (plotted horizontally).

The four quadrants are given evocative labels and the BCG made recommendations about the product range based on its position in the matrix. Products in the low growth, high competitive index quadrant are called *cash cows*. These can generate – be milked for – cash. Above these, in the quadrant for high growth, high competitive index products, are the *stars* – the company's success stories. Stars may generate some cash but they are equally likely to need investment in order to protect them from competitive attack. In the high market growth, low competitive index quadrant are the *question marks* (sometimes called *problem children*). These are products about which a decision must be made – to invest in improving the competitive position (to make them stars) or to divest (to drop the product). The final quadrant contains the low market growth, low competitive index products. The products here – called *dogs* – are said to be cash sinks. They take up more cash than they generate and have poor prospects for the future. The recommendation is to divest these.

The dividing lines between the quadrants are to some extent dependent on industry conditions. Often a 10 per cent growth rate is used to separate high from low growth. A competitive index of one is used to separate a good from a bad competitive position. More information can be obtained by means of the BCG matrix if products are represented by circles of different sizes reflecting the sales or profit contribution that they make.

The BCG matrix offers broad recommendations. However, like any analytical method, its recommendations should not be followed blindly, but interpreted in light of the particular features of the company's situation.

◆ The directional policy matrix

The directional policy matrix (DPM) was defined by three strategists in the chemicals industry, Robinson, Hitchens and Wade, in 1978. In principle, it is similar to the BCG matrix, but it uses more general factors to determine market attractiveness (plotted vertically) and competitive position (plotted horizontally).

Important factors in determining market attractiveness are market growth rate, profitability, stability of profits, customer strengths and environmental conditions (defined by means of the PEST analysis – *see* Section 17.3).

Important factors in determining competitive position are market share, production and technical expertise and relationships with distributors and buyers. Different factors can be weighted if they differ in significance.

Each axis is divided into three levels – labelled high, medium and low – giving nine sectors in total. The DPM enables recommendations to be made on investment and divestment on the basis of the position of the product in the matrix. As with the BCG matrix the recommendations should not be followed blindly but used to provide insights in the light of the context of the business.

◆ Pareto analysis

Every business is different. However the contribution to sales (or profits) of different lines in a multiproduct firm follow quite a consistent pattern. This is that a (relatively) small number of leading lines will make a large contribution while a (relatively) large number of low volume lines will make a small contribution. This is called the Pareto rule. It is sometimes called the '80–20' rule, because often the top 20 per cent of lines make a contribution of 80 per cent to sales and profits.

A Pareto curve can be drawn by listing the product lines in order of sales (or profits), with those that make the highest contribution being first. A graph can then be drawn with the cumulative contribution on the vertical axis and the percentage of total product lines on the horizontal axis. The curve will look something like that in Figure 17.2.

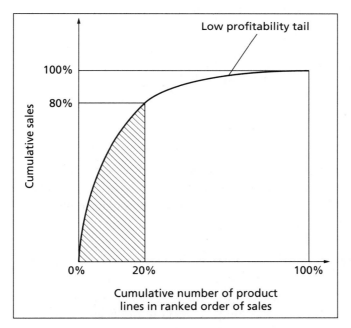

Figure 17.2 The Pareto Curve

A Pareto analysis is useful if a firm is considering rationalisation. Whereas different product lines make different levels of contribution, each line accounts for a fairly similar level of costs, particularly fixed costs. In general, profitability will be increased by divesting of product lines in the 'tail' of the curve. As with any general recommendation, though, this should be judged in light of the business, its situation and the product concerned.

17.6 Market positioning

A business will, as far as it is able, avoid head-to-head competition. Head-to-head competition is expensive and means that organisations dedicate resources to beating others rather than serving the customer. It is usually better to differentiate the firm's offerings so that it presents a face to the customer which is both attractive and unique. *Market positioning* is a concept which enables managers both to explore such distinctions and to use them to create competitive advantages.

Position suggests location and location suggests a map. In effect, the positioning of a business is the location it has on a map of the competitive situation in the sector in which it operates. As with any map, it is essential to define the coordinates appropriately. The most meaningful coordinates are those that buyers use to distinguish between the offerings of different firms in the sector. Any significant distinguishing feature can be used. Important ones are:

◆ high price or low price;

◆ high quality or emphasis on economy;

◆ upmarket or downmarket appeal;

◆ younger or older appeal;

◆ simple product or complex product;

◆ high-performance or basic performance.

A market map can be created using these factors. If just two (the two most significant) are selected the map can be drawn in two dimensions. If more than two factors are used then some statistical manipulation will be needed in order to project the map on to two dimensions. These methods are covered in many texts on market research.

The position of different firms on the map will give an indication of the level of competition at different positions. If individual firms are represented by circles, then the size of the circle can be used to indicate sales at that point. The map can give the consultant a clear guide as to how the firm should position itself in the market. The map illustrated in Figure 17.3, for example, indicates that the cheap and simple product position is crowded and that a move to a higher cost, more complex product might be a good strategic option.

Further details on these techniques and information on how to use others is given in many books on strategic analysis. *Corporate Strategy* by Richard Lynch (1997) provides a good source from a modern perspective. *Contemporary Strategy Analysis* by Robert Grant (1995) is also highly informative.

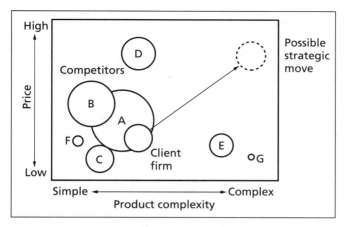

Figure 17.3   A market map

Team discussion point

Read the following short case study.

Halifax Foods is an upper-medium-sized supplier of own-label canned goods to major supermarkets. It has ten key product categories. The firm is concerned about its costs and a consulting team has been called in to help the company develop a rationalisation plan. The team has held a brainstorming session with key players in the firm. Using the factors discussed above, the team have established the following ratings (out of 10) shown in Table 17.2 for market attractiveness and competitive position for each product category. These are listed with the sales for each category.

Table 17.2

Category	Annual sales (£m)	Market attractiveness	Competitive position
Fruit	11	5	4
Baked beans	2	4	2
Traditional soups	39	7	8
Ethnic soups	1	10	2
Mixed vegetables	24	3	7
Carrots	7	2	4
Peas	6	1	3
Stir-fry vegetables	1	8	1
Broad beans	2	6	4
Flavoured beans	1	8	2
Total sales	94		

Construct a Pareto analysis and a DPM for the firm. What strategic recommendations would these analysis methods suggest?

Summary of key ideas

A number of techniques are available to the consultant to aid analysis of a business and its environment. A basic audit should include the following:

◆ the *SWOT* analysis: a summary of the business's abilities and the environment it operates in;

◆ the *PEST* analysis: an analysis of the factors which define the business's environment;

◆ *financial* analysis: an evaluation of the firm's financial performance and its financial stability;

◆ *portfolio* analysis: an evaluation of the firm's product range and how different parts contribute to the business as a whole;

◆ *positioning* analysis: an analysis of how the business fits into its market in relation to competitors.

18

Evaluating business opportunities

Learning outcomes

The learning outcomes from this chapter are:

◆ to understand the value of market information to effective decision making;

◆ to recognise the *qualitative* market research techniques that can aid decision making;

◆ to recognise the *quantitative* market research techniques that can aid decision making.

18.1 Opportunity, innovation and information

Managers make decisions about the direction their organisations are to move in. Those decisions relate to the selection of strategic options, the implementation of plans and the allocation of resources. If those decisions are to be the right ones they must be informed. Managers need information if their decisions are to be good ones. Market research is a discipline which has developed a number of very powerful techniques for evaluating the market context of a business and giving managers clear insights into the dynamics of the markets in which they operate and the behaviour of the customers they serve.

Market research falls into two types. *Qualitative research* aims to answer questions about individual attitudes and orientations. It answers the 'who?', 'why?' and 'what?' questions. *Quantitative research* aims to answer questions about collectives of individuals. It answers the 'how much?' and 'how many?' questions. The two forms of research work together. In combination they can provide a picture of the market in which the firm operates and flesh out the details of a market opportunity. Qualitative methods define the nature of the opportunity. Quantitative methods give an indication of its worth. Market research calls on a variety of techniques, many of which are very sophisticated. Market research is a specialist area of which few managers have the relevant knowledge. Supporting managers in developing an insight into market opportunities is something which consultants are often called on to do.

Market research can be expensive. It is an investment in the business. Like any investment it should only be undertaken if the returns are appropriate. Managers must consider the nature of the decisions they are facing, the value of the resources involved and the risks to which they will be exposed and then decide what it will be worth to invest in information that will improve those decisions. A sales representative visiting a new prospective customer may dedicate an hour or so to brushing up on the company, reading the annual report and a few newspaper articles. A business making a major launch of a new consumer brand may spend millions in analysing market potential, customer buying behaviour and perhaps advertising effectiveness. A firm aiming to buy another will undertake an extensive programme of evaluation – called due diligence – which will involve marketing, finance and legal specialists in order to be sure of its fit and potential.

When the level of expenditure available for market research has been decided it is important that that investment be used wisely. The objectives of the research must be clear. The questions it aims to answer must be made explicit. The right techniques for answering those questions must be selected. The appropriate groups of customers must be selected for investigation.

Consultants may or may not themselves be conversant with the details of various market research techniques, though it is certainly useful for them to be able to undertake some of the more straightforward methods. What they must be able to do, however, is recognise how market research can illuminate a management issue and be used to support better decision making. They must be able to help managers formulate their problems so that a cost-effective, informative marketing research exercise can be devised.

The following is only intended as an overview of market research techniques: an indication of the approaches available. It is recommended that should they be called upon to implement an extensive market research programme students consult a specialist market research text such as *Contemporary Marketing Research* by McDaniel and Gates (1991).

18.2 Secondary research

Secondary research is that which uses already published information. The amount of information in the world relevant to business is vast. And it is growing. Already published information, because it has not been undertaken specifically for the task in hand, varies enormously in its relevance. But it is of low cost. And it can be very informative. It should always be the first source consulted by the researcher. Some of the most valuable sources are as follows.

◆ Newspaper articles

Quality newspapers regularly feature articles that are of relevance to a consulting project. The *Financial Times* not only covers ongoing events in the world of business; it also includes regular surveys dedicated to specific business areas, topical issues and geographic regions. The weekly newspaper, *The Economist* (which actually has a magazine format) provides a good, succinct and very accessible guide to what is going on in the world of international politics, finance and business. This also has regular business and geographical surveys. Profiles of publicly traded companies can be found in the *Investors Chronicle* along with commentary on general developments in the world's stock markets.

Most consultants read these publications regularly. Many keep a cuttings file on topics of interest. Business libraries keep back copies and have key word indexes.

◆ Company annual reports

Company annual reports serve a very specific and legally defined function. They must inform investors of the financial state of the business through the balance sheet and profit and loss account. However, most annual reports go beyond just fulfilling this basic function. They are exercises in public relations promoting the company as a whole to all its stakeholders. They are a mine of information, not just on the company but on its industry in general. The chairman's statement gives an indication of the prospects for the sector. There may be information on political, technological and social developments in the business's spheres of operation. The annual report may also provide an insight into those areas where the business is investing in the future.

Much information relevant to a small business client will be gleaned through a detailed and insightful reading of the annual reports of some of the large players in its sector.

◆ Market sector reports

A number of companies routinely publish reports on market sectors. Mintel covers important areas of consumer spending. Euromonitor looks at developments in European markets. In addition there are a number of *ad hoc* reports on specific sectors. Many of these are held by the British Library and can be accessed through listings in a good business library.

◆ The Internet

The Internet is proving to be one of the most valuable tools for the secondary researcher. Many companies, and most of the larger ones, now have their own sites. Financial data are published regularly. Broad searches can be conducted through key words.

18.3 Who, why and what? Qualitative methods for evaluating opportunities

Markets are made up of individual decision makers. The dynamics of a market must be understood in terms of both the influences on individual decision making and the way individuals aggregate to generate overall demand.

A number of techniques are available to explore the nature of individual needs, buying and product selection.

◆ Depth interviews

Depth interviews are one-to-one interviews in which the investigator gets the potential customer to explain how he or she makes buying decisions. The interview may be partially structured but the investigator will keep open the option of exploring interesting avenues as they are revealed. Examples of products and other stimulus materials might be used to encourage the discussion.

◆ Focus group discussions

Focus group discussions involve a small group of potential customers (usually about four to seven people) who are invited to explore their views on a product category. The session will usually last between two and three hours. The discussion is led by a facilitator who will be responsible for interpreting the findings afterwards. Again, product examples and stimulus materials may be used.

◆ Telephone interviews

Telephone interviews are conducted on a one-to-one basis. The interview will be fully or semi structured. This approach is (usually) cheaper than depth interviews but the lack of contact limits the communication. The opportunity to use stimulus material is limited unless it is sent to the interviewee first.

◆ Postal surveys

With this technique potential customers are asked to complete a written questionnaire relating to their buying habits. The questions must be well constructed and interesting if a meaningful response is to be obtained. This technique is of low cost but has limited flexibility to explore interesting avenues that open up unless a follow-up is made (for example, as in the Delphi technique – *see* Section 15.8).

◆ Product placements

With product placement the customer is exposed to the product in a normal usage situation before being questioned via one of the above techniques. This technique can give a very insightful picture of the customer's reaction to the product on which to base further development and promotion. It does, however, demand that a product, or a prototype, be available. This can prove to be expensive and may present security issues if the product is in a development stage.

Each of these techniques has its own strengths and weaknesses. They may be used in combination to give a full picture of the buying behaviour of potential customers. Often a small number of flexible, but relatively expensive techniques (e.g. depth interviews, focus groups) will be used to establish broad issues which can then be explored in more depth using less expensive but less flexible techniques (e.g. postal and telephone surveys).

18.4 How many, how often and how much? Quantitative methods for evaluating opportunities

Once the character of the individual buying process has been established the researcher must move on and establish how buyers as a group present an opportunity to a particular business. This calls for quantitative techniques. Some of the most important are as follows.

◆ Postal surveys

A representative sample of customers are mailed a questionnaire. This will include questions relating to what products they buy, from what suppliers, how often they buy, how much they use and how frequently they use them.

◆ Telephone surveys

In telephone surveys, a representative sample are asked the same questions as are used as in the postal survey but the individuals are contacted by telephone. There may be more potential to open up new lines of enquiry here than in the postal survey. On the other hand, consumers may not have time to reflect on their consumption (as they will have with a postal survey) and a follow-up call may be needed.

◆ Distributor audits

Distributor audits are a particularly important source of information on markets, their structure, size and growth. The technique used requires a representative sample of distributors (who may be wholesalers or retailers) to keep a record of their purchases and sales. This information, which can nowadays be kept electronically, can be supplemented by direct outlet audits. A distributor audit allows a market to be broken down in a number of ways. The overall market can be represented as the product of *rate of sale* (the number of units a typical distributor sells) and *distribution* (the proportion of distributors selling the stock). Other information includes *stock holding* (the amount of a product a typical distributor holds) and forward stocking (the amount on display to the buyer). Information of this type allows the business to make very subtle decisions about its distribution strategy and how to manage its relationship with distributors.

A meaningful distributor audit is likely to be time consuming and expensive. A number of companies offer store audits on a commercial basis. A. C. Nielsen and Audits of Great Britain (AGB) are the leaders.

| *Team discussion point* | Consider the decision you made to undertake your course in management consulting. What market research methods would you adopt to evaluate the interests of your colleagues in such a course within your institution? How would you measure the overall demand for such a course? How would you investigate ways in which the course might be modified to make it more attractive in the future?

Discuss your ideas as a group. |

Summary of key ideas

◆ Effective decision making demands good information.

◆ Decision makers need two sorts of information about a market:
  – how individual buying decisions are reached; and
  – how groups of individual buyers add up to make a market opportunity.

◆ The first is investigated by qualitative market research techniques; the second by quantitative research techniques.

◆ A number of market research methods are available. They vary in the type of information they offer, their flexibility and their cost. A full market investigation may demand that more than one be used.

◆ The consultant does not need to know how to use all the market research techniques available. However, he or she should be informed enough to work with market research professionals.

19

Analysing decision making in the client business

Learning outcomes

The main learning outcomes for this chapter are:

◆ to understand the traditional model of decision making in organisations;

◆ to recognise the limitations of this model and be sensitive to how decisions are really made in organisations;

◆ to recognise the types of *decision-making roles* managers undertake;

◆ to recognise the ways managers *influence* each other's decisions;

◆ to understand the *dimensions* that can be used to define a particular decision.

19.1 Decision making in organisations

For an individual, a decision is a choice between two or more courses of action. Individual decision making is influenced by complex psychological processes involving recognition of personal need, cognitive style and strategy and motivation.

Organisations must also make choices between different courses of action. Organisational decision making goes beyond the concerns of the individual, however. It involves interactions between individuals. These interactions include the passing of information, discussion about analysis and the negotiation of outcomes. Individual choices are only part of the process of organisational decision making. Organisational decision making occurs at a level above that of individual decision making.

The 'traditional' picture of decision making in organisations sees it as an open process in which the manager seeks information, analyses it in a rational way and then implements the decision through the organisation. Such a picture is represented in the general model of organisational decision making. The origins of such a model go back to the work of T. T. Patterson (1969). Models of this type, as illustrated in Figure 19.1, highlight six stages in the organisational decision-making process.

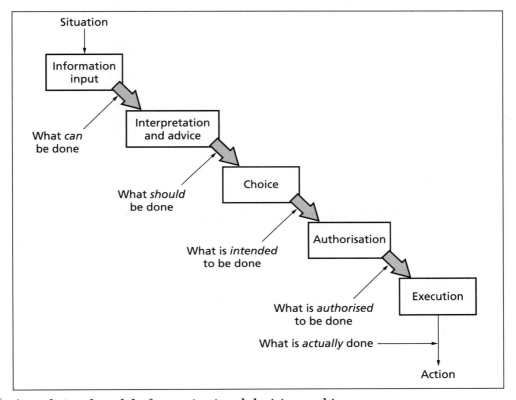

Figure 19.1 **A traditional model of organisational decision making**

Such models are valuable in that they suggest ways in which decision making may be accessed and influenced. However, they present a somewhat idealised picture of how decision making really occurs in organisations. As with many models of organisational life they depict the 'essence' of a process rather than its reality. The details of decision making are often much more complex than such models suggest. Decision making is complicated by human issues. For instance, managers do not always sit and plan decisions in detail. Information may be limited. Advice, even good advice, may not be appreciated. Not all decisions are instigated by the manager; some are forced on to him or her. Not all decisions are rationalised through a formal interpretation of choices. Some are impulsive and based on intuitive understanding. Authorisation may not always be 'official'. Execution may be hindered by political concerns and internal infighting.

The consultant aims to influence decision making in the organisations with which he or she works. It is important that the consultant understands how decisions are made in practice. Every organisation has its own style of decision making. If the consultant is to be effective in supporting the client organisation in achieving its objectives then he or she must be sensitive to this style: the way in which decisions are *actually* made, justified and implemented within a business. To do this four levels of insight are valuable:

◆ an appreciation of the *types* of decision a manager is called on to make;

◆ an understanding of *who* is involved in decision making;

◆ an understanding of the way in which a decision may be *defined*;

◆ an ability to define the *styles* of decision making an organisation can adopt.

This chapter develops models which provide a guide to gaining these insights and using them to influence decision making in the client business.

19.2 Types of management decision-making role

Not all decisions are the same. As we discussed in Chapter 6, Henry Mintzberg (1973, p. 77) has defined four distinct types of decision-making role for managers. These are the *entrepreneurial*, the *disturbance handler*, the *resource allocator* and the *negotiator*. We can now reflect on the type of decisions these roles entail.

◆ The entrepreneurial

Entrepreneurial decisions are those aimed at generating controlled change for the organisation. They involve the manager in actively seeking out new opportunities and identifying problems which, although not pressing at present, may limit the organisation in the long term. The manager who initiates entrepreneurial decisions and actively promotes them in the organisation is often called an intrapreneur, a term introduced by Gifford Pinchot in his 1985 book, *Intrapreneuring*. Formal evaluation techniques may or may not be used to evaluate and justify entrepreneurial options.

◆ The disturbance handler

Disturbance-handling decisions are those which are forced on the manager by some crisis or organisational 'disturbance'. Such disturbances take three broad forms. They may result from (a) conflicts between individuals within the organisation; (b) some change in the external environment which affects the way the organisation operates; or (c) a sudden loss in some important resource. Real organisational crises often result from a combination of these three things. Disturbances must be handled quickly and often in a situation of panic and political intriguing. The manager must often act on impulse and insight and may not have time for much formal evaluation of the decision. Decision making in a crisis is often based on a manager's intuitive knowledge and understanding.

◆ The resource allocator

Resource-allocation decisions are those which involve the dedication of resources to specific projects on behalf of the organisation. These decisions may relate to capital investment, the purchasing of the factors the organisation uses or the delegation of particular tasks and work programmes to individuals and groups. The way in which such decisions are made and justified depend on the significance of the decision to the organisation and its culture.

◆ The negotiator

Negotiation decisions involve debate about and the agreement of outcomes on behalf of the organisation with the other organisations and individuals with which it comes into contact. Important outcomes include the commitment of resources to and the sharing of rewards gained from joint projects. Negotiations take many forms. Some are seen as 'zero-sum' games in which one party must lose if another wins. The negotiator sees a 'pie' of fixed size which can only go so far. The aim is to get the biggest share. Alternatively, they may be more positive and be driven by a win-win attitude. In this case the negotiator sees the parties to the negotiation as able to work together to make the pie bigger for all.

19.3 The decision-making unit

Mintzberg's four roles relate to individual managers. They represent only one dimension of decision making. A business decision also involves the interaction of managers in groups within the organisation as a whole. The group involved in making a decision is called the decision-making unit (DMU). The key players in the DMU are the decision maker, the authoriser, information providers, the resource provider, influencers, implementers and gatekeepers.

◆ The decision maker

The decision maker is the person called upon to actually make a decision. He or she will be the person who is seen as responsible for the *outcomes* of the decision.

◆ The authoriser

The authoriser is the person who is called on to authorise, modify or sanction the decision made by the decision maker. In hierarchical organisations the authoriser is often the decision maker's line manager. In team-based organisations it will be the project leader.

◆ Information providers

Information providers give the decision maker the information which he or she will use to analyse possible courses of action and then to justify the decision eventually made. Information providers may be part of the organisation but are often external experts called in when needed. Consultants are often information providers.

◆ The resource provider

The resource provider is the person who authorises the use of any resources that are required before the decision can be implemented. The resource provider can be the same person as the authoriser but this is not inevitable.

◆ Influencers

Influencers are individuals who are in a position to change the opinion of other members of the decision-making unit and develop their attitude towards particular decisions. The influencer's role may be formally defined or it might be informal.

◆ Implementers

Implementers are those individuals who must put the decision into effect. Important implementers are production staff, research and development specialists and sales staff.

◆ Gatekeepers

Gatekeepers are those people who control access to other members of the DMU. Personal assistants, secretaries and receptionists are often important gatekeepers.

Different decisions call on different DMUs within the organisation. The extent of the DMU will depend on the scope and significance of the decision being made. Routine decisions may be controlled by long-standing DMUs. Non-routine decisions may require the setting up of an *ad hoc* DMU. Some DMUs are recognised formally. The board of directors, special committees and project teams for example. Others may be quite informal, the clique of managers who meet for a drink after work for example. It is possible that the organisation may not even recognise that some informal DMUs are functioning, though their impact on the business may be considerable.

19.4 The dimensions of a decision

The decision-making roles outlined above suggest that all decisions can be described in terms of a small number of features, in particular, the significance of the decision, who is involved in making it, how it is justified within the organisation and how it is communicated to the organisation.

◆ The significance of the decision

What impact will the decision have on the business? Is it a major decision defining the future of the business or is it a relatively minor one? What proportion of the organisation's resources will be affected by the decision? How many people within the organisation will be affected by the decision? In general, the more important the decision the more extensive, and formal, will be the involvement of a DMU.

◆ Who is involved in the decision

Who is involved in making, authorising and implementing the decision? In other words, what is the structure, function and membership of the DMU that will judge the decision? (*See* Section 19.3.)

◆ How the decision is justified

How does the decision maker go about justifying the decision he or she is advocating? There are a number of ways a decision can be promoted within the organisation. For example, it can be through a process of logical analysis (presenting detailed market data, cost analysis and option evaluation, for instance); it can be advocated on the basis of the decision maker's expertise and past successes ('Trust me – I know what I'm doing!'); it can be insisted upon on the basis of the decision maker's authority ('I'm the boss and I say it's going to happen!'); it can be made to happen through political manoeuvring ('Help me on this and you'll get my support later!').

In practice, many decisions are promoted in different ways to different members of the DMU. Typically, the consultant will be more formal in his or her decision justification than the organisation would expect its internal managers to be. This is for two reasons. As an outside expert the consultant will be expected to work as an expert – and for many people this means formality. Second, the consultant, lacking internal experience of the internal situation and formal authority, must rely more on overtly logical justification. Process consulting, though (*see* Section 6.4), may deliberately avoid an excessively formal approach.

◆ How the decision is communicated

How will the members of the DMU be informed about the decision? It might be through a formal meeting or presentation. The decision might be communicated in a written format, perhaps by way of a memorandum, or be part of the recommendations in a report. Alternatively it may be talked through by the decision maker on an informal one-to-one basis with members of the DMU. It may also travel through the informal grapevine in the organisation. Normally, a consultant will be called on to communicate his or her ideas in a formal way, through a report or presentation, though effective consultants also know how to use informal channels of communication as well.

We can picture a particular decision as located in a three-dimensional space with the axes defined by the decision-making role, the functioning of the DMU and the features of the decision. This decision-making space is depicted in Figure 19.2.

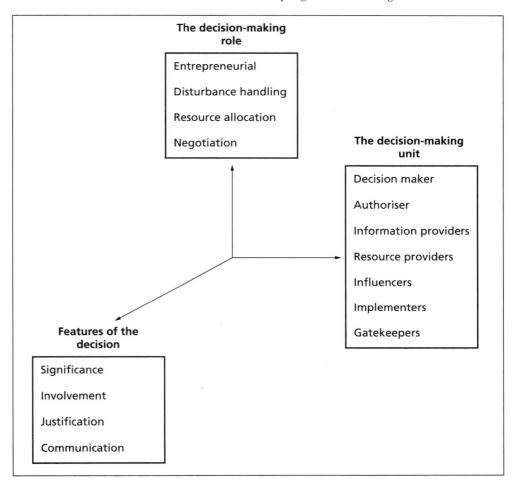

The decision-making role

Entrepreneurial

Disturbance handling

Resource allocation

Negotiation

The decision-making unit

Decision maker

Authoriser

Information providers

Resource providers

Influencers

Implementers

Gatekeepers

Features of the decision

Significance

Involvement

Justification

Communication

Figure 19.2   The dimensions of a business decision

Team discussion point

Reflect on the decision making in your consulting team. What is the style of decision making? What decision-making roles are being undertaken? By whom? How is the DMU constituted?

Can you envisage a better decision-making structure? Discuss your ideas as a group. You will find your project log a useful aid to reflection and analysis.

Summary of key ideas

◆ Decision making in organisations can take a number of forms. It may be explicit, open and rational; or it can be implicit and based on management intuition.

◆ Businesses adopt a variety of styles of decision making. If the consultant is to see his or her ideas take shape he or she must work with the client's decision-making style.

◆ Managers take on four distinct decision-making roles:
  – the entrepreneurial;
  – the disturbance handler;
  – the resource allocator;
  – the negotiator.

◆ Decisions in an organisation are controlled by decision-making units (DMUs). The key roles in a DMU are:
  – the decision maker;
  – information providers;
  – influencers;
  – gatekeepers;
  – the authoriser;
  – resource providers;
  – implementers.

◆ The four features of a particular decision are:
  – its significance;
  – who is involved in making it;
  – how it will be justified;
  – how it will be communicated.

Together, these three dimensions form the basis of decision analysis.

20

Understanding the decision-making environment

Learning outcomes

The main learning outcomes from this chapter are:
- to be able to analyse the decision-making environment the client organisation presents;
- in particular to recognise how decision making within the organisation is influenced by the following factors:
- *organisational orientation* and the prioritisation of technical, selling and marketing activities;
- different types of *organisational culture*; and
- different styles of *strategy implementation* process.

20.1 Decision-making style and influence

Every organisation has its own style of decision making. The consultant must recognise this and be ready to use it. Consultants should not challenge the organisation's style of decision making (not in the first instance anyway – though this may be the objective of change management programmes). They are most influential when they present their arguments in a way which is sympathetic to the organisation's decision-making style. Even if they are involved in a change management project dedicated towards developing organisational decision-making skills they must still work with the organisation's initial style, not against it. In short, a consultant should go with the flow!

This presents the consultant with a challenge. How is he or she to understand the decision-making style in the client organisation and then use it? There are a number of models which help provide such an understanding. Three which are particularly valuable are the ideas of *organisational orientation*, *organisational culture* and *strategy process*. The following three sections explore each of these.

20.2 Organisational orientation

Businesses are sometimes described as having an orientation. This orientation defines the priorities the organisation sees itself as having and the kind of issues it must address. Three orientations are described: the *production orientation*, the *sales orientation* and the *marketing orientation*.

◆ The production orientation

The production-orientated organisation is primarily concerned with how it makes the things it sells, or delivers the service it offers. The business will prioritise decisions which relate to the developing of products, the setting up of production and the solving of operation problems. These things will be seen to be more important to the organisation than actually creating demand for what it offers. For a business with a production orientation, generating demand for products is secondary to actually making them.

The production orientation is often found in new businesses and those which are adopting an innovative approach to production and service delivery. Technologists and operational specialists tend to be important players in decision-making units (DMUs).

◆ The sales orientation

The sales-orientated organisation is primarily concerned with actually *selling* its goods or services to customers. It is interested in creating short-term demand and gaining immediate sales revenues. The business is usually very confident in its belief that what it sells is attractive to its customers – it just needs to get them to buy it! The sales-orientated business can sometimes give the impression that it is seeking power over the customer. Priority is given to decisions focused on sales strategy and (short-term) promotional tactics.

The sales orientation is often found in businesses which are in highly competitive markets and those which are underperforming financially. Sales managers are usually key players in the business's DMUs.

◆ The marketing orientation

The marketing-orientated business gives priority to understanding customer demand and developing a means to satisfy it. The business will profess that the customer lies at the centre of the business and that addressing the customer's real needs is the key to performance. It will eschew what it sees as 'hard selling' techniques as unnecessary. The business is usually concerned with developing a strategic approach to its marketing and to product development. These factors will feature strongly in the decisions it makes. Marketing and development people play key roles in DMUs.

Many management thinkers advocate the marketing orientation as the 'highest' or 'best' orientation and the key to long-term success. It has been suggested that a business evolves from the production to the sales to the marketing orientation as it grows, matures and learns.

This may be so, but the marketing orientation can only really establish itself in a business which can free its managers to take on the entrepreneurial decision-making role and engage in long-term, self-instigated projects. Hence, the marketing orientation is often found in innovative businesses which have enjoyed a degree of success and in which there are no immediate crises. If a critical issue arises and the disturbance decision-making role is demanded then the marketing orientation can often be dropped in favour of one of the other two. The marketing orientation may be seen as 'unrealistic' or too 'long term' whereas the sales orientation will seem to offer an immediate solution to demand-based problems and the production orientation solutions to supply-based problems that challenge the business.

It is a valuable exercise for the consultant to assess the business and determine what its orientation is. Different parts of the business may have different orientations. This is often the case in larger organisations which have separate production, sales and marketing functions.

20.3 Organisational culture

The idea of organisational culture is one of the most important to enter the management lexicon over the past twenty years. It has been advocated (most notably, by Tom Peters and Robert Waterman in their 1982 book *In Search of Excellence*) as *the* most important facet of the business, which can be used to differentiate it from competitors and establish a base for success. Others, it must be added, challenge the way the concept is used by management thinkers and suggest it cannot provide a meaningful management tool.

It is not possible to engage in this debate here. All that will be said is that the idea of culture as a description of the 'way a business does things' can be used to give a good picture of the decision-making environment in a business. Charles Handy has described four types of organisational culture in his book

Understanding Organisations (1993). These are the power culture, the role culture, the task culture and the person culture (or people culture). Consideration of culture in this way can provide a particularly useful insight to the consultant.

◆ The power culture

The power culture is characterised by a strong, central figurehead who dominates the business. He or she is the source of all authority in the organisation. Often the authority is based on ownership of the business combined with person charisma and leadership. Tasks other than the most routine are delegated by this central figure on a 'need to do' basis. Planning is *ad hoc* and largely concerned with short-term issues. There is little formality in the business. Procedures are ill-defined and bureaucracy low. It is likely that communication will, in the main, take the form of informal discussions.

The central figurehead will dominate any DMUs in the business. He or she may even *be* the DMU. Power cultures often occur in small, privately owned and entrepreneurial businesses. Power cultures only work in an organisation which is small enough for one person to make all the important decisions.

◆ The role culture

The role culture is characterised by structure and procedures. Individual roles are defined through job descriptions and specifications. An individual's position in the organisation is defined in an organogram. Position bestows authority. The business is likely to be broken up into well-defined departments or functions such as finance, marketing, production and so on. The organisation may engage in formal planning and use it to specify definite goals and future situations. Officially, communication is formalised by the use of regular meetings, reports and memoranda. Informal grapevines are often important as well, though.

Decision making in such organisations is routinised as far as possible. DMUs are extensive, with individuals taking on recognised, official roles. Organisations with role cultures are often quite bureaucratic. They are typically well-established medium to large firms operating in a stable environment.

◆ The task culture

A task culture is characterised by the need to get certain jobs done. Achieving objectives is seen as more important than defining what one's job is. The business is often structured around multidisciplinary teams rather than departments. Authority is based on expertise rather than formal position. Teams may be permanent fixtures or may be set up when needed to undertake a particular project. Long-term planning may be engaged in but it is likely to be seen as offering a way of gaining insights rather than specifying a definite path. The organisation attempts to keep bureaucracy to a minimum though formal procedures may be established to monitor and provide resources for the activity of the task teams.

Decision making is centred on the project team who largely constitute the DMU. The authorisers and resource allocators may nominally stand outside the group, but they will be susceptible to advocacy by the group.

Businesses with task cultures are often innovative and fast-growing entrepreneurial businesses which are too large for a power culture. They are effective in unstable and rapidly changing environments where decision making must be 'pushed down'.

◆ The person culture

The person culture is characterised by a prioritising of the needs of the individual over those of the organisation as a whole. Organisations with a person culture resist the imposition of formal structures and procedures though informal ones may emerge. The main concern is with the internal environment rather than with the organisation's relationship with the wider world.

Decision making is informal. DMUs tend to cluster round influential individuals who may exercise unofficial authority based on expertise and/or personal charisma.

This type of culture is hard to sustain as it can be hard to reconcile the needs of the organisation as a whole with those of the individual. Organisations with person cultures can be hard to focus on well-defined objectives and may tend to fragment. They often need support in obtaining resources.

Person cultures can be found in some non-profit organisations (public health care, charities and so on) and in religious groupings. Some unorthodox profit-making organisations such as co-operatives may profess or aspire to a person culture. A person culture may also be found in some 'professional' organisations which have a small number of 'highly valuable' people who must be handled with care. Important examples include business support agencies such as advertising agencies, legal firms and management consultants.

20.4 Strategy processes

A business strategy has two sides. One side is the *content* of the strategy. This is what the business actually does. The other side is the strategy *process*. This is the way in which a business decides what to do. Strategy process is the way a business organises its decision making. Henry Mintzberg (1973) has described three basic modes of strategy process: the *entrepreneurial*, the *adaptive* and *planning*.

◆ The entrepreneurial mode

The entrepreneurial mode of strategy process is typified by four main features. First, it is focused on identifying and exploiting new opportunities. Second, entrepreneurial decision making is concentrated into the hands of a powerful individual. Third, it is concerned with major moves forward rather than incremental or gradual change. Fourth, it concentrates on decisions which offer the possibility of business growth. An entrepreneurial mode of decision making has resonance with a power culture.

◆ The adaptive mode

The adaptive mode of strategy process is characterised by its being reactive rather than proactive. It represents a response to short-term and immediate opportunities and threats. Four characteristics arise as a consequence of this. First, adaptive decision making is made by individuals and small groups and is not co-ordinated by the organisation as a whole. Second, it is not aimed at achieving well-defined long-term organisational goals. Third, adaptive decision making is incremental. It is concerned with small changes, not with major leaps forward. Fourth, it is disjointed. It may be difficult to relate the logic behind one adaptive decision to that behind another.

◆ The planning mode

The planning mode of strategy making is characterised by systematic analysis and formality. Three features of decision making arise from this. First, and foremost, individual decisions are integrated into and related to an overarching strategy for the business. Second, alternatives are carefully evaluated to assess costs, benefits and risks. Formal techniques may be brought in to do this. Third, not least as a result of the need for the application of formal planning and decision analysis techniques, expert strategic analysts play an important role in the organisation's DMUs.

P. J. Idenburg (1993) has built on these insights by Mintzberg and others and proposed a two-dimensional matrix which defines four types of strategy development process. The axes of this matrix are defined by goal orientation and process orientation. These are defined as follows.

◆ Goal orientation

Goal orientation is the *what* of strategy development. It is concerned with the definition of goals, targets and desired future states for the business. It considers the actuality of decisions and their outcomes. Goal orientation decisions are of the 'where do we want to go?' type.

◆ Process orientation

Process orientation is the *how* of strategy development. It is concerned with the rules and procedures by which strategy making is guided, evaluated and monitored by the organisation. It considers how decision making will be controlled, rather than what the actual decisions are. Process orientation decisions are of the 'how are we going to get there?' type.

Each orientation may be strong or weak in the way it influences organisational decision making. The options define the 2 × 2 matrix illustrated in Figure 20.1. This matrix has four quadrants, each of which represents a distinct strategy-making style.

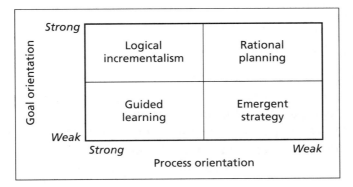

Figure 20.1 **The Idenburg Matrix for Strategy Process**

Source: Reprinted from *Long Range Planning*, 10(2), P.J. Idenburg, 'Four styles of strategic planning', pp. 9–15, Copyright (1993), with permission from Elsevier Science.

◆ Logical incrementalism

The logical incrementalism style results from the organisation having both a strong goal orientation and a strong process orientation. There is a concern both with *where* the organisation is going and with *how* it will get there. Decisions are monitored and evaluated by pervasive control functions in the organisation. The justification of decisions may be formalised by both systematic analysis and review procedures. Critically, decisions are related to each other. The organisation moves forward in a pattern characterised by small (incremental) and logical (rational) steps. The business may well mistrust 'entrepreneurial' decisions which demand significant leaps into the unknown.

◆ Guided learning

A guided learning style results from an emphasis on the process of making strategy at the expense of what the strategy is meant to achieve. The business may be active in delegating decision making to local managers. Rather than give them targets the business expects them to set their own and perhaps to engage in planning activity. However, this will be seen as a way of getting managers to explore their environments and the possibilities the business faces and perhaps even their own thinking modes rather than as a procedure for simply defining objectives.

A guided learning style does not mean managers are free to make any decision they wish. Controls still exist. The organisation will be active in developing managers so that they make the 'right' decisions. This control can be explicit, say through training programmes. It can also be implicit. The organisation may rely on its culture – its 'how we do things around here' – to define and limit management decision making.

◆ Rational planning

The rational planning style is characterised by an emphasis on meeting definite goals rather than worrying about how managers go about achieving them. In many respects it parallels Mintzberg's planning mode. It is defined by definite commercial targets imposed on managers from the top. Planners adopt systematic decision-evaluation techniques and decisions are reviewed using formal procedures. The achievement of objectives is carefully monitored by top management.

◆ Emergent strategy

In the final quadrant of the Idenburg matrix strategy development occurs in the absence of both strong goal and process orientations. The business's strategy 'emerges' rather than being explicitly developed. As discussed in Section 19.2, managers do not always have the luxury of being able to sit down and plan every decision. Some must be made on the spur of the moment in response to a crisis. Some decision making may not be guided by consideration either of the organisation's goals or of how it should best go about making decisions. Managers just use their intuition and make them. Entrepreneurs starting a new business rarely consider their decision making in an abstract sense. They are likely to be more interested in using their decision-making skills to chase opportunities and get the venture off the ground. If they are successful and the business grows (perhaps through a power culture, then a task culture phase) they may never explore, in isolation from the actual running of the business, the way in which the business makes decisions about where it is going and how it is to get there.

This is not to say that emergent decision making is a free-for-all. It is just that decision making is controlled by being embedded in the experiences, knowledge and culture of the business rather than by location with reference to externally considered goals and processes.

Organisational life is rich and complex. Decision making is an integral part of the organisational tapestry. These three approaches to understanding organisational decision making, organisational orientation, organisational culture and strategy process, simplify the complex picture of decision making. By simplifying it, they make it easier to understand. However, they also present the risk of caricaturing it. They are best used as frameworks which can guide the consultant's experience of the client organisation rather than as rigid boxes into which 'facts' about the organisation must be forced. Used in this way they can be a valuable tool which can help a consultant convince the client organisation that his or her ideas are worth putting into practice. Evaluation of decision-making style is a critical first step to developing a strategy to communicate ideas to the client organisation.

Group discussion point	Consider the following short case study.

Sarah had worked with a small manufacturing company as part of a team on an undergraduate consulting project. The firm produced in-flight entertainment systems which they supplied to the aircraft-manufacturing industry. The project she had worked on had been instigated and then co-ordinated by Isobel, the firm's business development manager. Isobel held a middle-ranking position in the firm.

Sarah's project involved assessing the potential for developing the firm's presence in the Chinese market. Based on what she had heard about the country Isobel had a feeling it might offer a lot of potential in the future.

Sarah's team had investigated this. Their final report confirmed Isobel's feelings. They had found that, though at a low base, the average number of air-miles flown by a Chinese citizen was doubling every year. The government was also committed to developing China's own aircraft-manufacturing business. This meant a great many new aircraft would be built in China. And, as China grew wealthier through economic growth, the demand for luxuries such as in-flight entertainment would grow. It seemed a golden opportunity for the business. The team established some contacts via the Chinese Embassy and found that a trade fair concerning the right sort of product areas was to be held in Beijing in the near future. In the final report they recommended that Isobel's business give priority to development of the Chinese market and start by making representation at the trade fair. Isobel had been pleased by the report and agreed that a good opportunity had been identified.

After Sarah had been invited back by Isobel to do some vacation work one of her first questions was how the Chinese project had gone. Isobel just smiled and said that it had stalled. Sarah asked why.

Isobel explained what had happened. Her manager had been enthusiastic at first. He agreed that China looked like a good opportunity. He asked Isobel to cost out going to the trade fair in China. It proved to be quite expensive, more than her manager was authorised to spend on a single project, and so it had to be taken to a full board meeting for a decision.

Isobel was invited to present the project and what it had to offer to the board of directors. The board was impressed with the analysis Isobel had done but a number of issues were raised. First, the finance director made the point that he had attended a seminar on developing markets where it had been said that the Chinese market, though attractive because of economic growth, was proving more difficult for western businesses to break into than many had predicted. 'If you want to develop a real presence in China, it's a long haul and takes a lot of investment,' he had said. Then the sales director had insisted that any trade fair must be attended by a trained sales representative ('so we can be sure the right image of the firm is given'). When the dates of the fair were announced he had said that this was during the main campaigns of the year for the launch of a new entertainment system and that he couldn't possible spare anyone.

Isobel concluded by relating that, in the end, the MD decided that China should wait until the proper level of resources could be made available to invest properly. The project was 'on hold'. Sarah said she thought this was a pity because China had seemed like a real opportunity for the business. Isobel agreed.

Using the evidence available from the case study discuss the following issues as a group.

1 The type of management decision-making role that Isobel was undertaking when she instigated Sarah's project. (Use Mintzberg's framework described in Section 19.2 as a guide.)

2 The DMU roles of each person mentioned in the case study. (Use the framework described in Section 19.3 as a guide.)

3 The nature of the decision to move into the Chinese market. (Use the framework described in Section 19.4 as a guide.)

4 The orientation and culture in the firm.

5 The nature of the strategy process operating in the firm.

**Summary
of key ideas**

◆ A number of frameworks can be used to analyse organisational decision-making style. Three particularly useful ones are:

◆ *Organisational orientation*: Important types include:

- production orientation;
- marketing orientation;
- sales orientation.

◆ *Organisational culture*: Important types include:

- power culture;
- task culture;
- role culture;
- person culture.

◆ *Strategy process*: Important types include (after Mintzberg):

- entrepreneurial mode;
- planning mode;
- adaptive mode.

and (after Idenburg):

- logical incrementalism;
- rational planning;
- guided learning
- emergent strategy.

Bringing people along
Developing relationship-building skills

21

Communication skills

Learning outcomes

The key learning outcomes from this chapter are:

◆ to recognise the importance of effective communication to consulting success;

◆ to understand the process of communication;

◆ to be able to establish objectives for communication;

◆ to recognise that communication has rational and emotional aspects;

◆ to appreciate the advantages and disadvantages of verbal, written and visual mediums for communication.

21.1 The nature of business communication

Communication is a fundamental aspect of our lives. The facility to communicate subtle and complex messages is what enables to us organise tasks: to decide what needs to be done, to allocate different jobs to different people, to discuss how they should be undertaken and to agree how the rewards of that co-operation are to be shared. In brief, communication allows us to build organisations and use them to create value – to manage and undertake business. It is not surprising that understanding communication and being an effective communicator are critically important to success as a consultant. A consultant aims to develop and promote a new course of action for a business.

If the business is to take the consultant's advice, the consultant must communicate his or her ideas effectively. Communication is about informing people but it is not just about informing people. It is also about motivating them to act in a particular way. Successful management is not just about understanding the business one is in, or even about being able to make the right decisions. It is also about inspiring people, motivating them, of developing the power to push ideas forward and of taking a leadership role. These skills may seem elusive but a major part of them is understanding how to be a proficient communicator. To be effective as a communicator one needs to understand communication at several levels. This is a theme that is developed in the next chapter which considers rapport building. Communication is not just about transferring information: it is about influence as well. Good consultants not only relate their ideas but actively *advocate* a course and *motivate* others to follow it. People are social beings and when they communicate they interact at many levels. People act as a result of the information they are given and those actions are coloured by the nature, tone and context of the communication as well as its content. Consultants must understand the *how* of communication as well as *what* is to be communicated. As we will see later (in Chapter 24), effective communication is an integral part of leadership.

Communication can be thought of as a process. As is often the case when relating ideas it is helpful to create a model which can describe and be used to explore them. A general model of communication has been developed which highlights some of the important features of the process.

In this model there is a distinction between the sender of the message and its receiver. The first stage involves the decision by the sender on what they wish to include in the message that has to be sent, that is, what information they wish to send. The next stage involves encoding the message in some form; that is, expressing it in some way using a symbolic system – a language of some sort. The third stage involves transmitting the message through some medium. It is possible that the message may be confused by 'noise' interfering in the communication medium at this stage. The fourth stage involves the receiver of the message actually receiving it and decoding it. The fifth stage involves the receiver interpreting and acting on the message. The whole process is governed by a feedback mechanism. The act of communicating is modified in response to the reactions of the receiver. We may illustrate this process in the form of the diagram in Figure 21.1.

This model, though quite simple, actually tells us a lot about the nature of communication and how we can go about managing it. In particular it highlights:

◆ the fact that we never send information directly; it must be encoded in some way first;

◆ that communication can only occur if the sender and receiver both understand and share the rules of encoding/decoding the message – the language used;

◆ that the message may be interfered with by noise in the medium through which it is being transmitted – the message may be misunderstood;

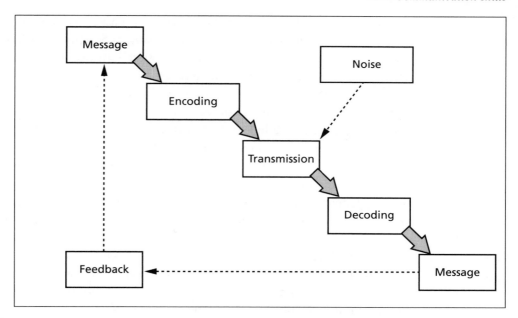

Figure 21.1 The communication process

- that receiving a message is an active part of the communication process, not a passive one;
- that actions are taken as a result of communication.

These are important points which we will need to keep in mind when we start to consider the management of the communication process.

21.2 Communication as a business tool

Communication is a fundamental aspect of business life. But business communication is not something which is undertaken for its own benefit. Communication is effective only if it leads to the right decisions being made and, as a result, the correct courses of action being followed. People cannot make the right decisions unless they have the right information to hand. Communication is the means by which people obtain and transmit information and indicate what information they need in order to make decisions.

Actions are a result of the decisions that people make. Communication can encourage them to take one particular course of action over others. Communication is a process governed by feedback. Once initiated, communication leads to further communication. We judge other people's perceptions of our actions by the feedback (response communication) we get. In general, positive feedback encourages or reinforces particular actions. Negative feedback discourages them. Communication, information, decision making and action taking are then linked in a loop. Managing communication effectively, using it as a business tool, is about managing this loop in its entirety.

Communication is not just a passive, background, aspect of organisational life; it is the very thing that makes organisations happen. It is therefore important that communication is looked upon as an active part of business activity. And, as with any business activity, the objectives of communication need to be considered. Of course, the extent to which formal and explicit objectives are set will depend on the nature of the communication. A major presentation to the client will demand a formal consideration of objectives. A telephone call to check on some facts will have objectives which are implicit and will not need much explicit consideration.

None the less, all communication should be undertaken with some objective in mind. The following is a quite general framework for setting communication objectives. They apply to any communication: not just those between the consultant and client but those between members of the consulting team.

The critical objective is:

◆ What do I want to happen as a result of this communication?

In other words, the question to be answered is not, 'What do I want to say?' but, 'What do I want to happen as a result of saying it?'

Once this objective has been resolved the following questions need to be asked:

◆ Who will be the recipients of the communication?

◆ What information needs to be conveyed?

◆ What actions should the recipient(s) take as a result of the communication?

One of the key actions that the recipient might take is to provide you with some information, so it is also important to consider:

◆ What information should they give as part of their response? (In other words, 'What do I want them to tell me?')

People act on emotional as well as rational grounds. People emerge from communication encounters feeling motivated or demotivated. So consider:

◆ How should the recipient *feel* as a result of the communication?

A further question that should be asked is:

◆ What information do the recipients need in order to act in the way desired?

Don't flood the listener(s) with information. Consider what is the minimum information the audience will need to complete the actions that are needed. Consider whether it will be a hindrance if the recipients have to come back for more information. Or will this in fact help? This question is related to a further one that must be asked:

◆ What level should the information be at?

How deep is the audience's understanding (and desire to understand) specific details. Do they want a broad picture or a highly detailed account? How technically competent are the audience? How much technical detail do they need?

Don't forget that communication is a continuous process not a one-off exercise. Consider what follow-up actions will be needed as a result of the communication to ensure the desired actions occur. The consultant is engaged in a continual process of communication with the client. This process does more than just transfer information. It is the basis on which an effective and rewarding working relationship is built.

We can integrate these questions into the model of business communication illustrated in Figure 21.1.

21.3 Verbal communication

If the written word is the skeleton of organisational communication then the spoken word is its flesh. Oral communication is so pervasive that we often forget that it constitutes a distinct aspect of organisational life. The types of spoken communication vary enormously and the situations in which it occurs are diverse. Oral communication can occur between just two people, within a small group (the consulting team) or to a large audience. The communication can be one way or be interactive. The forum in which the communication takes place can be either formal or informal. It can occur with the communicators located together, or with the assistance of modern communication technology, separated by enormous distances. Teleconferencing allows long-distance group communication to occur. The spoken word can be 'stored' but this requires the use of sound recording technology.

The advantages of oral communication are:

1 It is flexible: communications can be generated quickly.

2 It is of relatively low cost.

3 The communication can be supported by personal contact: persuasion may be easier.

4 The meaning of messages can be complemented and modified by paralanguage and non-verbal communication (*see* below).

5 It allows instant feedback.

There are, however, a number of disadvantages:

1 It does not (usually) leave a permanent record.

2 It can be difficult to control and direct (especially when large groups are involved).

3 Responses are expected quickly: there may be little time to plan and think ahead.

4 It can easily be dominated, especially where there are strong-willed people with opposing views.

The fact that verbal communication is 'instantaneous' and that it is 'inexpensive' leads to such communication often occurring on an *ad hoc* rather than a planned basis. We can be called upon to respond to an oral communication (say, to give an immediate answer to a question via a telephone call) in a way which we are not with a written communication. We can have time to think before responding to a memo or an e-mail. Indeed, as social beings, we are required to indulge in oral communications to a much higher degree than in other forms of communication. Note that every human society has access to a spoken language though, historically, only a minority have found the need to develop written versions of that language.

This insistence that we engage, almost instantaneously, in verbal exchanges means that there is a particular challenge in planning for oral communication. However, there is still a great deal to be gained from planning and a little time dedicated to this can reap enormous benefits in terms of its effectiveness.

Some situations, particularly those which are formal and those that involve communication to larger groups – presenting the final report, for example – are relatively easy to prepare for. With a presentation or a speech, the planning has a great deal in common with that of written communication. Indeed the words spoken may be from a written script. With less formal communications, or those to small groups where the oral interaction is highly iterative and built on feedback, the planning may have to occur while the conversation is unfolding.

Planning for oral communication falls into two types: *prior* planning where what is to be said is decided before the conversation occurs and an *ongoing* planning which occurs while the conversation is taking place. This second form of planning is, in a sense, more natural, in that – to some extent or other – we all do it anyway. Yet, because we are not being given much time to think, it is perhaps the more difficult. It can be made much easier by a little prior thinking about the conversation that is to take place.

Oral communication has the same objectives as other forms of communication and the same questions, such as the following, should be considered:

◆ What actions do I wish the recipient of the conversation to take?

◆ What information should be given?

◆ What should be the tone?

◆ How should the recipient feel?

Additionally, however, some consideration should be given to the kind of response the recipients might make:

◆ What kind of questions are they likely to ask?

◆ What additional information will be requested?

◆ What kind of problems and objections might be encountered?

Prior planning, so that answers to these questions have been considered before the communication starts, will aid ongoing planning during the communication and enhance greatly the effectiveness of that communication.

The meaning transferred through verbal communication is not just encoded in the words used. It is also related by how the words are used. The impact of a verbal communication is governed at several levels. The meaning encoded in verbal communications must be considered in terms of *paralanguage* as well as formal language.

Speech carries information through the sounds that are made (language). But it also carries important information in the way in which that language is used. Those aspects of spoken language which are not related to the actual content of what is being said are collectively known as *paralanguage*. As an old saying goes: 'It's not what you say but the way you say it.' Paralanguage includes aspects of spoken language such as:

◆ *Tone of voice* – indicating emotions, for example, anger, expectation, etc.:

They sounded very positive about the idea!

◆ *Timbre of voice* – indicating attitude, for example, trembling with apprehension, sneering with condescension, etc.:

It's a complicated idea. I don't understand it. It certainly doesn't help when experts talk down to you about it!

◆ *Timing* – particularly important for indicating degree of consideration and conviction, for example:

The client has finally agreed. Mind you she took some convincing. She paused for ages before she said yes to the budget we proposed.

Paralanguage is particularly important in communicating the emotional context of what is being said. Consider how flat and unemotional a voice synthesised by a computer can sound. This is because such a voice contains no paralanguage signals.

A challenge in planning oral communication that is not encountered in planning written communication is the consideration of non-verbal and paralanguage aspects of the communication. We do, of course, deal with these aspects constantly without really thinking about them. We are to a great extent instinctive communicators. If, however, we wish to effectively manage communication and its effects the ability to consciously control these aspects of our communication is a powerful tool.

21.4 Non-verbal communication

The fact that there are rational and emotional aspects to all communications means that the effectiveness of communication is an intimate mixture of content and context; of what is said and how it is said. With verbal communications paralanguage and body language are particularly important signifiers of context.

Non-verbal communication includes such aspects of communication as the following:

◆ Facial expression

Particularly expressive elements of the face, changes in which constitute forms of non-verbal communication, are the eyes, eyebrows and mouth. Consider:

It was a radical idea – he raised his eyebrows at the thought of it.

She was a bit critical – but with a smile.

◆ Body language

Body movements add to and extend spoken communication. It is easy to send both positive and negative messages with body language. Most body language signals are sent and received subconsciously.

◆ Posture

The positioning of the whole body with respect to what is being communicated can be a form of expression. An open posture (arms relaxed by the side of the body) is more inviting than a closed, defensive posture (arms folded across the chest).

◆ Gestures

Specific movements may add emphasis, for example, pointing, arm opening (indicating welcome), looking at the watch (indicating boredom), bringing the hand to the chin (indicating consideration). Gesture can mirror meaning. Relaxed body postures are more inviting than are tense ones. Facial gestures can indicate whether something is an enquiry or a statement. Open body postures are an indication that the debate is still 'open', closed body postures that it is 'closed'.

As discussed above, the objective of business communication is not so much one of delivering information but one of eliciting action. The management of communication can then be considered in two interrelated parts: first, making people receptive to the communication – that is, building rapport, and second, encouraging them to act on the message – that is, motivating action.

21.5 Written communication

Written communications are the backbone of organisational communication systems. The consultant's report, whether backed up with a presentation or not, is often seen by the client as the 'product' of the consulting exercise – the thing that is actually being paid for. The use of a written medium has a number of advantages in a business context:

1 With the written medium there is time to plan the communication before it is delivered.

2 Written communication is permanent; it can be stored.

3 It is unambiguous: what's written is written!

4 Written communications are easily copied.

5 The receiver has time to analyse the content of the communication at leisure.

6 It can be supplemented with visual communications (e.g. diagrams, graphs, etc.).

There are, however, a number of disadvantages to written communication:

1 It is slow compared with verbal communication.

2 There is little opportunity to modify the communication with paralanguage.

3 Feedback is restricted: there is a limited opportunity for the receiver to explore the communication with the sender (unless verbal communication is used as a supplement). Modern communication technology such as e-mail makes feedback easier. However, it is still slower than verbal communication.

The most important pieces of written communication the consultant makes are the initial project proposal and the final report.

21.6 Visual communication

The visual image is a very fundamental form of communication. It has a number of advantages:

1 The visual image can be very powerful.
2 It can be used to simplify complex ideas and relationships. (This is an idea discussed earlier, in Section 15.3.)
3 It can be used to support and add impact to other forms of communication.
4 Images are remembered (more so than words).

There are, however, a number of disadvantages:

1 Without supporting explanation the image may be ambiguous.
2 It may require special interpretation skills.
3 Production may be costly.

Visual images used in communication are very diverse: diagrams, graphs, photographs, sketches, drawings. Some techniques for visualising information so that patterns and relationships become clear were discussed in Section 15.3. Visual stimuli can be three-dimensional, for example, models. The visual image can be used in a variety of communication scenarios:

♦ when the subject of the communication is primarily visual;
♦ when complicated ideas need to be simplified;
♦ when complex relationships need to be demonstrated;
♦ when the communication requires emotional impact;
♦ when the message needs to be remembered: we remember information in the form of images much better than in a verbal form.

Given its strengths and weaknesses, visual communication really comes into its own when it is used in conjunction with other forms of communication. Some particularly important forms are:

♦ with written text:
  – diagrams, graphs and charts in reports;
  – images and pictures in product guides;
  – images and pictures in printed advertisements;

◆ with the spoken word:
  - slides and overheads used in presentations;
  - images in sales presentation materials;
  - images in television and print advertising;
  - models used with small group forums. Particularly important here are stimuli for brainstorming, focus group and other creative sessions.

The visual medium is very effective at representing information in a way which is memorable, draws attention to relationships and has impact. Take it as a rule of thumb that people will remember five to seven pieces of information from a visual image. Try to organise the information that you wish to communicate so that each image has about this number of key points. Key points include not only facts but also relationships between facts; so not only that this year's sales are £2 million but also that they are larger than last year's and smaller than is hoped for next year.

Be creative with visual images. Graphs are a good way of illustrating facts and the relationship between them but their impact can be made greater by customising them with bespoke images. Complex arguments can be made clearer by the use of flow diagrams which indicate how different aspects of the argument are logically interrelated.

Images can also indicate the way the audience is expected to feel about the information. Imagine a graph of a company's sales performance to which has been added the illustration of a rocket soaring away in flight – or the illustration of a sinking ship!

As a test for a visual image ask the following questions:

1 If the audience were asked to summarise the image what five facts would they indicate?

2 How would they feel about those facts? (That is, would they react positively or negatively? Consider the points made in Section 16.2.)

These points will be developed in Section 25.3 which considers the formal presentation of findings.

<table>
<tr><td>

Team discussion point
</td><td>

Go back to the project proposal you have made to the client. Analyse it as a piece of communication. Ask the following questions:

1 What was the objective of the communication?

2 Does this objective meet the criteria set for objectives discussed in Chapter 11?

3 What actions did you want the client to take as a result of reading the proposal?

4 What is the mix of 'rational' and 'emotional' elements in the communication?

5 Did you talk the client through the proposal on a one-to-one basis? If not, do you think this might have added to the impact of the proposal?

Discuss these issues in your team.
</td></tr>
</table>

Summary of key ideas

◆ An ability to communicate effectively is a critical skill for a consultant.

◆ Communication is not just about passing information: it is about getting the recipient of that information to act in a particular way.

◆ Communication has an impact at a rational and emotional level.

◆ Objectives should be set for communication.

◆ Communication can take place through verbal, written and visual mediums. Each has its own advantages and disadvantages.

◆ Verbal communication is influenced by more than just content: paralanguage and body language are also important.

22

Rapport-building skills

Learning outcomes

The key learning outcomes of this chapter are:
- to recognise the importance of rapport in building managerial relationships;
- to understand how rapport can be built and used.

22.1 Rapport and influence

Decisions are made with an eye to what will follow as a consequence of their being made. Decision making may be formalised – for example by using probabilities and decision trees. However, human decision making cannot be reduced to a simple procedure of calculating outcomes and expectations.

Understanding business decision making requires more than the assumption that managers will always act in a way which is completely rational and predictable. Assumptions about rational behaviour can only be a starting-point for considering decision-making behaviour in the real world. For a start, managers do not have access to all the information that is available about a situation. Such information, even if it is available, may be expensive to obtain. In any case, human beings are limited in the amount of information they can handle at any one time. So managers make decisions, to some extent or other 'in the dark'.

We must also recognise that the objectives of managers are much more complex than simply maximising economic returns. As was noted in Chapter 16, a problem demanding a decision has cognitive and political dimensions as well as its rational dimension. Concerns for social well-being and cultural values may limit profit-maximising activities that are deemed to be unacceptable behaviour. Additionally, managers may not attempt to optimise their organisation's performance because it is not in their interest to do so. They may divert resources from the owners of the firm (the shareholders, say) for their own internal use.

These diverted resources are called agency costs. Further, not all decision making need be rational in the sense of being directed towards improving material well-being. Decisions may be aimed at satisfying emotional as well as physical wants and needs. Decision making needs to be understood in terms of emotive as well as rational factors. It is this, which makes not only *what* is said, but the *way* in which it is said an important part of managing business communication and making it effective.

This said, it is true that managers, on the whole, do attempt to improve the performance of their organisations. When managers work together they take this as a starting assumption. Managers who explicitly work against the interests of their organisations are at best regarded as perverse and at worst as criminal. Working together positively is the explicit 'rule of the game' as far as organisational management is concerned. However some of the rules of the game are *unwritten*, as Peter Scott-Morgan, the Arthur D. Little consultant. points out in his book of that name (1994).

There are a number of reasons why some rules are unwritten. Managers enhance performance in a way which is limited. It must reflect their less than complete knowledge of the world, their inability to process information perfectly, their concern for things other than just the organisation's profits and their interests outside the organisation. Behaviour such as this is referred to as satisficing rather than profit maximising. Peter Scott-Morgan's book is recommended to any student who wants to understand how managers *really* work together.

The fact that there are rational and emotional aspects to all communications means that the effectiveness of communication is an intimate mixture of content and context; of *what* is said and *how* it is said. As noted in the previous chapter, the actual substance of verbal communications is modified by the delivery context. Factors such as paralanguage – the tonal quality of verbal delivery, and body language – gestures that are used to support verbal delivery, are important. This implies that effective communication not only requires that a message be sent but that it be sent in a way, and in a context, that encourages the receiver to actively absorb, interpret and understand the message and then to act on it in a certain way. This can be illustrated by the model in Figure 22.1.

Ensuring that the context of the message is one which makes it likely that the receiver will understand it, be sympathetic to it and respond positively to it is called *building rapport*. Good rapport should mean that the receiver of the message not only understands the information in the communication but also has a good perception of the sender and his or her intentions. Additionally it should mean that the receiver has a positive attitude towards the message and the actions it calls for. In everyday use the term 'rapport' is usually employed to refer to a situation of verbal communication where the speakers are said to be

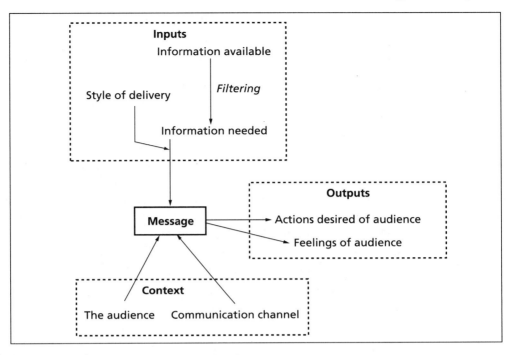

Figure 22.1 Content and context in communication

'hitting it off' or 'on each other's wave length' or 'speaking the same language'. In this kind of situation the speakers are at ease with each other, the conversation is creative and flows easily. The speakers are receptive to and understand each other. They are comfortable exploring problems as well as successes and, critically, they are motivated to act on the messages they are sending to each other. Such aspects of a relationship may be summarised as its *congeniality*. The value of congeniality in an effective business partnership is considerable. The problems that occur when its opposite – a failure to build congeniality or simply 'to hit it off' – happens will be appreciated!

Rapport, although particularly important in relation to verbal communication, is not confined to such communication; it is a feature of communication generally. Consider how we feel when we read something and we appreciate how sympathetic the writer has been to our level of understanding of what is being discussed, or how we feel when presented with a diagram we do not understand. These are also aspects of building, and failing to build, rapport.

Rapport may seem to be quite elusive. It is something we recognise when we see it (and notice when it is missing), but which is difficult to define. The ability to build rapport may appear to be a part of personality – something one either possesses or does not. In fact, building rapport is a skill that can be learned. Like any management skill, rapport building is something which can be developed with practice and which, in time, becomes quite automatic. The following are some general points to remember which will help with building rapport when communicating.

◆ Vocabulary

Use words that the audience both understand and will have resonance with. Use short words rather than long ones. Avoid technical terms if there is any doubt that the audience will not understand them. If a word the audience is unlikely to have met before must be introduced then take care to clarify its meaning. Never think that there is anything to be gained by 'blinding the audience with science'.

The consultant should be particularly cautious about talking in terms of the models and frameworks used to analyse and resolve business problems. In many cases, these will be meaningless to the client. Furthermore, these are the tools of the consultant's trade. The client will be interested in the work done with them, not in the tools themselves.

◆ Syntax

The word syntax refers to the overall grammatical structure of the sentences. Consider the audience. Which is more appropriate: a dynamic, 'bullish' style or a more 'reserved' style? If a dynamic style is required, consider the following points.

◆ Short sentences combined with imperatives (demands, commands, instructions) are particularly potent. Compare:

> *This is a good opportunity. We won't get another chance like this one. Let's get on with it!*

with

> *This is a good opportunity and another is unlikely to occur in the near future so we should progress it.*

◆ Active rather than passive constructions are better where a dynamic effect is wanted. Compare:

> *This will really improve company performance.*

with

> *The company's performance is something which will be improved by this.*

◆ Logical structures

It is very easy to get too close to the argument you wish to make. Its logic may appear to be so obvious that the validity of the argument should be clear to everybody. Unfortunately, to other people, the argument you wish to make may appear to be anything but obvious.

Consider the logical structuring of the argument you wish to make. Use mind maps or flow diagrams to decide how ideas should be linked (*see* Section 15.6) Consider questions such as:

◆ What information does the receiver need?

◆ At what stage in the argument?

Be selective, emphasise and highlight key points.

◆ How should the elements of the argument be progressed?

◆ What objections might be made at each stage?

◆ How can they be dealt with?

Try to recognise the receiver's cognitive style, as discussed in Section 15.5 and resonate with it.

◆ Imagery and metaphors

Verbal and written communications can be given great impact by the creative use of metaphor. A metaphor is a figure of speech in which one thing is compared to another. The objective is, by emphasising that something is like something else, to suggest parallels and new relationships. It also creates a mental image which gives impact to an idea. Together these can suggest a potent theme about which an argument can be hung. Consider, for example:

> *We're all pulling in the same direction now.*

> *I know the sales force are working hard but they're catching the little fish. We need to help them go after the big ones!*

> *I agree, there is a window of opportunity and I can see how we can open it. But our competitors won't be slow in following us. If we open the window can we close it behind us again?*

Again, the impact of imagery and metaphor will be a function of the receiver's cognitive style. Actively listen and make note of the metaphors and images the client uses. Adopt them and develop them to make your point. The student who is interested in a detailed discussion on the use of metaphor as a communication technique is referred to the excellent paper by Tsoukas (1991).

◆ Style

The style should be appropriate for the communication taking place. On the whole informality is usually better for creating rapport. But be careful. Too much informality, too early may be interpreted as disrespect. Some organisations are careful to keep a high power distance between management levels, whereas others encourage informality.

When two people begin to communicate for the first time the level of formality is usually high. As the communication (and the relationship generally) develops, the level of formality tends to drop. This process is largely automatic, with subtle changes in language, paralanguage and body language occurring. But it is also punctuated with conscious decisions to move the relationship on to a less formal footing; for example the decision to use someone's first name for the first time. With a little practice it is possible to actively manage the level of formality with language and body language signs. An experienced consultant will manage the level of formality, bringing it down to build a more open relationship with the client.

◆ Using body language

With verbal communications a great deal of context information is provided by body language. 'Open' body language gestures rather than 'closed' are better for building rapport. In general, avoid protective gestures which send the signal, 'I am protecting myself from you'. (One such gesture is the folding of the arms in front of the chest, an action that is very easily taken when one is giving formal presentations!)

One subtle, but powerful device in developing rapport with one-to-one communication is that of posture mirroring. This technique involves imagining that there is a mirror between you and the person with whom you are communicating. The idea is to consider how that person's image would appear in a mirror to them and then adopt a posture appropriate to this image. A related technique is that of gesture resonance. Everybody uses gestures and body language to some extent.

With a little observation we can observe the gestures and body language people use to emphasise a point or indicate that something is particularly important. The trick is then to use the same gestures to emphasise our points and indicate what we feel to be important. This body language will have particular impact for and resonance with the listener.

To some extent we tend to do these things naturally and we certainly feel more comfortable with people who share these aspects of our (subconscious) communication. With a little practice this posture mirroring and gesture resonance can be used to 'open up' someone's body language and (remarkably) their receptiveness to our message. A word of warning, however. These techniques take practice and there is a fine (and dangerous) line between mirroring and mimicry; the latter will be very poorly received!

Rapport is a very powerful way of getting someone to be receptive to the message being delivered and leaving them with a good perception and a positive attitude. But in terms of motivating action it is only a starting-point. To ensure that the receiver of the message will pursue the actions desired by the sender, credibility, confidence and expectation need to be managed as well.

Rapport is to a great extent a cultural phenomenon. It depends on a cultural context. Rapport may be difficult to build with a person from a different culture – not because that person is being difficult but because he or she is not reading and responding to signals in the way you intended. (It is worth considering this in terms of the communication model developed in Section 21.1.)

This is a complex area. There are no formulaic rules. Gestures may be important. (For example, blowing one's nose is considered very rude in Uzbekistan, whereas spitting is not!) Formalities matter (e.g. the way you handle a business card in Japan). Power distance – the social separation between people of different 'ranks' in the organisation – affects the extent and speed with which formality moves on to informality (low in Australia but usually quite high in the rest of the Pacific Rim).

As when dealing with any new challenge, the consultant is advised to obtain advice from an expert. If a project in which a consultant is involved takes on an international perspective he or she should try to talk to someone who has experience of working in the country concerned. He or she should seek to find out the nuances of the local managerial do's and don'ts. Business guides which provide briefings on managerial cultures in other countries are also highly informative.

Much can be gained by brushing up on the country's history – for good, brief overviews travel guides are valuable. It is amazing how people's behaviour makes sense when you understand even a little about their cultural and historical context. Read through some back issues of *The Economist* or *Financial Times* reviews to get a feel for current affairs. This will provide some useful talking points which will help to break the ice (and give the impression that you are informed and on-the-ball). The main thing is not to be intimidated! People from different cultures usually work well together and enjoy the experience of learning about each other as a positive to be enjoyed, not a problem to be dealt with.

22.2 Personal presentation

Situations in which it is necessary to brief the client or influential external people on some issue are common in consulting exercises. These can vary from an informal chat with the client to a formal presentation with members of the company's board or detailing the company's performance to a major investor. The situation can be one of explaining success or warning of some problem. The issue might be an emergency requiring immediate action or the development of a long-term view. The rules for dealing with these situations are, however, quite general.

As with any communication the first question that must be asked is, 'What actions do I wish to have taken as a result of the communication?' In particular:

◆ What actions do you wish the listener(s) to take?

◆ What support will those actions need in order to make them effective?

◆ What actions will you yourself have to take in order to provide that support?

With answers to these questions firmly in mind you can begin planning the briefing. The first stage is to analyse the situation that is to be the subject of the briefing:

1 Identify the key issues: what will the briefing communicate?

2 What is the logical order in which to present the issues?

3 What supporting information will be needed?

4 What recommendations would you make regarding the situation?

Try to understand the situation from the perspective of the listener(s).

◆ How important will the issue be from their perspective? How quickly will they need to act?

◆ What information are they going to need before they can act?

◆ Is it appropriate to propose your own recommendations for dealing with the situation?

◆ How can you encourage the audience to make their own suggestions?

With these issues resolved you can answer questions relating to the logistics of the briefing:

◆ Should the forum be formal or informal?

◆ What supporting mediums should be used for delivery (written, verbal, visual)?

◆ What supporting information needs to be provided? Should this be in a documented form?

Effective management briefing skills are relatively easy to develop and are an important dimension in giving the all-important impression of being competent and in control.

22.3 Questioning skills

Questioning is a fundamental part of communication. By definition, a question is a request for information. But its role in communication, especially business communication, goes far beyond this. Questioning is a way of leading and controlling communication. The person asking questions is not only gaining information; he or she is in control of the conversation. Questioning is a way of leading and focusing a debate.

There are two sorts of questions. *Open questions* invite a long answer. They can be used to open up the discussion. They give the respondent a good deal of latitude in what he or she reveals. *Closed questions* require a yes or no answer (ostensibly at least). They give the respondent little space. They can bring the conversation to a halt. Most conversations involve both open and closed questions. Effective questioning demands two things. First, asking the *right questions*, and second, asking them in the *right way*.

The first is a matter of preparation. Consider what you need to know. Develop a list of key questions in advance. Use open questions first. This opens up the conversation. You will find new issues coming to light as the discussion goes on. Further questions can be asked to explore these avenues. (Hint: if you are taking notes a mind map approach will give you flexibility in building the structure of the conversation.) Closed questions can be used later to confirm points and bring the conversation to an end.

Most business people are more than happy to talk about their business. They are usually flattered by interest. Asking questions is a matter of practice. Positive questions usually get a positive response. A positive open question is a good means of starting a conversation on a high note. Examples are:

What would you describe as the main factors behind the success of your business?

Your business has been successful. Why is that?

Try to avoid interrogating with what seems to be a stream of evident questions. This can be a little wearing for the respondent. Vary your style. Not all enquiries must be grammatical questions. A statement made in the right way (on a rising tone with a quizzical look) will be responded to as a question. Use body language to open up the speaker. Motivate him or her with active listening. Above all, use the questioning to build rapport.

22.4 Listening skills

So much is going on in a conversation it's a wonder we have any time to listen! Despite the fact that listening may seem to be a passive part of communication, that we just need to sit back and let it happen, listening is in fact a very active part of verbal communication. We positively set out to listen. How often have we felt that something has 'gone in one ear and out the other'? In a conversation we often use other people's speaking time to prepare what we are going to say rather than use it to listen to what *they* are actually saying. But if we don't listen to people and absorb what they have to say how can we engage in effective communication with them? As an active part of communication listening represents a skill that can be improved.

Some points to help with this are:

1 Actively concentrate on what is being said. It is easy for the mind to drift.

2 Keep track of, and mentally summarise, the key themes in what is being said.

3 Keep an ear out for particularly relevant ideas or facts.

4 Identify and mentally record key phrases.

5 Note the speaker's use of metaphor and imagery.

6 Use your own paralanguage and body language to encourage the speaker (this does help active listening – try it).

7 When appropriate, ask questions to explore key points further.

8 Summarise the speaker's points and ask him or her to confirm your understanding.

9 If possible support active listening with note taking. The project log is a good place to keep such notes.

10 Avoid concentrating on preparing your own response while the other person is speaking. Don't feel you must answer right away. It is perfectly acceptable to take a few seconds to reflect on what has been said and then respond. In fact, this will make it clear that you are concentrating on what the speaker is saying and will motivate them.

You will find that with a little practice active listening, far from detracting from your ability to prepare responses, positively enhances it, not least because your responses will be relevant to the other speaker.

22.5 Managing client expectations

An important aspect of successful communication is managing the expectations that are being developed. The main danger is that of creating expectations that cannot be met. It is particularly easy to 'over-promise' something when selling the project. If this occurs, the recipient will be disappointed – whatever is delivered – even though the recipient might have been highly satisfied with the same outcome if what is delivered had been slightly 'undersold'. Such disappointments will be hard to overcome in the future.

When communicating what the consulting project can do for the business bear in mind the following:

◆ Be clear as to what can be offered.

◆ Be positive about what can be offered, but be realistic.

◆ Be honest about the limitations of the project.

◆ When talking about limitations put them between positive statements – a kind of *positive-negative-positive* sandwich. (Consider this in conjunction with the discussion on problem interpretation in Section 16.2.)

When two people communicate, expectations are created on both sides. Expectations are, simply, beliefs about what will happen in the future, or what outcomes to expect. The extent to which actual outcomes are felt to be satisfactory is not so much a function of the absolute value of those outcomes as of how they compare with expectations. Put simply:

◆ Outcomes more than expectations = high satisfaction.

◆ Outcomes equal to expectations = satisfaction.

◆ Outcomes less than expectations = dissatisfaction.

An aid to building rapport and trust is to be confident, when discussing, as to whether these limitations are really significant for the recipient and, if so, how they can be overcome.

Credibility relates to the recipient's perception as to the sender's ability to satisfy the expectations being generated. In other words: 'Can this person (or organisation) make this happen?' Credibility is not a once-and-for-all thing; it is an ongoing thing which is built (and eroded) over time. Initially, however, credibility is provided through evidence. In particular this will centre on the following:

◆ Is what is being offered viable?

◆ Does the proposer have the expertise/ability to make the offer?

◆ Are the necessary resources in place?

◆ How satisfactory have previous experiences been?

◆ What is the proposer's reputation?

These issues do of course represent the rational aspects of decision making. As has been discussed in Section 22.1, decision making is also built on emotional perceptions and attitudes.

Confidence is a function of credibility and expectations but it also involves a further dimension: the importance or significance of what is being considered. Higher demands will be made on credibility if something is highly important than if it is relatively trivial. This links to the ever-present concerns about what will happen if the outcomes are not achieved, and introduces the idea of the risk inherent in acting on the communication.

Confidence occurs if the level of credibility suggests that expectations will be achieved to a degree that satisfies concerns about those outcomes not being achieved. The ability to consider and manage expectations, to develop credibility and engender confidence, is crucial in getting people to take actions which they believe to have some element of risk.

The management of credibility begins at the start of the consulting exercise. Credibility comes from satisfying realistic expectations. Expectations are managed through the consulting proposal (*refer back to* Section 9.1 for a discussion). If expectations are unrealistic at the start, credibility will be hard to manage later.

22.6 Maintaining client interest

Managers are busy people. They will have many commitments. The consulting exercise will be only one of the projects they are involved in. Events move on. As the project progresses, the manager's priorities will change. The opportunity to develop new business opportunities will loom. It is possible, even probable, that the importance of the consulting project to the manager will diminish. If the manager's interest is to be maintained then the consulting team must keep the manager informed and motivated about the project.

Keep up the communication. Give the manager regular updates on the project and how it is developing. Remind him or her of the outputs of the project and the value these will have to the business. Check on how the business is developing. What projects is the manager involved in now? How can the consulting exercise help with them? In short, keep communicating and keep building the consultant–client rapport.

22.7 Neuro-linguistic programming as a consulting tool

Neuro-linguistic programming (usually referred to as NLP) is a technique used in cognitive psychology. It was developed in the United States by Richard Bandler and John Grinder. It is used primarily as a therapeutic technique. It has however been advocated by some management practitioners as a powerful means of enhancing communication, building motivation (both in oneself and in others) and facilitating rapport. For this reason it is useful for the consultant to be aware of the technique and its potential.

NLP is based on the ideas that individuals have inbuilt mental filters which are used to process information about the world and to build representations of it and that these filters can be managed through communication of the right sort.

These filters are as follows:

◆ *Meta programmes*: these are cognitive facilities which process this information in three key ways: *deletion* (the paying of attention to some information while ignoring other bits); *distortion* (changing the nature of a piece of information) and *generalisation* (using a few pieces of information to develop generalised conclusion). Meta programmes have resonance with the idea of cognitive styles discussed in Section 15.5.

◆ *Values*: a core set of routines used to make judgements about what is good and bad or right and wrong.

◆ *Beliefs*: convictions about what is real or imaginary and true or false.

◆ *Attitudes*: values specific to particular issues, subjects and events.

◆ *Memories*: collections of recollections about the past.

◆ *Decisions*: which are a special category of memories about how we reacted to events in the past and the outcomes that resulted. Decisions feed back and create and reinforce beliefs and attitudes.

NLP makes a number of proposals. First, that these filters are fundamental to the way in which individuals see the world and respond to it. They even underlie self-communication. Second, that these filters are revealed through the way in which people communicate, often in very subtle ways (through eye movements, for example). Third, that these filters can be 'read' by an expert observer. Fourth, that the filters can be influenced and modified through a process of communication. This influencing can be directed at motivating an individual and encouraging him or her to act in a certain way – hence, the interest of management practitioners in the technique.

The technique is quite complex and needs practice to be used effectively. It is not without its detractors among mainstream psychologists. Some consider that its assumptions are not valid and that it is not based on rigorous observation and experiment. This debate will continue. The student interested in NLP and its possibilities is referred to the Suggestions for further reading (pp. 323–5) for further information on the technique. The works by Robert Dilts (1980), Steve and Connirae Andreas (1987) and Tad James and Wyatt Woodsmall (1988) are particularly recommended.

Team discussion point

Read the following short case study.

Holroyd Engineering is a private company founded some twenty years ago by David Holroyd. The main line of business is machining parts for the automotive industry. The company has 20 employees. David is now 63. He is in the process of passing over control of the business to his son, Donald. However, he still comes in most days.

Donald is in his early forties. He heads the management team which consists of four directors. The others are Graham Sullivan, the marketing director, Philip King, the production director and Tony Milligan, the finance director. Graham, 36, is new to the firm. He joined from a firm of consultants after undertaking a project for the firm. He was recruited by Donald. Philip, 59, and Tony, 61, were recruited by David Holroyd shortly after the firm was founded.

Donald Holroyd has called in a consulting team to undertake a full strategic review of the business. He is convinced that it has growth potential that his father has missed. He has asked Graham to lead the project.

The team have visited the site. Graham had arranged a short presentation on the company and its market. Graham then moved on to show them around. While on the tour they met with David. David rather took over and insisted on showing them the latest machine tools. He asked them about the project they were undertaking. When they mentioned marketing he grabbed a gear wheel that had just been cut. He held it up. 'Don't worry about marketing,' he said, 'a good product sells itself!'.

As a team, discuss the likely communication priorities for the consulting team in this case.

Summary of key ideas

◆ Communication has emotional as well as rational aspects.

◆ A consultant–client relationship works best if there is rapport between them.

◆ Rapport building is a relationship skill that can be learned.

◆ The secret of rapport is, in great part, a sympathy with the listener's communication needs.

◆ Rapport building depends on good questioning and listening skills.

◆ A consulting exercise will only be successful if the consultant actively manages both the client's interest in and his/her expectations of the project.

◆ Neuro-linguistic programming (NLP) may offer an approach to managing communication, motivation and rapport.

23

Team-working skills

Learning outcomes

The key learning outcomes from this chapter are:

◆ to understand the process of team formation and how it might be managed;

◆ to recognise how team conflicts are caused and how they might be resolved;

◆ to appreciate the way in which external people might be drawn in to support the team in its project.

23.1 The dynamics of team working

Teams are perhaps the most important feature of modern managerial life. Increasingly they are taking priority over traditional business departments. Departments are a good way of organising jobs around fixed functions such as marketing, finance and operations. They work well for established, medium to large businesses in stable, predictable environments. However, many types of business find such a departmentalised structure inappropriate. Small businesses do not have sufficient people. Allocating responsibilities to departments may not fit with the organisational style of the entrepreneur running the firm. A fast-growing firm or a firm in a fast-changing environment may need to change roles rapidly. Fixed structures may limit this adaptability. For organisations such as these, the small team structure offers a way of allowing individuals to specialise their contributions to the venture without creating structures which develop a life and a logic of their own.

Even established organisations are finding that an element of team working shifts emphasis from jobs to tasks: from what people assume they are paid to do to what needs to be done in order to progress the business. Bureaucracies are moving towards 'adhocratic' structures which combine the benefits of fixed organisation with the dynamism of entrepreneurial teams.

For these reasons, management experts have taken a keen interest in the way in which teams form and function and what influences their productivity. An important part of these studies has been investigation into the factors which influence the structure of teams and the way in which they work. A useful approach is to classify these variables into two groups: intrinsic, which are features of the group itself and extrinsic, those factors which come from outside the group.

◆ Intrinsic factors

The important intrinsic factors are as follows.

Group size

The larger the group, the more latitude there is for individuals to specialise their roles. However, larger groups are more difficult to manage than smaller groups and it is harder to maintain cohesiveness. The dynamics of a group are a function of the way in which individual members interact with each other. The number of possible interactions between group members increases dramatically as group size increases. Above a certain size (probably around 10–15 members) a balanced pattern of individual interactions becomes impossible and subgroups with their own pattern of interactions will tend to form. The management challenge will be to keep all the subgroups focused on the overall group objective. Typically, consulting groups have a size of 4–7 people. This is a good size as it provides adequate resources, but it is relatively easy to keep the members focused. Some larger projects may involve larger numbers.

Stage in group formation

The function of a group changes over time. Groups, like individuals, learn to do their tasks. As discussed below, groups undergo clear stages in their development. The productivity of the group depends on the stage it has reached.

Individual expertise and specialisms

Groups offer individuals an opportunity to specialise their contributions to the overall venture. The shape and function of the group will be affected by the expertise and specialisms of individuals. The development of the group will be influenced by the way in which individuals are allowed to enhance their expertise within the group. The kind of specialisms individuals can develop within the consulting group have been discussed in Section 12.2. Group roles represent the formalisation of the contributions individuals can make. Groups in which all members share a specialism are called homogeneous. Groups formed from members with widely differing specialisms are referred to as heterogeneous.

Group norms and culture

Groups are formed by individuals who have their own social experiences and expectations. The group operates in a social environment. Social norms influence the way in which the group works. The group itself will develop its own 'local' culture. A culture can be thought of as the set of rules (formal, informal, explicit and implicit) which define what is allowed as behaviour within the group and what is not. An important element of group culture is the way in which the members of the group distinguish between themselves and outsiders. Groups which exclude outsiders are referred to as closed. Those that easily include outsiders are called open.

Leadership

Effective leadership is essential if the team is to maintain its coherence and to be focused towards its objectives. The leader plays a crucial role in organising tasks, allocating resources and resolving conflicts. The leader may play a symbolic role, giving the group an identity and representing it to the outside world. However, leadership should not be thought to be just what the leader does. Leadership is a group activity that takes on many guises. Leadership does not emanate from the leader. It occurs when leaders and followers interact with each other. Active leadership demands the participation of the whole team.

Individual personalities

Groups are made up of individuals. Although groups offer individuals a chance to integrate their efforts the group does not subsume the individual personality. The way the group functions will, in part, depend on the personalities of the individuals who make it up. Individual personalities give the group its character. They can make it fun to work with. There is no such thing as the 'right' group personality. A good team has a mix of personalities. Extroverts and introverts, the articulate and the reflective, all have a role to play. The cognitive style and strategy of individuals are elements of personality that are pertinent to the way team members interact, identify issues and solve problems.

Group motivation

A critical dimension in the cohesiveness and performance of the group is the motivations of its members. A number of models provide an insight into the factors which motivate individuals to be part of a group. They share the common assumption that individuals are motivated at a number of levels. Abraham Maslow provided one of the most famous formulations in 1954. It describes five levels. Maslow suggests that individuals are motivated to address each of these levels in turn. The first level is physiological needs: the basics of human survival – food, air and water. The next level is safety – the need for a basic level of comfort and protection. The third level represents social needs – the desire to be part of a community of fellow people. Once these are addressed, the individual is motivated to satisfy the higher needs of esteem – standing within the social group, and self-actualisation – the desire to develop in an intellectual and spiritual way.

Frederick Herzberg with co-workers (1959) suggested a two-factor model of motivation. Satisfaction was not merely at the opposite end of a spectrum from dissatisfaction. In fact, he proposed, the two worked independently to characterise an individual's approach to a task. Motivators are positive factors which attract; hygiene factors are negatives which, if present, will demotivate. Herzberg found that addressing hygiene factors alone will not motivate. Positive motivators must also be present.

David McClelland in a seminal study of entrepreneurial motivation (1961) found that three motivation factors were important for driving entrepreneurs. These are a need for achievement – to make a difference, a need for power – to be in control, and a need for affiliation – to interact socially with others. People with these needs found the move to entrepreneurship attractive if the option of working for themselves offered a means to satisfy the needs more effectively than they could do working for an established organisation.

Douglas McGregor (1960) suggested that managers adopt one of two overarching views – or paradigms – about the nature of human motivation which determined their approach to managing. His Theory X held that people basically dislike work and that if workers can get away with it, they will shirk their responsibilities. A consequence of this view was that managers must be vigilant and keep up the pressure on their workers. His Theory Y held that individuals basically enjoy work and that if given the opportunity people will be motivated and show initiative. A consequence of this view is that the manager must create an environment in which the individual is given freedom to contribute. There is evidence to support both views and it is likely that each may be valid in different circumstances. The consultant, who usually lacks formal authority in the client organisation, must learn to rely predominantly on Theory Y assumptions.

These intrinsic factors interact with a range of external, extrinsic factors in defining the group form and function.

◆ Extrinsic factors

The critical extrinsic factors are as follows.

Group task

The issue that defines the team and draws it together is the task it exists to address. The nature of the task is an important shaping force. The task provides a challenge. The team is motivated to meet that challenge. A number of aspects of the task are relevant. The *familiarity* of the team with the task type is important. The more experience the team has, the more individual roles and interactions will have been defined. It is likely the team will be more confident in its abilities. This will be especially so if the team has had earlier successes with tasks of this type. On the other hand, a new task will present new challenges which will generate new interest, especially for those with a cognitive style which seeks new experiences. The *complexity* of the task will drive role differentiation within the team. If complexity is high there will be an encouragement to specialise. Complexity is especially relevant to information processing and communication tasks. A third task factor is the *significance of outcomes*. A task which is important to the client organisation, one which has outcomes of significance, will lead to pressure on the team. It will also increase the team's power to gain resources and drive change. A meta-study by Mark Tubbs (1986) supports the view that motivation is increased by well-defined and accepted goals which stretch the individual and team.

Every consulting project is different. Each offers its own unique challenges. However, consultants develop familiarity with managing the overall consulting process (*see* Chapter 8). Consulting tasks vary greatly in their complexity. As far as the student consulting project is concerned, it is important that the team accept a project which is of the right level of complexity, that is challenging but realistic – a point discussed in Chapter 12. The significance of the project will vary according to the needs of the client, expectations and the level of trust in the team's ability. In general the best student consulting projects are those that relate to information that it would be 'nice to have'. They are of value to the client and are projects that the client would like to undertake if the resources were available. However, they will not be critical to the survival of the business.

Resource availability

A team needs resources in order to pursue the task it is required to address. The level of resources made available will influence the way the team works. If resources are too low it will be difficult to meet objectives. On the other hand, if resources are made too freely available, the team may become complacent. The optimal level of resources is one at which the objectives are attainable but which demands that resources be worked hard to achieve them. Both a too-high and a too-low level of resources can foster discontent in the team and lead to conflict.

Group rewards

People work together in teams because in this way they can achieve more. The rewards made available are greater than if the individual members worked alone.

The way in which the members of the team work together will depend on the individual motivations, the rewards available and how those rewards are shared between team members. Individuals seek a variety of rewards from work situations. One level is *material*, at which work is undertaken for the financial benefits to be gained. Another level is *social*: team working is a way for people to interact and share a social experience. A good, well-formed and functioning team certainly offers the prospect of rewarding comradeship. A third level of reward is that of *personal development*. The consulting experience offers an opportunity to develop real and valuable transferable skills. This is particularly important for the student consulting project – a point that will be developed in Chapter 26.

Interaction with other groups

A team does not work in isolation. It is part of a wider organisation. A business may consist of a series of interlocking and interacting teams. Individuals may be members of more than one team. Teams may make presentations to each other. Teams exchange and share resources, information and members. Teams in an organisation are part of a wider cultural system. The way in which the team integrates within the wider organisational context will influence the way it works with that organisation.

23.2 Types of groups

Teams take a variety of forms. Some of the more important defining characteristics are as follows.

◆ Formal groups

A formal group is one which is defined and legitimised by the wider organisation. The team is recognised by the organisation and its power comes from authorisation of its role and responsibilities. An example of a formal group is the company's board of directors. This is a key group for the consultant to influence positively.

◆ Informal groups

An informal group is one which is not explicitly recognised and authorised by the organisation. Informal groups are sometimes known as 'cliques'. Cliques may be horizontal (made up of managers from the same level) or vertical (made up of members at different levels within a function or department). The fact that they are informal does not mean such groups are not powerful. They may be very influential 'behind the scenes'. A consultant needs to recognise the existence of informal groups and how they may be co-opted in the implementation process. If they are not co-opted they may present a considerable resistance to change.

◆ Primary groups

Primary groups are those whose members interact on a regular basis in pursuit of a particular task or task type. They are coherent and usually quite small. A project team is usually a primary group.

◆ Secondary groups

Secondary groups are usually larger than primary groups. Though the individuals who make up such groups share characteristics and may ostensibly pursue a common goal, individual interaction is limited. The store managers in a retail chain, for example, are likely to constitute a secondary group.

◆ Permanent groups

A permanent group is one which has a long-term existence in the organisation. It becomes a fixed feature of the organisational landscape. Individuals may interact on an ongoing basis in a permanent group or may come together at set intervals or intermittently to undertake the group task.

◆ Temporary groups

A temporary group is one which is brought together to address a specific task over a specific period. It is not intended that the group be maintained once the task is complete. This is often the case with consulting teams. A group which is temporary in a formal sense may often have more permanence in an informal sense, especially if the experience of members is a positive one.

23.3 The process of group formation

The interactions between individuals in a primary group change over time. Any team has both a history and a future. Observation of groups suggests that teams undergo four stages of development. These stages may be labelled: forming, storming, norming and performing.

◆ Forming

In the forming stage the members of the group come together for the first time. There is considerable uncertainty about the goals of the group, the roles of individual members and how the group will function. There may even be doubt about the need for the existence of a group at all. Individuals will be concerned with testing each other out.

◆ Storming

Once individuals have got to know each other and accepted the existence of the group the debate about goals, roles and process will start. At first this may be quite heated. People will be jostling for position in the group. Several may be claiming the leadership role. There will be disagreement about goals and how they should be pursued. If the group is large enough subgroups and short-term coalitions may form. There may be a call for outsiders to step in and arbitrate on issues.

◆ Norming

Provided the group survives the storming stage (and whether it does so depends on individual personalities, group motivations and environmental factors), a consensus will emerge. This consensus will recognise the roles individual members will play (including that of the leader), the overall goals for the group and the process through which individuals will interact. The detail in this will vary. Some groups are formal and define the group contingencies in detail upfront. Others are less formal and are willing to let contingencies emerge and evolve over time. The consensus will gain general acceptance though some members will be happier with the norming outcomes than others.

◆ Performing

Once the group contingencies have been agreed through norming the group can move on to undertake the tasks it exists to perform. It may continue to develop incrementally as it learns to do its job better.

There is no guarantee that the team will stay in the performing stage. As discussed in Chapter 14 a project shock, for example the introduction of new members, changes in resource availability or changes in goals, may cause the group to revert to an earlier stage. If the group does not meet for some time, it may have to proceed through the whole sequence again.

As with any model of a process care should be taken in using the model predictively. The length and intensity of each stage will vary between groups and situations. Some stages may be long and memorable; others may be short and may not be noticed.

23.4 Managing team conflicts

Conflicts are an inevitable feature of team working. Conflicts are a normal part of the storming stage of team formation. They may emerge later in the performing stage of the team's development. Conflict may be defined as a situation in which the goals of one party are incompatible, or at least are seen as incompatible, with those of another party. As a result one party blocks, or attempts to block, the actions and pursued outcomes of the other. Conflicts can arise over a host of issues in a consulting project. There may be disagreement over the roles individuals must play, the overall goals of the project, the details of objectives and decision-making processes.

Traditionally, conflict was seen in unambiguous terms: it was bad. It was something that disrupted the functioning of the team. A more modern approach to conflict takes a more dispassionate view. Conflict need not always be negative. *Functional* conflict may be a necessary aspect of change processes, especially if the team is set in its ways and has adopted an inflexible style of groupthink. *Dysfunctional* conflict, however, is negative, does distract from goal achievement and must be managed out if the team is to be successful. Managing conflict is something which must involve the whole team. However the leader has a critical role. Every conflict presents its own challenges but some useful general ground rules for its management are as follows.

◆ Address the issue

It is very tempting to ignore conflict and hope it will resolve itself. It rarely does. It may be pushed below the surface. But it will undermine effort and will surface again later. At this point it will be more difficult to manage. The team leader must grasp the nettle and manage conflict early.

◆ Identify parties

The first stage of conflict management must be to recognise who is involved. It may go beyond the obvious and vocal members of the team. Such people may just be the tip of the iceberg. They may represent informal subgroups. It is important to recognise all who have an interest in the conflict and its resolution.

◆ Assert the need for resolution

The first responsibility of the leader is to the team as a whole and its objectives. If the conflict is dysfunctional and threatens the achievement of goals and group integrity, then the conflict must be resolved even if the outcomes are not those one or both parties would wish. The leader must assert the need for resolution and the fact that it will, one way or another, be achieved. This will encourage the parties to the conflict to accept a compromise.

◆ Understand both sides

Conflicts are rarely black and white: one side right and one wrong. Both may have virtue on their side in at least some aspects of their position. Listening to the views of both sides is important. This is a time when listening skills are particularly useful.

◆ Look for common ground

In a conflict situation individuals tend to see their own position in terms of what makes it different from those of others. A dispassionate perspective may reveal that the parties have more in common than they think. Indeed, a synthesis of the views of the two sides may be stronger than either position alone. The conflict may be a 'problem' which actually presents an opportunity (think back to Section 16.2).

◆ Give parties a back-out route

Often, what matters to a party to a conflict is not so much the position they have taken (especially if its limitations have been pointed out to them) as their credibility. This, they may feel, will be compromised if they 'back down'. If they are given a way of moving to a new position without being seen to lose credibility the process of achieving compromise will be easier.

To this end, it is important that triumphalism by one party is discouraged. Further, emphasis should be given to the positive elements of both positions that are included in the final synthesis.

◆ Be prepared to impose a solution

Ultimately, the progression of the project is more important than the concerns of individuals. If no compromise can be achieved the leader must be prepared to impose a solution. Clearly, this should be a last resort. But if it has to be undertaken, neither party to the conflict should be seen to win. If a win-win scenario cannot be achieved a lose-lose situation is better than a win-lose. Imposing a solution calls upon all the leader's authority and power.

23.5 Working with external supporters and experts

No team will have all the skills, expertise and insights to tackle every issue it might face. It may be advisable to call on outside experts for advice and support. If this is done, the following are some basic ground rules which will make the process more successful.

◆ Understand what issue you need advice or support on

As the project progresses a number of issues will become apparent. The team may find it is working under conditions of considerable uncertainty, especially in the project's early stages. It can be very tempting to 'throw up one's hands' and call in an 'expert' to resolve the whole thing. This temptation must be resisted. The project belongs to the team. There is no expert to which it can be passed. There *are* people who might be able to offer advice and support on specific issues, though. Spend time as a team resolving the broad morass of problems into a series of specific issues that are amenable to resolution.

◆ Define objectives

Once specific issues have been identified be clear as to the objective of their resolution. How does the resolution fit with the overall project? How will it assist the delivery of the project's main objectives? What priority has it? How much resource (time and, if appropriate, money) should be dedicated to it?

◆ Identify who can help

Who will be able to offer advice with the resolution of the issue? In an academic institution there are enormous intellectual resources which can be drawn on at low cost. Check the library and ask business information specialists. They will be able to direct you to valuable sources for secondary research. Look for experts. Experts in quite specific areas may be identified through academic articles and books. If the issue is one which demands primary research, surveys of customers or firms in a particular sector may be needed. If possible, get the advice of a market research specialist.

◆ Approach positively

Experts are usually busy people. You will be making a call on their time. They are more likely to respond well if you approach them positively. This means that your communication (probably in writing) must be clear and succinct. Explain your objectives and why you think the expert can help. Be definite about the information or opinions you want. Tell the recipient which institution you are based at and explain how the information received will be used. Be careful, though, not to reveal the name of your client if there is an issue of confidentiality. Ask the expert if he or she knows of anyone else who might be approached to provide further information.

◆ Ensure understanding and integrate findings

Once advice has been offered make sure that its implications are understood. How does it influence the progression of the project and the recommendations to the client? Often advice will offer insights which open up new avenues of enquiry. Ask if further investigations might develop the understanding gained.

Team discussion point	Using your project log review the process of your team's formation. Can you identify each of the stages described in Section 23.3? How did you feel at each stage? How satisfied were you with the consensus that emerged?
	Compare your findings as a team exercise.

Summary of key ideas	◆ Effective team working is a critical relationship skill and is an essential to delivering effective consulting exercises.
	◆ The shape and function of groups is subject to number of intrinsic and extrinsic factors.
	◆ Teams undergo definite stages in their development. Four key stages are forming, storming, norming and performing.
	◆ Conflicts are a normal part of team working. Functional conflicts may lead to positive change. Dysfunctional conflicts are disruptive and must be managed out. The management of conflict is a leadership responsibility.
	◆ External experts may be called in to support the working of a consulting team.

24

Leadership skills

Learning outcomes

The learning outcomes from this chapter are:

♦ to appreciate the importance of leadership to the successful delivery of the consulting project;

♦ to recognise the nature of leadership;

♦ to understand how leaders behave;

♦ to recognise the responsibilities of the team leader.

24.1 The nature of leadership

Leadership is one of the most important factors in business success. It is also one of the most elusive. A 'commonsense' view is to regard leadership as 'what leaders do'. This merely moves the issue on. What then is a leader? To say 'someone who leads' invites circularity. Management thinkers are concerned with more than just defining leadership. The prize is to understand how leaders behave and to develop means for managers to develop their leadership skills.

This is a great prize and the literature on leadership is vast. Unfortunately many contributions share few points of agreement. Understanding on leadership has progressed, though. Four main approaches – or paradigms – have been adopted. The first regarded leadership as the result of some personality factor or trait. Leadership was a feature of the leader. If a person had a 'leader's' personality then people would follow him or her. Although this view might resonate with popular perceptions it has many problems. The first is that there does not seem to be one personality feature which predetermines leadership. Many studies have sought one, but not successfully. It is true to say that leaders tend to show drive, dedication and a range of task-orientated skills. But so do many non-leaders. Possession of these traits is not a predictor of leadership. Second, it presents a developmental dead-end. If leadership is a feature of personality it is fixed: one is, or is not, a leader. There is no prospect of learning to be a leader.

The second paradigm – that of a behavioural approach – takes the view that leadership is not about what leaders are but about what they do. Leaders are leaders because they behave as such. This is a move forward. Leadership is learned and behavioural theories offer managers the possibility of enhancing their leadership. However, despite their differences trait and behavioural approaches share an assumption: that is, that leadership is centred on the leader. Neither takes account of the situation in which the leader is operating. Contingency theories attempt to bring environmental and organisational factors – the stage on which leadership is played out – into consideration.

The most recent approaches to leadership bring in an actor who is largely neglected in the previous three paradigms: the *follower*. Interaction theories move the spotlight away from the leader to the relationship he or she develops with those who follow them and the web of relationships followers develop among themselves. A consequence of this view is that the leader is responsible for managing the working environment in its totality – the organisational culture – as much as people.

The question that must be asked by the consultant leading a team is what practical insights into effective leadership practice these theories have offered. The answer is: quite a few. Before moving on to consider these it is important to consider the role and responsibilities of the leader.

24.2 The role and responsibilities of the leader

Leadership as a functional aspect of the managerial role has been considered earlier (*see* Section 6.1). All managerial roles require some leadership elements. Clearly, the formally recognised leader of the team makes a particular call on them.

◆ Communication of objectives

The leader does not have to decide on objectives. This may be something about which a team consensus is achieved. However, once they have been decided the leader must take responsibility for communicating them to the team. This is not a one-off exercise. It is a continuous process. It is easy for the team to become distracted, for priorities to slip. The leader must keep the whole team focused on its essential goals and ensure that activities are directed towards their achievement.

◆ Delegation of tasks

To some extent tasks fall naturally into place if role differentiation (*see* Section 12.2) has been successful. Some tasks, though, fall between roles and the leader must step in to ensure that a team member has clear and unambiguous responsibility for the delivery of that task.

◆ Motivation of team members

It is a primary responsibility of the leader to ensure that all team members are motivated and feel positive towards the tasks in hand.

◆ Distribution of rewards

Working as a team can bring great rewards, material and otherwise. People are motivated to work as part of a team because of the possibility of these rewards. In many instances it is the team as a whole that is rewarded and the fruits must be distributed to team members. The team leader has responsibility for this distribution. If motivation is to be maintained and discontent avoided the allocation of rewards must be seen to be transparent, fair and equitable.

◆ Allocation of resources

The leader is usually called upon, in the last instance at least, to allocate the resources between different options for their investment. A number of control mechanisms exist for this. It may be done through the imposition of a strategic plan, a procedure for the agreement of budgets or the authorisation of immediate expenditure.

◆ Resolution of conflicts

To an extent, conflicts are an inevitable and necessary part of team working. The team leader has an important role to play in managing and resolving conflicts. (*Refer back to* Section 23.4 for a discussion of the practicalities of this.)

◆ Representation to the outside world

The team operates in a wider organisational context than its own environment. There are times when the team and its interests need to be represented in that context. Obtaining resources for the team will be especially important.

24.3 Leadership behaviour

The one thing that has become apparent from the study of leadership is that there is no one formula that can guarantee leadership success. Leadership is an event that is dependent on a range of individuals and situational contingencies. No two leadership events are exactly the same. Nevertheless, there are behavioural characteristics which effective leaders exhibit. These provide some useful ground rules for the team manager who wishes to enhance his or her leadership.

A number of models of correlation between leadership behaviour and situation have been proposed. Important contributions are the managerial grid of Blake and Mouton (1982), the autocratic-democratic continuum model of Fiedler (1967), the path-goal model of Robert House (1974) and the leadership participation model of Victor Vroom and Philip Yetton (1973). The interested student is referred to the Suggestions for further reading for details of these. Each of these models develops its own subtleties and offers different insights. However, all have a common theme: the fact that leaders must concern themselves simultaneously with two things – the *task* they aim to deliver and the *people* who work under them.

◆ Concern with tasks

Teams exist to deliver specific outcomes. A leader must be dedicated to the delivery of the team's goals: this is the point of the existence of the role of leader in the first place. Clearly, all members of the team must be concerned with goals. The leader must take particular responsibility for ensuring that goals are clear and communicated. Ultimately, the leader must take responsibility for the successful outcomes of the project.

◆ Interest in people

Goals are not achieved by themselves. They are achieved by the team members. Leadership means leading people. A leader must take an interest in the members of the team as individuals who have individual interests and concerns. These are distinct from the concerns of the group as a whole.

Although a variety of terms are used, all the models essentially differentiate leadership styles in terms of the balance of concerns for these two elements, task and people. The two dimensions of concern are complementary, not exclusive. Both can be addressed at once. A good leader can show a simultaneous concern for both. However, there are times when one must take priority. The priority depends on the leadership situation. For example, in the management of conflicts discussed in Section 23.4, the leader must ultimately decide the priority to be given to different goals.

In short, effective leaders do two things. First, they know *how* to express concerns for goals and people; second, they know *when* to express them. These two aspects of leadership resolve themselves into a series of concerns which, properly addressed, can offer the basis for a leadership strategy.

Effective leaders demonstrate the following behavioural characteristics.

◆ Focus on team goals and objectives

The team leader should be clear as to the goals and the objectives of the project. He or she must also be clear on the distinction between them. As noted in Chapter 11, it is valuable to draw a distinction between broad goals and specific objectives. Goals provide a reference point which can aid the negotiation of specific objectives and outcomes between different team members and with the client.

◆ Demanding targets

Effective leaders make demands on their followers. Targets set should be achievable but should stretch both the team and individuals. The objectives set should also be well defined, relevant and realistic, and should be signposted. This aspect of objective setting is discussed in Chapter 11.

◆ Setting an example

A leader must set an example to the team. It is no use setting challenging targets for the team if the leader is not seen to set such targets for him or herself. To fail to do so threatens credibility.

◆ Offering support

Having set demanding targets a good leader does not leave the team to flounder. He or she is active in establishing the support team members will need in order to achieve that target. The leader then makes sure that that support is forthcoming. Offering support and then not delivering it is a sure way to lose credibility. Leadership drives people through a process of both pull and push: objectives provide the pull; support to achieve them the push.

◆ Communication

Leaders learn to communicate with their followers. They are sure of the message they want to send (in both its rational and its emotional aspects) and the best means to deliver it. Leadership is, in great part, built on the communication skills discussed in Chapter 21.

◆ Being informed

A good leader knows what is going on! He or she is informed about the project and the people working on it. It is only through this understanding that the right leadership actions can be decided upon. This does not mean that leaders must control all information and its flow! There is little credibility in insisting that one must be informed about everything. If this is done it is likely that information overload will occur and poor decision making will result. An effective leader knows what information is important and where it can be obtained. Effective leaders develop questioning skills so that information can be obtained from those whose proper job it is to know it. Questioning before making a decision is a characteristic of true leadership behaviour. Questioning skills are considered in Section 22.3.

Student consulting teams sometimes ask if the leader should be appointed, either by the team members or by an outside agent. There is no simple answer. If no formal appointment is made a leader will usually emerge out of the storming phase of team formation. It should be remembered that, even if the appointment procedure is accepted by all in the team – a big if, formal appointment does not in itself confer leadership. At best it confers (a degree of) *authority*. This is not the same thing. Authority may potentiate leadership: it will open a window of opportunity to be a leader. But true leadership comes from behaving as a leader. Leadership behaviour is not exclusive to the formal leader. All team members – whatever their role – can enhance their performance by adopting it.

Team discussion point	Using the project log as a source reflect on the leadership roles adopted by yourself and other team members. How does the leadership behaviour match up with that described above? How might you use the above framework to enhance your leadership behaviour in the future? In particular, how might you integrate it into an experiential learning cycle? (Refer back to Chapter 3 if you need to refresh your memory of this concept.)

Discuss your ideas as a team.

Summary of key ideas

◆ Leadership is a very powerful management idea. Leadership delivers value.

◆ A number of approaches to leadership have been developed.

◆ In essence, leadership is concerned with integrating a concern for task delivery with a concern for people.

◆ Leadership can be enhanced by observing a number of simple behaviour rules.

◆ A leader cannot be simply 'appointed'. A leader is someone who *behaves* like a leader. All team members have some leadership responsibility.

25

Presenting your ideas

Learning outcomes

The learning outcomes from this chapter are:

◆ to recognise the importance of delivering your findings to the client;

◆ to understand the means by which those findings can be delivered;

◆ to appreciate some rules which will make the communication of findings more effective.

25.1 Planning the communication

The communication of the findings of the consulting exercise to the client is an event of great importance. The client is likely to see this as what he or she has 'paid for'. If the consulting exercise was an information-gathering exercise then the communication is the means by which the information is delivered. If the project is offering advice on a business development strategy then the final communication is the means by which that advice is made known. Even if the consulting has taken a process approach and the outcomes delivered are a result of the consultant–client interaction, the final report provides a tangible 'capstone' to the project.

The consulting project will have generated a lot of information and ideas. The main challenge in producing the communication is organising that material so that the message you want to send is delivered in a coherent and convincing way. One very effective approach is described by Barbara Minto in her book, *The Pyramid Principle*. Barbara Minto was a consultant for McKinsey & Company who went on to specialise in communication. The basis is to organise ideas into a hierarchy (a pyramid) so that they are sorted and interrelated. Minto lays down three rules for connecting ideas:

1 Ideas at any level in the pyramid must be summaries of the ideas below them; conversely, ideas at any level may be expanded upon at a lower level.

2 Ideas in each grouping (pathway in the pyramid) must be ideas of the same kind – that is, they must relate in some way and can be grouped together.

3 Ideas in a grouping must be ordered according to some internal logic.

Minto's ideas apply to business communications in general. There are a number of ways in which they might be applied to the challenge of producing a consulting report. The following is my own approach. You may interpret directly Barbara Minto's ideas to devise your own. I use four levels. These are illustrated in Figure 25.1.

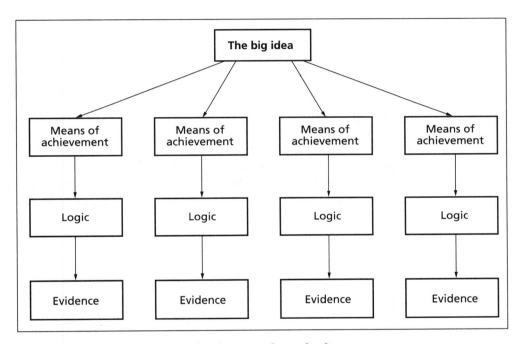

Figure 25.1   **The pyramid of ideas for relating consulting findings**

◆ The 'big idea'

The 'big idea' is what the whole consulting exercise is about. It is the central theme that unifies the exercise. It should be related to the original aims and objectives of the project. So, the 'big idea' might be 'to expand the business' or 'to improve profit margins' or 'to enter an international market' and so on.

◆ Means of achievement

How can the big idea be achieved? Expanding on this is where the consultant adds value. So, if the big idea is to expand the business, this level must expound on the options for expanding the business. It might include increasing market share in existing markets, developing new products or entering new markets. If the big idea is to increase profit margins the means of achievement level might consider increasing prices, altering the portfolio mix or reducing costs. This level may also be used to close off options which it is felt will not deliver the big idea.

◆ Logic

This third level connects the means of achievement to the big idea. It provides the explanation of why the big idea will be achieved by the means described in the second level. In some cases the logic will be 'obvious' (to you at least). In others it will rely on subtle interpretations. If in doubt, assume your audience would like to have the idea explained!

◆ Evidence

This final level contains any evidence that is available to justify the logic. It might include internal data on sales or costs. It might be data obtained through market research on the market, its potential and the opportunity it presents. It can include discoveries made through creative sessions and explorations of the type reviewed in Chapter 15.

Any of these levels can be expanded into sub-levels if this helps clarify communication of findings. The pyramid of ideas can be developed as a team exercise through a brainstorming session. An example is shown in Figure 25.2.

Don't forget, this expansion should be undertaken with a clear view of the objective of the communication. As discussed in Chapter 21, a communication objective relates to what you want the recipient to do; not just what you want him or her to know. Presumably, you will want the client to be impressed by your ideas, recognise their value to his or her business and to make an effort to implement them. No good consultant would want less.

25.2 The consulting report

A report provides a tangible, accessible and permanent communication of the findings of the consulting exercise. It need not be a long document. In fact, it is a safe assumption that managers do not like to read long reports. What it should be is a succinct and impactful presentation of the opportunity you have discovered for the business. Remember your objectives: it should be a call to action.

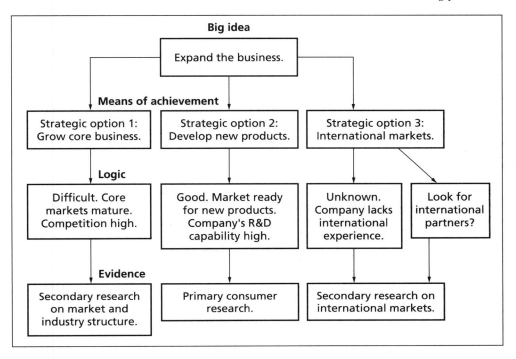

Figure 25.2 An application of the pyramid of ideas

The report may comprise the following sections.

◆ Executive summary

This is a summary of the findings of the consulting project. But it must be more than *just* a summary. The executive summary is the gateway to the report. It must be short, but inviting. A good rule is a one-page maximum. Use bullet points to isolate and summarise your ideas and recommendations. Use an active language style. Be positive. Talk about what the business might achieve if the ideas in the report are implemented.

Ask two questions about the executive summary. First, does it invite the reader in? On reading the executive summary will the reader be motivated to delve further into the report? Second, if the reader reads only the executive summary what is the message he or she will get? Briefly, will the executive summary deliver your objectives for the communication? These two questions may seem contradictory but they are not. If the executive summary is both complete in itself and an invitation to go further it will have impact and set the scene for the expansion of the ideas it relates.

◆ Introduction

The introduction should illuminate the context of the report. It should give any relevant information on the business and its situation. It should also specify the goals, objectives and outcomes that were agreed originally. The introduction will repeat much of the ground covered by the original project proposal. The original project proposal will provide a template for the introduction. The introduction might be used to give a flavour of what is to come: a further invitation to move into the body of the report.

◆ Body of the report

This is the part of the report where you can expand on your ideas and develop your case. The body of the report can be given an appropriate title. It may be broken down into subsections if appropriate. Don't forget, it is generally better to have a lot of short, well-defined and titled subsections than long sections. They make reading and later accessing easier.

The pyramid discussed in the previous section can be used to organise the material for the body of the report. It is better to work your way across the levels rather than down the groups. You don't need to provide logic and evidence upfront for every idea. Lay out the skeleton of your overall case first, then flesh out the details later. Be explicit. Tell the reader what your case will be and promise to support it later. Layer your ideas. The written page must be linear. But our thinking is not: it is hierarchical. Expand your themes in a hierarchical manner. Use internal references to signpost where your ideas are going. If the reader feels tempted to jump from one section to another, fine.

You may also want to use visual representations of ideas and information. Some techniques are discussed in Section 15.3. A picture really is worth a thousand words!

◆ Summary and recommendations

Remember your objectives. You should close your report with a final call to action. A good way to do this is with a succinct summary of findings and the recommendations listed as bullet points. This format not only repeats the message, but makes the recommendations accessible.

We value originality. Some people feel uncomfortable with this approach to report writing. They feel that they are repeating themselves by saying the same thing in the executive summary, the body of the report and then again in the summary of recommendations. So what! It has been observed that a good business communication tells the reader what it will say, says it and then tells the reader what has been said! If the message is a good one, don't be afraid of getting it across.

◆ Appendices

The trick with appendices is to be cynical. Assume they won't be read! They are a good place to put any information that you have used to make your case and that might be of interest to the reader in the future. If the information is valuable to your case then a summary of it (perhaps using a visual representation) should be in the body of the report.

Information which will be of use in the implementation of recommendations (say a list of potential customers) should not be hidden away in appendices. It should be highlighted and accessible in the body of the report.

Clearly, the report will speak for you. It will be a representation of your efforts. You should be proud of it. Make time for its planning and preparation. Check the copy, make sure that typographical, spelling and grammatical errors have been removed. Be warned. Many people find it difficult to check their own copy. It is better to have someone other than the report writer do the copy editing.

Modern word-processing technology makes report writing easy. Sections can be added, revised and moved with ease. Spellcheckers take the strain out of copy checking. Impressive visuals can be edited in. A variety of graphics can be used to decorate the report. But, at the end of the day, it is the substance of the report that matters. A simple, well-written, well-laid-out report relating ideas that will have a real impact on the performance of the business is much better than a report rich with graphics but lacking substance.

25.3 Formal presentations

A formal presentation is a very effective means of getting your message across. It allows the message to be finetuned using both verbal and visual communications, to get instant feedback from the client and to respond immediately to points and questions. Formal presentations are being used increasingly as a means of inter- and intra-organisational communication. The formal presentation is, however, a challenging mode of communication. To be effective it must be well organised and delivered with confidence. This confidence comes through preparation and practice.

It is worth while to take time to plan the visual aids to be used. The images that are to be used need careful consideration if they are to have an impact. They can be relatively expensive and take time to produce and copy so plan ahead. Some useful points to remember are as follows.

◆ Analyse the audience. What images will they find relevant and impactful? What interpretative skills do they have?

◆ Don't make the images too complicated. Clear, simple images have much more impact.

◆ Consider the relationships you need to communicate. Use images which emphasise the relevant relationships.

◆ Don't forget you can use a sequence of images to build up ideas.

◆ Use the pyramid principle to organise your message.

The images in the presentation should be used to support the presentation. They are *aides-mémoire* for the presenter and add impact to what the presenter says.

There are a number of technologies for producing visual material. The oldest, and simplest, is just a pen and paper. With a little care and attention quite professional diagrams and graphs can be produced. Word processing and desktop publishing systems and drawing packages are now easily accessed. With a little practice they can be used to produce sophisticated and very professional visual material.

Colour is a very effective stimulus in visual communication. Colour can be used to differentiate relationships (say, by the use of different coloured lines on graphs). Primary colours have most impact. Desktop publishing packages usually have colour facilities. Colour is reproduced well on overhead acetates and in 35 mm slides. Beware, however, if it is intended to photocopy the overheads for later distribution. Colour information is lost in black and white copies! A good deal of information can still be represented in black and white by using broken and dotted lines and different cross-hatching styles for areas.

The most common devices for visuals are the overhead projector which uses A4 sized acetates and the slide projector which uses 35 mm photographic slides (which are better for large audiences and more formal presentations). The following are a few points for producing effective visual support of the presentation:

◆ Remember that the visual material is supporting the presentation not making it! Don't put text on the screen and read from it.

◆ Keep the images simple. They should add impact to the presentation, not distract from it.

◆ Put up bullet points to indicate to your audience the key issues you are identifying. These will also act as *aides-mémoire* if you are presenting without notes.

◆ Use lower-case text. Upper-case text is austere and can be difficult to read.

◆ Use a pointer (either a traditional stick or one of the new laser type).

◆ If using an overhead projector try to point at the screen rather than the acetate. Pointing at the slide casts distracting shadows on the screen.

◆ Consider your positioning relative to the overhead projector. You wish to face the audience, not the screen, so position yourself so that you can see the screen with a slight turn of the head. Avoid blocking the audience's view and don't block the image by standing in the light path.

◆ When changing overhead acetates turn off the overhead projector first. The moving image projected overhead can be distracting. Also, turning on the projector will allow you to control exactly when the audience sees the new image.

Effective presentations are not difficult. Figure 25.3 gives a few tips to make them better.

The audience may find it useful to retain copies of the overheads you have used. Photocopies may be provided. You must decide if you wish to give the copies out at the beginning or at the end of the presentation. Giving them out beforehand allows the audience to annotate them during the presentation. However, the audience will inevitably flip through them. The audience may feel that all they need is in the handouts and so they don't need to follow the presentation in detail. Also you will lose control of when the audience sees particular images for the first time. For these reasons the presentation may lose some of its impact if handouts are distributed first.

The formal presentation can however be quite a nerve-racking experience for the inexperienced. Planning, preparation and practice are great builders of confidence. The rules for a presentation are the same as for any other communication. Think about what you want to achieve from it. Be sure of what you want people to do as a result of the communication. Analyse the audience. (*See also* Figure 25.3, which illustrates the points made in the text about effective presentation.)

Some simple rules for an effective presentation are as follows:

◆ Rehearse and practise the presentation. This is best done as a team. Not everybody need be involved in the actual delivery, but all can add to it.

◆ Use notes as *aides-mémoire* but try not to read from a script. It is better to consider the points you wish to make and learn them using the visual stimuli as a prompt.

◆ Time your presentation. Make sure it is the right length for the time available (Normally a presentation should be 15 minutes or less. Longer presentations

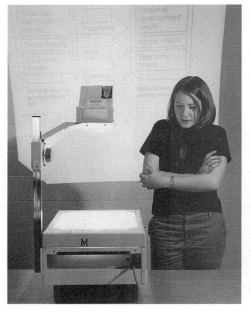

Avoid 'defensive' body language.

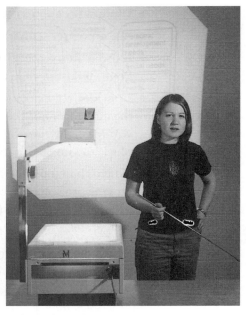

Relax. The audience is not out to get you!

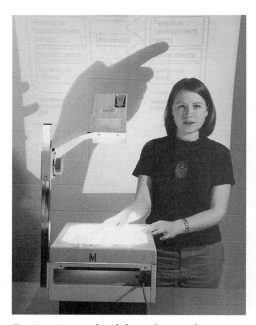

Don't point at the slide with your finger. It is very distracting.

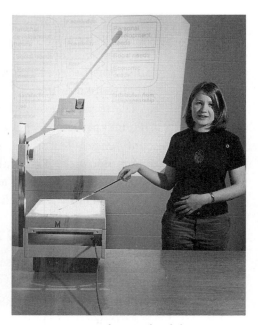

Use a pointer – either on the slide or at the screen.

Figure 25.3   **Some do's and don'ts for effective presentations**

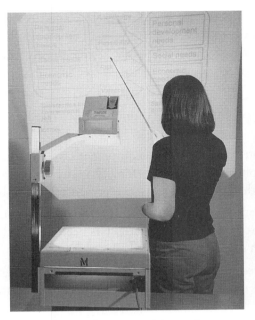

Don't obscure the projected image from the audience.

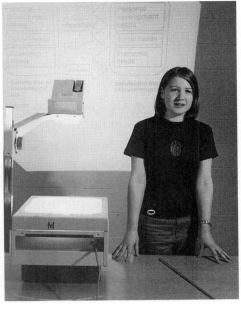

Stand clear. Make sure everyone can see.

Avoid passing in front of the projected image. If you must move in front of the projector, turn it off first.

Figure 25.3   continued

tend to lose their impact.) Make mental notes of some time-points to enable you to time the presentation and make sure it is on track. Place a watch or clock where you can see it discreetly (say, beside the overhead projector). Avoid looking at a watch on your wrist. It sends a bad message to the audience!

◆ On the day, dress appropriately, but comfortably. You'll feel much more confident!

◆ Before the presentation check that the equipment, e.g. overhead projectors, slide projectors, microphones etc., are working. It is stressful to have to sort out equipment in front of the audience before the presentation can begin!

◆ Make sure that the overheads you intend to use are in the right order and the right way up. Make sure any backing material has been removed. (Peeling it off during the presentation can irritate the audience!)

◆ When making the presentation use confident body language: make open gestures and avoid the temptation to cross your arms in a protective gesture. Try to make eye contact with the audience. Smile!

◆ Pace your speech. Take regular deep breaths. This will help control nervousness.

Try not to be anxious about the presentation. The audience is not out to get you! They are interested in what you have to say. With a little practice effective presenting becomes second nature – then you can concentrate on what you want to say! Increasingly, being able to give an effective presentation is a key skill in the modern business world.

25.4 Making a case: persuading with information

Information is needed for making decisions but decisions are not made on the basis of information alone. How it is presented and the context in which it is presented are also important in influencing decision making. In business, information is usually presented with the intention of encouraging the recipient to take a particular course of action (the 'what do you want the audience to do as a result of receiving the information?' objective). Being influential with information is a matter not only of identifying that information which makes your case but also of delivering it sympathetically to the audience.

Information will be more influential if it:

◆ is relevant to the decisions the recipient needs to make;

◆ is pitched at the right level of understanding;

◆ is presented in a form which makes it easy to understand and digest;

◆ is supported by impactful visual stimuli;

◆ is placed in appropriate opinion and feeling contexts;

◆ is delivered in a situation of good rapport (*see* Section 22.1);

◆ is part of an interactive process where the recipient is encouraged and supported to explore the information;

◆ has key points signposted and highlighted.

Don't forget, if you need to organise the information before presenting it use the pyramid principle described in Barbara Minto's book.

25.5 Answering questions and meeting objections in presentations

Formal presentations usually end with an invitation for questions to be asked. It is useful to develop some skills in dealing with the questions – and their close relative: objections!

After having invited questions look around the audience for signs of someone wishing to ask one. As the presenter you are in control. Even after you have invited questions potential questioners may still be looking for a sign from you that they have a right to speak. Eye contact and a 'yes' will usually be sufficient to elicit the question.

When the questioner speaks really listen to the question being asked! Use active listening (*see* Section 22.4). Consider the nature of the question being asked as well as the question itself. Is it a 'head' question, a rational seeking of further information, or a 'heart' question, a more emotionally rooted seeking of reassurance?

Some useful points to remember in answering questions are:

◆ Summarise the question being asked before attempting an answer. This will ensure that you have understood the question and that the rest of the audience have understood it. It will also give you some thinking time!

◆ If the question is complex and, in fact, contains more than one question then break it down into individual questions. Indicate that you will answer each in turn.

◆ Answer the question to the best of your ability. You can do no more! If you do not have necessary information to hand then say so. Take the questioner's details and offer to get back to him or her with the information. But don't forget to do so!

◆ After answering a question don't just move on to the next questioner. Close the answer by asking the questioner if the answer is satisfactory: 'Is that OK?'; 'Does that answer your question?'; 'I hope that's a little clearer', etc.

Objections are a little more difficult to deal with but there are a few good points to remember. Objections may be more heart than head. They may be individual or may summarise what might be the concerns of the entire audience. Meeting objections may require more than fighting fact with fact. If you come up against an objection try the following.

◆ Start by recognising (and even welcoming) the objection: 'Thank you. I'm glad you raised that'; 'Right. I can understand your concerns there'; 'An interesting point. Let me see if I can deal with it'.

◆ Consider the speaker's feelings when meeting objections (even if they don't seem to be considering yours). If they are seeking reassurance rather than information then give reassurance.

◆ If the objection is clearly emotional or no answer is obvious then ask a question back. 'This is obviously a major concern for you. Why is that?'; 'Have you encountered this kind of problem before?'; etc. This will get the objector to explore his or her objection (forcing him or her to put it on a rational footing). It will also give you some thinking time!

It may sound difficult, but learn to regard objections as an opportunity to make positive points!

Team discussion point	Prepare a short formal presentation (of five minutes with one or two overheads) on the theme of what you feel you have gained from the consulting project experience in terms of learning outcomes, transferable skills and enhanced career prospects.

Each member of the team should give this presentation and invite (positive) criticism from the other members of the team. (This is a good chance to practise the criticism technique described in Section 16.2.)

Summary of key ideas

◆ The final communication of the consulting findings is the 'product' the client is 'paying for'.

◆ The communication may take the form of a report, a personal presentation or a combination of the two.

◆ The communication should be planned with the objective of positively influencing the client and getting him or her to implement the ideas presented.

◆ Organise your message using the pyramid principle into four levels: the big idea, means of achievement, logic and evidence.

◆ The most important part of the report is the executive summary: this sells the report to the reader and invites him or her in.

◆ A presentation should be planned in advance. Impact will be gained if the presentation is pitched to the audience, their level of understanding and interests.

◆ Visual materials should support the presentation, have an impact and reinforce the key ideas.

Capitalising on the consulting experience

26

Learning from success

Learning outcomes

The key learning outcomes from this chapter are:

◆ to recognise your success in the consulting exercise;

◆ to recognise how these successes provide evidence of transferable learning;

◆ to be able to document those successes on a curriculum vitae and use them to support career development.

26.1 Recognising the successes

If undertaken with enthusiasm and with the application of the approaches described in this book a consulting exercise will provide a positive experience. Value will be created at several levels. It will be an opportunity to develop valuable and transferable skills. It will provide a chance to gain evidence of those skills. A high-level contribution will be made to the progression of a business venture. The consulting experience offers an insight into key senior management responsibilities: decision making at a strategic level and influencing the course of the business.

A successful consulting exercise – indeed any successful managerial experience – has three aspects. First is the *experience* itself – the actual activities engaged in. These will include elements of the three skill areas essential to effective consulting: analysis, project management and relationship building. Second is the *learning* that is gained as a result of that experience. This is best achieved through the experiential learning cycle: the application of ideas gained through analysis and then active reflection on the outcomes. Such learning is valuable because it is *transferable*. The third aspect of the exercise is the *evidence* that that learning has been used to create value and that it can be used to create new value in the future.

26.2 Success and transferable skills

The successes achieved in the consulting exercise will provide positive and motivating memories. Yet they have meaning beyond this. They are evidence of having developed valuable and transferable skills. Some experiences that will be of value in the future are as follows.

◆ Objective definition

Managers are directed towards objectives. Objectives will only be of value if they are good ones. Indeed, bad objectives will lead the venture down the wrong path and reduce value. The consulting exercise will have provided practice in creating objectives which are relevant, well defined, achievable and signposted.

◆ Problem analysis

Usually a business's managers will wish to see it grow. This presents a challenge. Businesses are limited by both external and internal factors. The external ones arise from market and competitive conditions. There is a ceiling on the economic value that can be created, given the business's assets. Internal limitations stem from the way in which managers use those assets. It is rare that a little more value cannot be squeezed out of them by working them harder. The things that limit a business will be recognised by managers as 'problems'. Yet problems do not present themselves. If they are to be managed problems need to be highlighted, defined and rationalised.

◆ Strategy development

A strategy is, at one level at least, just a way of using assets. In particular, a strategy is a way of creating value out of those assets. The development of an effective strategy is one of the great challenges of management. It demands consideration of the internal competencies of the business and the potential of the environment it is operating in.

◆ Project planning

A strategy will only create value if it is put into practice through the right plans. Plans are recipes for action. Plans must be driven by the project leader, or better, its *champion*. Planning has formal aspects which assist in resource allocation and budgetary management.

◆ **External relationship management**

Firms only prosper if they can attract external resources. This demands that relationships be built with the external parties who control those resources: customers and investors. Clearly, the ability to manage such relationships is very valuable. A consulting project will only be successful if a good relationship is built and maintained with the client. It presents an opportunity to develop such skills and gain evidence of their possession.

◆ **Team working**

When employers are asked what they consider to be the most essential managerial skill the answer most often given is the ability to work as part of a team. The growth in team working is one of the most prominent features in the development of management practice in recent times. Team working demands an ability both to integrate with and to motivate fellow team members.

◆ **Leadership**

Leadership is perhaps the most precious managerial skill. It is certainly in demand and there are good rewards for managers who possess it. Leadership is a skill. It is not a fixed aspect of personality. Leadership is about behaviour: it is what leaders *do*. It can be learned. But like any valuable skill it takes practice. The consulting project offers an opportunity both to recognise your own leadership style and to put it into practice.

Any manager who can combine these skills is offering a great deal to any organisation he or she works for.

26.3 Recording successes on your CV and relating them in job interviews

The curriculum vitae (CV) is a piece of communication. It is a particularly important one. It communicates you and what you have to offer to potential employers and clients. A CV should be thought of as an advertisement. It records your experience and achievements; but its *function* is to get you a job – or at least an interview. The important information to include is as follows.

◆ **Personal information**

Include your name, age, date of birth, nationality and contact address(es) and telephone number(s).

◆ Education

Give details of formal qualifications (date, subject, grade, awarding institution).

◆ Experience

Outline details of any employment undertaken. This should include the employer, the position and a brief summary of key responsibilities. Avoid verbosity. Use bullet points. This is also the place to refer to the consulting project.

◆ Achievements

A potential employer is interested not so much in what you have done as in what you might do. Past achievements are evidence of what might be achieved in the future. Achievements should be documented in a positive manner. If possible, quantify the achievement. To illustrate, the following are examples of achievements of a consulting project which might be included:

> *Key achievements of the consulting project were:*
> *– the development of a strategy which increased sales by 20 per cent;*
> *– a plan which enabled the business to enter an international market worth over £100 million;*
> *– an increase in productivity of 30 per cent;*
> *– a sales brief that was instrumental in gaining new customers worth over £100 000.*

And so on.

◆ Referees

A referee is someone who has experience of your work and who is willing to make a positive statement about it. A satisfied client makes a good referee. Include details of the person's title, name, position, employer and contact details.

26.4 Learning from failures

Not everything goes right. A consulting exercise is a complex experience. It presents a rich tapestry of intellectual and human engagements. Many experiences will be positive. But some, inevitably, will be negative. Mistakes and errors of judgement will be made. Information will be misinterpreted. Not all relationships will be good ones. Some people never seem to develop a rapport with each other

– to hit it off. There will be disagreements between members of the team over objectives and courses of action. There may even be disagreements with the client.

Such experiences are part of managerial life. They cannot be avoided. But they can be managed. And they can be learned from. Errors that result from the misinterpretation of information or poor judgement present opportunities to challenge the conceptual models and frameworks being used. Some of these will be explicit. These are easy to revise. Others will be locked into the cognitive strategy being used. These must be reflected on and actively revealed. A good consultant is active in revealing his or her own cognitive approach and recognising how it might be developed.

Errors that result in misunderstandings and conflicts with other people must also – although they may be more painful than simple interpretive mistakes – be used as learning experiences. Again the challenge is to analyse the experience and see what it says about how the person should be approached in the future and what it says about how people in general should be dealt with. Consider the message sent. How was it interpreted? How might it have been misinterpreted? Don't forget, a message has paralanguage aspects as well as a formal meaning. Also consider the other party's motivation. What did he or she want out of the situation? What did he or she get out of it? The key thing when interpreting a personal exchange is to avoid the temptation to allocate blame – either on oneself or the other party. It doesn't help. Analyse dispassionately.

Team discussion point	Consider the following questions: ◆ What career options have you considered? ◆ What skills are going to be valuable to success in these careers? ◆ How has the consulting experience given you an insight into these skills? ◆ What evidence of their possession have you gained? ◆ How might you document this in a CV? Draft a CV and review each other's as a team.

Summary of key ideas

◆ A consulting project is a great opportunity to gain things which will be valuable in your future career: managerial experience, active learning, achievements and evidence of achievements.

◆ Use the consulting experience to sell yourself: document (quantified) achievements on your CV.

◆ Not all experiences on the consulting exercise will be positive. Accept the negatives as a proper part of managerial life – but learn from them.

27

Consulting as a career

Learning outcomes

The learning outcomes from this chapter are:

◆ to appreciate the structure and dynamics of the global consulting industry;

◆ to recognise the opportunity to develop an internal consultant managerial style;

◆ to understand the value consistency skills offer for non-consulting jobs.

27.1 The consulting industry

The consulting industry is large. Just how large depends on definitions of what is or is not a consultant. Even on conservative definitions fee revenues are in excess of $15 billion world-wide. It is a significant employer. The larger US-based organisations alone employ over 100 000 consultants. It is also growing strongly. Over the past ten years the sector has grown in excess of 10 per cent per annum. Some leading firms have enjoyed growth over twice this rate. Indeed, industry insiders suggest that the main limit on the industry's growth is not the demand of customers but the supply of good quality consultants.

The industry's growth is driven by three main factors. The first is the increase in core demand from business organisations. Here demand has expanded as trends such as globalisation have increased the complexity of the environments in which businesses operate and managers have recognised the importance of knowledge rather than simply products or price as a basis for competing. Technology, especially information technology and computing, has changed the way managers work. Businesses now want to stick to their core expertise. Increasingly they wish to bring in specialists to manage non-core activities when they are needed.

The second factor is the growth in business organisations in the emerging economies of Asia and Africa and the transitional economies of the former communist world. Managers in these regions are looking to consultants as a source of experience. Many leading consultants see these as critical regions for future growth.

The third factor in the growth of consulting has been the increasing demand from governmental organisations. The last twenty years have seen the boundary between the private sector and the state being pushed back and becoming blurred. This is a world-wide phenomenon. Increasingly, it is accepted that government only has a role where the market cannot operate. As a result, government departments are putting work out to tender. This work includes support with information gathering and decision making, areas where consultants can add value.

Will the growth in the sector continue? This is an important question. Many in the sector assume it will. There is no reason why it should not. The main driving factors behind growth will remain in place for some time. Managers will continue to need advice and support in managing the ever-increasing complexity of tasks they face. Business activity will increase in the developing and former communist world. Politicians seem set to seek votes by pushing back the state. However, a market does not create itself. It is developed by its suppliers working with customers. Managers will only demand the services of consultants if the service they offer enhances their business. A growing market attracts many new entrants. Consultants must now, more than ever, be sure that they are creating value for their clients and are managing expectations.

All types of business call on the services of consultants. According to *Consulting News*, the sector's leading in-house journal, financial services make the most calls, accounting for nearly a quarter of the business of the 40 largest firms. Consumer products and manufacturing follow, with 11 per cent each. Utilities and high tech industries are not far behind. Government and health care are also important, accounting for about 9 per cent each. Retailing and wholesaling only accounts for some 2 per cent. This means it is under represented given its significance to the economy as a whole.

The services offered by the top 40 companies match this customer demand. In the lead is process and operations management, at nearly a third of service offering. Corporate and information technology strategy each account for 17 per cent. Organisational design makes a call on another 16 per cent. Marketing and sales strategy accounts for only 2 per cent of services offered. Given the importance of these activities to the modern business this suggests that these areas offer an opportunity for consultants to develop in the future.

The consulting industry has a relatively low concentration. It is fragmented and includes a number of different sectors. In general, the trend is for players to be large with a global reach or small and offering a specialised service. The main types of consultant firm are as follows.

◆ Accountancy firms offering consultancy

These are large firms with a global reach. Their traditional business has been in the accountancy area but they have recognised the opportunity that consulting offers to add value to the service they deliver. In short, they see the value in helping their customers create value, not just add it up. Important players here are Ernst & Young, Deloitte & Touche and the now merged Coopers & Lybrand and Price Waterhouse, PriceWaterhouseCoopers. The consulting business of these firms is separate from their accountancy work. This prevents conflict of interests.

◆ Large non-accounting consultancies

Again these are large firms with a global reach. However, their core business has always been in consulting. The big names here are McKinsey & Co., Arthur D. Little and Andersen Consulting.

◆ Small specialist 'boutiques'

These are firms which are (relatively) small and which offer a specialist service in, say, information technology or process re-engineering. Some important players are Gemini Consulting, the Boston Consulting Group and the Hays Group.

◆ 'Gurus'

'Gurus' are academics who have created a name for themselves by researching and developing ideas on how business might be approached. The term guru is taken from Sanskrit, the language of ancient India. It refers to a religious teacher. Gurus often promulgate their ideas through popular books. They may combine active consulting with teaching and seminar work. Well-known and influential management gurus include Tom Peters in the USA, Charles Handy in the UK and Kenichi Ohmae in Japan.

◆ Independents

Many individuals run their own consulting service as sole traders, as small limited companies or together as partnerships. Independent consultants offer a range of services, often quite specialised. They are often supported by professional bodies such as the Chartered Institute of Marketing and the Institute of Human Resource Management. These bodies offer professional training and accreditation and provide a forum for all-important networking.

A number of leading consultancy firms issue magazines or journals (*see* Table 27.1). These provide a medium for communicating new ideas on themes in management and are promotional devices. They are often available in business libraries and are worth reviewing both to keep track of development in management thinking and as a good source of information on individual consultancies – particularly their specialisms and style of working.

Table 27.1   Journals produced by leading consultancy firms

Journal	Consultancy	Style
Transforming	Gemini Consulting	Large-format magazine with short articles on a variety of subjects.
Prism	Arthur D. Little	Journal format with technical articles by ADL consultants.
McKinsey Quarterly	McKinsey & Co.	Journal format with technical articles by McKinsey consultants.
Strategy & Business	Booz-Allen & Hamilton	Journal format mixing technical articles with shorter articles and reviews.
Executive Agenda	A. T. Kearney	Mixed format with technical articles and more accessible shorter articles
Consulting Matters	KPMG Peat Marwick	Articles developed from interviews with consultants. Each issue is dedicated to a particular topic.
Mercer Management Journal	Mercer Consulting Group	Journal format with technical articles by Mercer consultants. Each issue is dedicated to a particular topic.

All major consultancy firms now have informative pages on the Internet. A list of web sites is given in Table 27.2.

Table 27.2 Major consultancies' Internet web sites

Consultancy	Web site
Andersen Consulting	www.ac.com
Bain & Company	www.bain.com
Booz-Allen & Hamilton	www.bah.com
Boston Consulting Group	www.bcg.com
Deloitte & Touche	www.deloitte.com
Ernst & Young Consulting	www.eyi.com
Gemini Consulting	www.gemcon.com
A. T. Kearney	www.atkearney.com
KPMG Peat Marwick	www.kpmg.com
Arthur D. Little	www.arthurdlittle.com
McKinsey & Co.	www.mckinsey.com
Mercer Consulting Group	www.mercermc.com
PriceWaterhouseCoopers	www.pwglobal.com

27.2 Career structure in consulting firms

All management consultancies organise themselves in their own way. But they are often quite hierarchical in their structures, especially the larger firms. This provides a definite ladder for gaining experience, building expertise and developing a career. In practice, most consulting projects are undertaken by teams which cut across levels of responsibility. Being team based, most consultancies operate with a professional, informal culture. Job titles vary, but some of the common roles (in ascending order of seniority) include the following.

◆ Analysts

Analysts are responsible for gathering information and processing it for the consulting team.

◆ Consultants

Consultants undertake the evaluation of the client business and make recommendations on its behalf.

◆ Senior consultants

More experienced consultants have responsibility for leading a consulting team undertaking a project on behalf of a client.

◆ **Business development managers**

Business development managers within the consulting business are responsible for developing the firm's products and building its relationship with clients.

◆ **Directors (or partners)**

Directors (or partners) are the most experienced consultants, who take on responsibility for the development of the organisation as a whole and who lead its strategic development.

27.3 The internal consultant

The changes which are driving the demand for consultancy services are also changing the way in which internal managers work. The old way in which businesses worked, with fixed structures defining hierarchies in which people work, are no longer appropriate. In today's fast-changing and unpredictable environments businesses need to be flexible and responsive to developing customer needs. Old structures must be flattened. Multifunctional teams with open membership must replace monolithic closed departments. Managers must forget about the jobs they are *supposed* to do and look towards the tasks they *must* do in order to make their businesses more competitive. Today's manager cannot simply look to a historical (and therefore out-of-date!) job description. William Bridges has suggested in his book *Jobshift* (1995) that managers must learn to thrive in a workplace without jobs, or at least jobs as they were understood. This presents both an opportunity and a challenge. The strategies and skills of the effective consultant allow those challenges to be met and those opportunities to be exploited.

The internal consultant is simply a manager who develops the role and approach of a consultant while employed in a permanent capacity. Some managers have always taken advantage of this opportunity, whatever their official job title. Many organisations now recognise the role, though. The following characterises the approach of the internal consultant.

◆ **Awareness of the resources needed by the organisation**

All organisations need external resources if they are to survive and prosper. These include the goodwill (and hence spending) of customers, investors' valuable capital, the support of suppliers and distributors, human expertise and information. As discussed in Chapter 7, attracting these resources is the way in which the consultant creates value for the client. The internal consultant is as keenly aware as the external consultant of the resources he or she is obtaining for the organisation, the value of those resources and the management of the relationships critical to obtaining them.

◆ Constant redefinition of job

No two consulting projects are the same. The role of the consultant changes with the challenges he or she meets. For the internal consultant, the job he or she does undergoes constant evolution. This means a constant redefinition of role, responsibilities and relationships, both internal and external. External relationships are managed to maintain resource flows; internal ones so that the whole organisation recognises the developing role.

◆ Demanding change

Change is not always easy. But it is easy to resist. A different future offers uncertainty. To seek solace in what is known is a natural reaction. Yet change is a necessary facet of organisational life. The environment changes, competitors change, the business must change in response. The internal consultant will not only accept change positively, he or she will actively demand it. Indeed, the internal consultant will be in the vanguard leading that change. This is not to say that change for change's sake is good, but that well-thought-out, and well-managed relevant change is.

◆ Constant development of skill profile

Active learning demands that skills are seen not as something we have, but as something we are in the process of gaining. Internal consultants must evaluate the skill demands of the tasks they face, assess personal competencies, identify any skill gaps and source a means of developing those skills.

◆ Intrapreneurial planning

All managers create change. Entrepreneurs are managers who drive *significant* change. An *intrapreneur* is simply a manager who behaves entrepreneurially within an established firm. The intrapreneur is a manager who leads the organisation so that it can change to exploit significant new opportunities. Effective entrepreneurship demands planning. An opportunity must be identified and its value evaluated. A strategy to exploit that opportunity must be devised. That strategy must be put into effect. It is in this area, perhaps above all others, that the internal consultant comes into his or her own.

27.4 The value of the consulting experience in non-consulting careers

This book describes a set of skills that make consulting effective and are the basis for success as a consultant. But they are not exclusive to consulting: they are general management skills. An ability to use information and analyse it to identify valuable options, to make plans that use resources efficiently to exploit those options and to build relationships so that people follow is a skill that will make any managerial career successful. This will be so in technical roles, specialist roles or general management roles. The skills of the consultant will be particularly evident when leadership and team working are called for. It is for this reason that successful consultants often move into high-profile permanent managerial positions, often on the invitation of satisfied clients.

Team discussion point

Each person in the group should seek out one or more of the web sites of the major consultancies. Imagine that you have been taken on to undertake a recruitment drive for that firm at the analyst and consultant level. What would you look for in prospective candidates?

Give a short presentation (of five minutes with two overheads) of your findings to the rest of the group. Give them a one-page summary advising them how to approach that firm to discuss career prospects.

Summary of key ideas

◆ Consultancy is a large and fast-growing sector.

◆ The growth drivers are set to continue.

◆ Changes in established organisations mean that the internal consultant will have an ever more important managerial role.

◆ Consultancy skills are general management skills. A person with consulting skills can look forward to success in a wide variety of roles and organisations.

◆ Consultancy skills will be of increasing relevance to managers in not-for-profit organisations.

Good luck in developing a successful consulting career, whoever you work for!

Appendix

Managing the management consulting exercise: a guide for the programme tutor

◆ Introduction

Undergraduate teaching is changing. Management educators can no longer confine themselves to the classroom. Helping the student achieve conceptual proficiency is not enough. Students now need the personal and social skills which will offer them success in a competitive business world. This is not without good cause. Employers are increasingly vocal in their demands for such skills. Students who have them (and who have *evidence* of them) are confident of claiming a premium in the graduate labour market. As a result, business students are demanding the opportunity to be exposed to the challenge of 'real business' situations as part of their learning programmes.

This presents management educators with a challenge. How can we allow the student to be exposed to the world of business outside the institution while retaining firm control of the learning experience and its outcomes? This is a challenge the management consulting exercise can help meet.

Management Consulting is a book that provides a detailed and comprehensive account of the skills necessary to undertake consulting projects successfully. It offers both conceptual understanding and practical advice. It deals in depth with:

◆ the *project management skills* needed to co-ordinate, organise and manage a high-level project in an effective manner.

◆ the *analytical skills* needed to develop an understanding of the client business, the issues it faces, the opportunities available to it and to develop innovative approaches in dealing with them;

◆ the *relationship skills* needed to work effectively with others, develop leadership potential, develop a good rapport with the client and communicate ideas in an effective and convincing way.

◆ Management consulting programmes

Management consulting can be undertaken with any sort of venture. Small businesses present excellent clients. They are numerous and offer broad-based projects. Their limited resources mean they are motivated to work with universities. Management consulting projects usually involve a small team of students (typically 4–6) working in conjunction with a local business undertaking a project which offers outcomes rewarding to both the students and the business.

The project is undertaken over a one-term or one-semester period and is subject to a formal assessment procedure. The students remain members of the learning institution and do not become employees of the business over the period of the project. Quite rightly, though, many students see the consulting exercise as a chance to create a future employment opportunity for when they graduate!

Such programmes offer opportunities for all the parties involved.

◆ The undergraduate gains a valuable, enriching and real management experience in a supportive, controlled environment which offers him or her the chance to develop recognisable and transferable skills.

◆ The business manager gains access to a consulting project which has outputs of real value to his or her business. This is particularly the case with small businesses that lack specialist internal management resources.

◆ The academic makes contact with the business community, creating a network of personal contacts that can be used to develop consulting and research links.

◆ The institution positively develops its profile with the local business community.

Management Consulting aims to be a learning resource that helps the student and the management educator capitalise on these opportunities.

◆ Objectives of this guide

Management consulting programmes present a number of administrative challenges to the management educator. These challenges go beyond the normal demands of running an educational programme. This guide aims to share some insights into the design and running of a small business management consulting programme.

This guide offers advice on:

◆ developing an effective teaching philosophy for a management consulting based teaching programme;

◆ the overall design of the programme;

◆ specifying formal learning outcomes for the programme;

◆ developing an assessment strategy which ensures that the students achieve the desired learning outcomes while the small business gets a consulting exercise of value;

◆ defining specific objectives for the consulting exercise in association with the client small business manager;

◆ motivating the student to become committed to the project;

◆ managing the student group and dealing with team conflicts;

◆ attracting the right sort of business into the programme;

◆ dealing positively with problems raised by the client business's management.

Running a management consulting programme is a learning experience, not just for the students but also for the management tutor. This guide is not intended to be definitive. It cannot be. It aims to present a framework for exploring the running of the management consulting programme and the building on the experiences of the programme tutor-manager.

◆ The role of management consulting in business education

Management is a craft. It depends on intuition and experience as well as formal knowledge. An ability to undertake analysis may enable the manager to see a way forward for the business. Actually taking the business forward demands an ability to influence and build relationships with people as well.

The days when the management educator could just offer students formal knowledge and leave it to their employers to nurture the relationship skills necessary to make them effective managers are long gone (if they ever really existed). The increasingly vocal demand by employers that students make a value-delivering contribution 'from day one' means they must practise using their complement of formal knowledge in a real business situation while they are still in the learning environment.

Undertaking a consulting exercise on behalf of a business presents students with an opportunity to develop management skills which are valuable and relevant. Doing so while at a teaching institution means they can develop those skills with definite and controlled learning outcomes in a safe and supportive environment.

Any size of business can offer a learning environment for the consulting exercise. However, small businesses offer a number of advantages as clients:

◆ They are numerous and are easily accessed.

◆ They face broad-based challenges which produce relevant and interesting consulting projects.

◆ They respond positively to the opportunity to work with a local teaching institution.

The management consulting project, particularly with a small business, offers a learning experience which is in many ways better than, and certainly complementary to, long-term industrial placements.

Table A.1 **Advantages of management consulting over placements**

Management consulting	Placements
Learning outcomes and content can be controlled by academic staff	Academics easily lose control of the placement experience
Student performance can be monitored and assessed through formal criteria	Formal criteria are difficult to apply and monitor
The students get to undertake a 'high-level' project of real value	Students often finish up doing 'odd jobs' for the business
There is no need for a formal contract of employment	A formal contract is required; this is bureaucratic and demands a legal commitment from the employer
It opens up the possibility of using small businesses	Small businesses are numerous but resist short-term placements because they demand a commitment of valuable time and are disruptive
It is cost effective and enables the progression of a large number of students; it utilises small team working and group teaching	It requires the management of individual placements

◆ Developing a teaching philosophy

Management consulting moves the learning experience beyond the constraints of classroom-based teaching. This offers both opportunities and challenges. The student is given the chance to develop real and transferable management skills. If the student is to take advantage of this opportunity in a meaningful way he or she must take personal responsibility for delivering the project outcomes. This does not mean that students must work in isolation. Responsibility is most readily accepted when support is offered to meet the challenge of taking it.

People cannot be forced to take advantage of an opportunity they are presented with. They can be shown its possibilities. They can be encouraged to exploit what it offers. But, ultimately, it is they who must make the move to capitalise on it. This applies to the opportunity presented to students by a management consulting project.

Students can be motivated to become involved in the programme (some practical tips for which are detailed below) but they must recognise that it is *they* who are responsible for capitalising on what it has to offer. This insight forms the basis of a teaching philosophy for the programme. In essence it is that the programme tutor-manager creates the opportunity for students to learn, but they must take advantage of that opportunity.

Not only is this an effective philosophy; it offers the programme educator-manager a means to drive the programme forward and sustain it in the face of the many challenges it will meet.

Programme teacher–managers cannot possibly deal with all the problems that students will encounter. Nor should they. Addressing the management challenges presented by delivering the consulting project is a valuable part of the learning experience for the student. Mistakes are as much a part of the learning experience as successes. This does not mean that students should be left floundering. Or that they feel they are out on their own. What it does mean is that the programme teacher-manager must offer support, guidance and counselling on how to solve the problem but not (in the first instance anyway) direct intervention to deal with routine problems.

The philosophy of the course must be that the educator-manager's role must be one of facilitating the project not doing it on behalf of the student group.

A number of issues arise while working on programmes. Conflicts within the team and misunderstandings with the client are common. *Management Consulting* provides the student with practical guidance for dealing with issues like these. 'Team discussion points' included in the book encourage students to explore and develop strategies to deal with the problems they are likely to encounter.

The book makes clear the students' responsibility to their projects and the outcomes they agree to. The book also makes clear that the role of the educator is one of providing support, advice and encouragement, not project management resource.

◆ Designing the programme

A small business management programme demands the same attention to design, learning outcome definition and content considerations as any teaching programme. The programme will have the following elements:

◆ delivery of a conceptual knowledge base to the student;

◆ progression of a well-defined project with a client business;

◆ fulfilment of a programme of consulting activities;

◆ engagement of the students with a small business manager;

◆ support of the project by an academic supervisor;

◆ delivery of project outcomes to the client;

◆ final assessment of the exercise.

These elements must be fitted together in an integrated way which fits with the overall teaching schedule and meets with resource constraints. The students can be free to arrange meetings with the client business on their own terms. Regular meetings in the form of tutorials or 'surgeries' can be used to deliver necessary knowledge, gain feedback from the students and provide support and encouragement.

◆ Defining learning outcomes

Learning outcomes provide a focus for a teaching programme. They concentrate the mind of the teacher and the student on the programme's key aims and objectives. Learning outcomes provide the 'selling points' for a programme of learning to the student. They are a valuable way of motivating the student to become committed to the exercise.

The learning outcomes for the consulting programme can be defined as follows.

As a result of successfully completing the programme the student will:

◆ recognise the importance of sound analytical thinking when approaching business opportunities and challenges;

◆ recognise the need for a proactive approach to business opportunities and challenges;

◆ recognise the rewards for effective team working in a business situation;

◆ develop an understanding of the value of effective communication in a business situation;

◆ recognise his or her own business skill profile, identify strengths and opportunities for development;

◆ develop confidence in promoting his or her own business ideas.

If the client organisation is a small business then the following outcomes may be added:

◆ to develop an understanding of the issues facing, and decision making in, small–medium-enterprise (SME) ventures.

◆ Assessment procedures

Assessment is a critical part of a teaching programme. It is not just a hurdle that the student must leap if he or she is to be credited with successful completion: it is an opportunity to focus the student and to motivate him or her to achieve the desired learning outcomes. It is suggested that the programme have three separately assessed exercises. These are in Table A.2.

Table A.2   Assessment

Exercises	Basis	Overall contribution (%)
Project proposal	Group assessment	25
Final report	Group assessment	50
Project log	Individual assessment	25

The assessment schemes for each of these stages takes the form of a contract offering the student a given level of reward for a given output. This emphasises the responsibility of the student to deliver the outcomes and is a reflection of the reality of rewards in business life.

Management Consulting offers the student advice on how to use these assessment exercises positively to guide the consulting project and to gain high rewards from it. Learning how to keep a project log is an important skill. It encourages active learning and personal reflection. It is given a chapter to itself, which deals with content and format in detail.

Assessing the proposal

Making an assessment of the project proposal at an early stage in the project offers the tutor a number of opportunities:

◆ it ensures that the project is on track;

◆ it reminds the student that he or she is responsible for the outcomes of the project;

◆ it reflects the reality that business rewards well-communicated, relevant proposals;

◆ it provides a chance to check that the students have negotiated the right type of outcomes with the client;

◆ it provides a focus for the progression of the project;

◆ it offers an opportunity to remotivate the students.

The project proposal should be reviewed with the students at an early stage in the project. The best stage is shortly after the initial meeting with the client business. A deadline of three weeks after the project is initiated is about right. Positive feedback at this stage is encouraging and gives the students confidence to progress. It is also a chance to spot and help heal any early rifts between team members.

Assessing the final report

Assessing the final report presents a challenge. The assessor must think beyond a simple consideration of the quality of the analysis performed and the recommendations made. Clearly, these are important. But they are standards that must be considered in the light of the student's expertise and experience at the stage he or she has reached in their management education.

The opinion of the client business manager on the project outcomes is useful. But avoid formalising the manager's input. It puts the manager in an uncomfortable position as he or she lacks training and experience to make a detailed comparative or normative evaluation of the student's performance. Nor is the manager in a position to compare the performance of different student groups.

Assessing the project log

The project log (described in Chapter 5) is a valuable tool which not only aids delivery of the consulting exercise but ensures that it is an effective and rewarding learning experience. Keeping the project log up to date makes sure not only that the consulting team are kept focused on the objectives they have set themselves, but also that they reflect on the exercise and use it as an active learning opportunity.

Details on the assessment strategy for each of these exercises are discussed in Chapter 4.

◆ What sort of businesses should be involved?

Why be restrictive? As noted, small businesses make good clients. The definition of 'small business' is fluid, though. When presented with a project opportunity ask, not 'Is this a small business?', but 'Is the project offered one that meets the learning criteria set for the programme?' If the business offers the right sort of project why reject it?

A business in any sector has the potential to present an interesting project. The tutor may select on the basis of his or her research interests or consulting experience.

Whatever the size of business and its sector look for projects which:

◆ have the potential to be well defined in terms of objectives and outcomes;

◆ relate to a well-defined part of the business or business unit;

◆ are sponsored by someone of seniority in the business;

◆ are meaningful to the business (this motivates the manager); but

◆ are not critical to its survival (which may put too much pressure on the students);

◆ offer a broad-based management experience;

◆ do not demand too specific and advanced a knowledge on the part of the student.

In short, do take positive projects which make a demand on general management skills, interest a senior manager and are 'nice to have' for the business but are not a priority given its current resources.

On the other hand it is best to avoid projects which concern 'make or break' issues for the business or demand specialised knowledge (unless, of course, this reflects a specialisation the students are exploring and the relevant academic resource is available to offer support).

◆ Attracting businesses into the programme

Management consulting programmes can only work if business managers offer their support to them. There are a number of means by which their interest can be gained. The immediate temptation may be to stress the aspect of 'low-cost' consulting. This approval should be used with caution, however. It offers a mixed blessing to the busy manager. There are a number of reasons why this is so.

◆ The manager may doubt the value of something which is offered free.

◆ The manager may (albeit wrongly) doubt the ability of students to offer insights of real value to the business.

◆ The manager may be suspicious about the value of consulting in general.

◆ The business may have access to low-cost consulting from other sources.

◆ The manager may be concerned about the time that will be needed for the exercise.

◆ The manager may be concerned about the disruption the students will cause.

The tutor must be aware of these concerns when promoting the programme. Unaddressed, they may prevent potentially valuable clients taking advantage of the scheme.

In many respects there is an advantage in being honest. Rather than offer the manager something he or she may not want, ask the manager for his or her support. Most managers will be flattered that a teaching institution is genuinely interested in their insights and experience and wants them to support a teaching programme. Asking the manager 'in' to support the teaching programme rather than sending the students 'out' to undertake something on behalf of the business also provides a sounder platform on which to manage the manager's expectations and deal with any problems that arise.

There are a number of mechanisms that can be used to promote the programme.

Institutional promotion

Many institutions have formal procedures for promoting themselves to private businesses. These should be exploited. Those involved in promoting the institution should have information on the management consulting programme and what it can offer. They should be encouraged to pass potential projects on to the tutor for consideration.

Direct promotion

The management consulting programme can be promoted directly. This may involve mailshots or telephone enquiries. This is effective and allows precise targeting of potential clients. It is relatively expensive, though.

Identification of projects by students

Students can be encouraged to identify clients for themselves. If they present a proposed business to work with, fine. Check that the client and the project are suitable for the learning outcomes and that the whole student team are prepared to work with the client, though, or problems may arise later. It is not wise to insist that the students find their own clients, however. It is time consuming for them and can put them under undue pressure.

Recommendation through business support agencies

Many business support agencies, for example the Training and Enterprise Councils (TECs) or Business Links, will be more than happy to recommend the consulting scheme to businesses enquiring about the support available. They can prove to be very good at selecting the right sort of business for the scheme. It is worth while making a formal briefing to decision makers in these organisations. This communicates what the scheme has to offer and confirms its professional approach. The consulting scheme offers a powerful way for the academic to network with these valuable organisations.

Recommendation through banks

The small business support of high street banks offers access to potential clients. They are good at selecting young, fast-growing businesses that approach them for capital. Businesses such as these are usually eager for consulting support. As with business support agencies, invest in a formal brief. Network and build up contacts.

Trade associations

Trade associations can be asked to promote the scheme to their members. This is a good way to target clients in a particular sector, reflecting perhaps the tutor's research or consulting interests. Again, a formal briefing works wonders.

Word of mouth

Encourage colleagues to pass on potential contacts. Encourage clients who have had a good experience to tell others about it.

Don't hunt – harvest!

There is no reason to discard a client after it has been involved in the programme once. A good experience with it means it will be amenable to offering support again in the future. Building up a collection of 'old hands' strengthens the scheme. The time needed to recruit new businesses is reduced, the client becomes practised in helping the student learn and the relationship built can be called on to deal with the problems that inevitably arise.

◆ Promotional literature

It is worth while spending a little time and money to prepare a leaflet which describes the scheme. This can be used to promote the scheme via mailshots or third party recommendations. It can be left behind after formal presentations.

Information included should include:

◆ the name of the institution and school or faculty running the scheme;

◆ a brief summary (selling points) about what it has to offer;

◆ some details about the scheme:
  – when it runs from, for how long;
  – what type of business should be involved;
  – any costs (direct costs, support with expenses);

◆ a contact name with telephone, fax and e-mail details.

It is advisable to include a prominent statement to the effect that the students will *not* need to be employed by the business. It is easy for the client to assume that they will be and this may discourage them from becoming involved.

◆ Dealing with issues in managing the programme

The management of the programme has several interconnected tasks. A number of issues can arise.

Delivering the conceptual base

The skills necessary for effective management consulting are eclectic. Analysis, project management and relationship-building skills are needed in equal measure.

> *Management Consulting* gives a comprehensive and accessible insight into these skills. It provides a basis for supporting the review and discussion of these skills through lectures and tutorials.

Motivating the students to become involved

A live consulting exercise is demanding. The student faces challenges – team working, self-organisation, developing a relationship with a professional manager – that do not arise in classroom-based teaching programmes. If they are to learn from the experience, students must be motivated to meet these challenges.

A 'pep talk' at the beginning of the programme sets the scene. Remind the students of what the programme offers: a chance to become involved in a real business situation, valuable CV points and an insight into an attractive and rewarding career path. Do tell them that, though they are responsible for delivering outcomes, they are in a safe decision-making environment and will be offered a high level of support by both the academic and the business client.

Running the surgery

A regular 'surgery' session can be used as a forum for delivering conceptual knowledge, for reviewing the progression of projects and for advising on dealing with issues.

In the author's experience it has been found valuable to split the surgery into three parts. Use the first for a formal teaching of ideas with overheads, etc. Use the second to talk to individual groups, to review progress, monitor group development and motivate individuals. The final part can be used for a plenary session in which common ideas and issues can be explored. The first part may form the basis of a formal lecture programme. In this case, use the surgery to concentrate on the team review and plenary session.

Managing the relationship with the small business manager

Managers are busy people. They work under considerable pressure. The project will be only one of the matters with which they will be involved. No matter how enthusiastic they are at the start it is easy for the priority of the project to slip. Meetings may be cancelled. Requests for information may not be dealt with promptly. Such experiences can easily demotivate the students.

The first point to make is that it is the responsibility of the student group to keep the client motivated. It is better to advise them how to do this rather than address the issue yourself.

Management Consulting offers the student some practical tips on how to maintain the interest and commitment of the client manager.

If the situation is proving beyond the capabilities of the student, it may be necessary for the tutor to move in so that the integrity of the learning experience is maintained. It is often easier to manage the situation if the manager has been 'brought in' rather than if the student group has been 'sent out'.

Maintaining group integrity and dealing with group conflicts

Conflicts are an inevitable part of group working. Disagreements arise over a number of issues. Intelligent, able students should be expected to take a stance on what the objectives of the project are and how it should be managed. If individuals differentiate their roles within the team (a process to be encouraged) then there will be debate, often heated, about the value of the contributions made by different team members. Personality clashes may exacerbate these conflicts.

Such conflicts eventually come to the surface. A member or members of the team often call on the tutor to 'deal' with the problem. The best approach is to offer the students support, but ensure that they accept responsibility for the maintenance of effective team functioning. The team should be reminded that conflicts are a natural part of team working, but that managers have a responsibility to deal with them. This responsibility falls particularly heavily on the shoulders of leaders.

Encourage the team to explore issues in an open way. Get them to recognise that conflict will inhibit the achievement of objectives. Identify the team leader (whether formally recognised or one who has simply emerged). If need be, take the leader to one side and advise on the counselling skills necessary to resolve conflicts (these are dealt with in Chapter 23).

A frequent source of friction is a team member who is felt to be underperforming. The project is assessed on a team basis. Members will be quick to spot what they see as 'freeloading'. The opening gambit is to pass the problem back to the team. Suggest that underperformance is usually a result of lack of clarity in relation to objectives and poor direction rather than a cynical attempt to get something for nothing. The team should consider the objectives given to every member and ask if these might be clearer. Have the objectives been assigned agreed signposts and are outcomes clear? If not, these should be put into place. Every member of the team should be encouraged to consider his or her own motivations and what motivates the other members.

If, eventually, the tutor is convinced that a member of the team is not making a sufficient contribution then one-to-one counsellling may be in order. Specific objectives in relation to the individual contribution can be set. Monitorable outcomes and the project log can be used to keep track of the contribution made.

Whatever the outcome, the students should be directed to reflect in the project log on the conflict, its causes and strategies for its resolution. In particular, they should consider the leadership skills needed to deal with it, how they used them and the opportunities they have to develop them further in the future.

◆ Assessment contracts

It is recommended that the basis of assessment be presented to the students as a 'contract': if the student aspires to a particular grade, the level of performance required to achieve that grade is defined. The author has used the following assessment contracts successfully. Clearly, there must be some latitude for interpretation in these. This can be used positively to negotiate outcomes based on drafts of proposals, final reports and logs which can be reviewed in the surgeries.

Assessment contract: Project proposal

The project proposal is a 2–3 page document which represents your agreement with the client business as to the objectives of the project, what it will achieve and the actions the business will be able to undertake as a result of the project.

This is a **group** exercise and holds a **25** per cent weighting.

If you wish to achieve the indicated grade you must:

Grade   Achievement

A   Provide a proposal which clearly defines the objectives of the project and unambiguously indicates the outputs that will be provided. Objectives and outcomes will be well defined and reflect clear thinking about the business and the situation it faces. They will be based on information gleaned from discussion with the client manager. Critically, the proposal will define *in detail* the actions that the business will be able to take as a result of receiving the final report.

B   Provide a proposal which clearly defines the objectives and outputs of the project. The definition of the objectives and outputs will reflect clear thinking about the business and the situation it faces. The proposal will define the actions the business will be able to take as a result of receiving the final report although these may not have the detail that would justify an **A** grade.

C   Provide a proposal which defines the objectives and outputs of the project. These will be appropriate for the business and the situation it faces but may not reflect the level of thinking that would justify an **A/B** grade. The actions that the business can take as a result of receiving the report may not be clearly defined.

D   Provide a proposal which defines the objectives and outputs of the project. These may not be particularly well defined or be seen to reflect clear thinking about the business and the situation it faces. The actions that the business will be able to take as a result of receiving the final report may not be clear.

E   Provide a proposal which fails to define the objectives and outputs of the project.

F   Make no submission.

Assessment contract: Final project report

The final report relates your analysis and recommendations to the business. Length and format will vary but it is typically 4000–5000 words long with a one-page management summary which makes a strong impact.

This is a **group** exercise and holds a **50** per cent weighting.

If you wish to achieve the indicated grade you must:

Grade   Achievement

A   Present a final presentation which develops logical and valid conclusions based on extensive, reliable and properly interpreted information. The analysis will be clear and based on a well-defined, appropriate and properly used conceptual framework. Key actions to be taken by the business will be clearly defined. Presentation will be professional and attention catching with ideas communicated in an impactful manner.

B   Present a final presentation which develops logical and valid conclusions based on well-researched, reliable and competently interpreted information. Analysis will be based on a well-defined and appropriate analytical framework. The conclusions will lead to the business being able to take positive actions, though these might not be as explicit as those that would earn an **A** grade. Presentation will be professional with an effective communication technique used.

C   Present a final presentation which develops generally valid conclusions. These will be grounded on effectively researched information but this may not be as extensive as that which would justify an **A/B** grade. Analysis will be competent though it might not draw on the kind of conceptual insights that would justify an **A/B** grade. Presentation will, on the whole, be professional. The business will be able to take positive actions as a result of the report but these actions may not be clearly defined by the report.

D   Present a final presentation which draws some useful conclusions but it will not be clear that these are based on wide-ranging or particularly reliable background research. Analysis will, on the whole, be competent but it may not be based on a clear conceptual foundation. The actions that the business should take as a result of the report will not be clear.

E   Present a final presentation which does not develop any useful conclusions. This is likely to be because insufficient background research has been undertaken and/or meaningful analysis has not been undertaken. The business will not be able to undertake any specific actions as a result of the project

F   Make no submission.

Assessment contract: Project diary

The project diary represents an opportunity for you to relate your personal experiences on the project, the kind of thinking used, the analysis undertaken, the active learning adopted and how you used the programme to develop a personal leadership and motivational style towards the rest of the group.

This is an **individual** exercise and holds a **25** per cent weighting.

If you wish to achieve the indicated grade you must:

Grade   Achievement

A   Present a diary which clearly defines all the major steps in the project, what the specific objectives of each step were, how the objectives were defined and how they were achieved. The diary will demonstrate reflection on how the team is operating and the group dynamics operating. The diary will have evidence of action learning techniques being adopted and will relate the analysis that was carried out. The diary will also make reference to the development of personal leadership and group motivational style.

B   Present a diary which clearly defines all the major steps in the project, what the specific objectives of each step were, how the objectives were defined and how they were achieved. The diary will demonstrate reflection on how the team is operating and the group dynamics operating. The diary may also have evidence of action learning techniques being adopted and relate the analysis that was carried out. The diary will, however, lack the kind of reflection on personal leadership and group motivational style being developed that would justify an **A** grade.

C   Present a diary which clearly defines all the major steps in the project, what the specific objectives of each step were, how the objectives were defined and how they were achieved. The diary will demonstrate reflection on how the team is functioning and the group dynamics operating. Evidence on action learning, group dynamics and leadership style will, however, be too limited to justify an **A/B** grade.

D   Present a diary which is a simple list of the main tasks, how they were defined and what was achieved. There will be no evidence of analysis or reflection on action learning, group dynamics, leadership or motivation.

E   Present a diary which merely lists the tasks carried out.

F   Make no submission.

Suggestions for further reading

Andreas, S. and Andreas, C. (1987) *Change Your Mind – And Keep the Change*. Moad, UT: Real People Press.

Ansoff, I. (1987) *Corporate Strategy* (revised edn). Harmondsworth: Penguin Business.

Beckhard, R. and Harris, R.T. (1987) *Organizational Transitions: Managing Complex Change* (2nd edn). Reading, MA: Addison-Wesley.

Bell, C.R. and Nadler, L. (1979) *Clients and Consultants*. Houston, Texas: Gulf Publishing.

Blake, R.R. and Mouton, J.S. (1976) *Consultation*. Reading, MA: Addison-Wesley.

Blake, R.R. and Mouton, J.S. (1982) *The Versatile Manager: A Grid Profile*. Homewood, IL: Richard D. Irwin.

Bourantis, D. and Mandes, Y. (1987) 'Does market share lead to profitability?', *Long Range Planning*, 20 (5), 102–8.

Bridges, W. (1995) *Jobshift: How to Prosper in a Workplace Without Jobs*. London: Nicholas Brealey.

Buzan, T. (1995) *Use Your Head*. London: BBC Publications.

Caloris, R., Johnson, G. and Sarnin, P. (1944) 'CEO's cognitive maps and the scope of the organisation', *Strategic Management Journal*, 15, 437–57.

Carroll, A. (1979) 'A three dimensional model of corporate performance', *Academy of Management Review*, 4 (4), 497–505.

Daniels, K., Johnson, G. and de Chernatony, L. (1994) 'Differences in managerial cognitions of competition', *British Journal of Management*, 5 Special Issue, S21–9.

Day, G.S. (1994) 'Continuous learning about markets', *California Management Review*, Summer, 9–31.

Dilts, R. *et al.* (1980) *Neuro Linguistic Programming*, Vol. I. Cupertino, CA: Meta Publications.

Dougherty, A.M. (1990) *Consultation; Practice and Perspectives*. Pacific Grove, CA: Brookes Cole.

Drucker, P.F. (1954) *The Practice of Management*. New York: Harper & Row.

Fiedler, F.E. (1967) *A Theory of Leadership Effectiveness*. New York: McGraw-Hill.

Floyd, C. (1997) *Managing Technology for Corporate Success*. Aldershot: Gower.

French, W.L. and Bell, C.H. Jr. (1990) *Organization Development*. Upper Saddle River, NJ: Prentice-Hall.

Gallessich, J. (1985) 'Towards a meta-theory of consultation', *Counselling Psychologist*, 13 (3), 336–54.

Golembiewski, R.T. (ed.) (1993) *Handbook of Organizational Consultation*. New York: Marcell Decker.

Guth, W.D. and MacMillan, I.C. (1986) 'Strategy implementation versus middle management self-interest', *Strategic Management Journal*, 7, 313–27.

Grant, R. (1995) *Contemporary Strategy Analysis*. Cambridge, MA: Blackwell.

Handy, C. (1993) *Understanding Organisations* (4th edn). London: Penguin.

Hayes, J. and Allinson, C.W. (1994) 'Cognitive style and its relevance for management practice', *British Journal of Management*, 5, 53–71.

Hedley, B. (1977) 'Strategy and the Business Portfolio', *Long Range Planning*, 10 (2), 9–15.

Helmer, O. (1966) *Social Technology*. New York: Basic Books.

Herzberg, F., Mausner, B. and Snyderman, B. (1959) *The Motivation to Work*. New York: John Wiley and Sons.

House, R.J. and Mitchell, T.R. (1974) 'Path-goal theory of leadership', *Journal of Contemporary Business*, Autumn, 81–97.

Idenberg, P.J. (1993) 'Four styles of strategic planning', *Long Range Planning*, 26 (6), 132–7.

Jago, A.G. (1982) 'Leadership: Perspectives in theory and research', *Management Science*, March, 315–36.

James, T. and Woodsmall, W. (1988) *Time Line Therapy and the Basis of Personality*. Cupertino, CA: Meta Publications.

Kakabadse, A., Ludlow, R. and Vinnicombe, S. (1988) *Working in Organizations*. London: Penguin.

Kast, F.G. and Rosenzweig, J.G. (1985) *Organization and Management* (4th edn). New York: McGraw Hill.

Kay, J. (1993) *The Foundations of Corporate Success: How Business Strategies Add Value*. Oxford: Oxford University Press.

Kolb, D.A. (1978) *A Learning Style Inventory: Technical Manual* (Revised edn). Boston: McBer & Co.

Langley, A. (1995) 'Between "paralysis by analysis" and "extinction by instinct"', *Sloan Management Review*, Spring, 63–76.

Lundberg, C.C. (1997) 'Towards a general model of consultancy', *Journal of Organisational Change Management*, 10 (3), 193–201.

Lundberg, C.C. and Finney, M. (1987) 'Emerging models of consultancy', *Consultation* 6, (1).

Lynch, R. (1997) *Corporate Strategy*. London: Financial Times Pitman Publishing.

McCann, A. (1995) 'The rule of 2 x 2', *Long Range Planning*, 28 (1), 112–15.

McClelland, D.C. (1961) *The Achieving Society*. New York: Van Nostrand Reinhold.

McClelland, D.C. (1975) *The Inner Experience*. New York: Irvington.

McDaniel, C. and Gates, R. (1991) *Contemporary Marketing Research*. St Paul, MN: West Publishing Company.

McGregor, D. (1960) *The Human Side of the Enterprise*. New York: McGraw-Hill.

Maslow, A. (1954) *Motivation and Personality*. New York: Harper & Row.

Minto, B. (1987) *The Pyramid Principle*. London: Pitman Publishing.

Mintzberg, H. (1972) 'Research on strategy making', *Proceedings of the 32nd Annual Meeting of the Academy of Management*, Minneapolis.

Mintzberg, H. (1973) *The Nature of Managerial Work*. New York: Harper & Row.

Mintzberg, H. (1975) 'The manager's job: folklore and fact', *Harvard Business Review*, July-August, 49–61.

Mintzberg, H. (1994) *The Rise and Fall of Strategic Planning*. New York: Prentice-Hall.

Patterson, T.T. (1969) *Management Theory*. London: Business Publications.

Peteraf, M. and Shanley, M. (1997) 'Getting to know you: A theory of strategic group identity', *Strategic Management Journal*, 18 (SI), 165–86.

Peters, T. and Waterman, R. (1982) *In Search of Excellence*. New York: Harper & Row.

Pinchot, G. III (1985) *Intrapreneuring*. New York: Harper Collins.

Plane, R.D. (1994) *Management Science: A Spreadsheet Approach*. Danvers, MA: The Scientific Press Series.

Porter, M.E. (1980) *Competitive Strategy: Techniques for Analysing Industries and Competitors*. New York: Free Press.

Porter, M.E. (1985) *Competitive Advantage: Creating and Sustaining Superior Performance*. New York: Free Press.

Prahalad, C.K. and Bettis, R.A. (1986) 'The dominant logic: A new linkage between diversity and performance', *Strategic Management Journal*, 7 (6), 485–501.

Quinn, J. B. (1977) 'Strategic goals: Process and politics', *Sloan Management Review*, Fall, 21–37.

Reger, R.K. and Huff, A.S. (1993) 'Strategic groups: A cognitive perspective', *Strategic Management Journal*, 14, 103–4.

Robbins, S.P. (1988) *Essentials of Organizational Behaviour* (2nd edn). Upper Saddle River, NJ: Prentice-Hall.

Robinson, S.J.Q., Hitchens, R.E. and Wade, D.P. (1978) 'The directional policy matrix – a tool for strategic planning', *Long Range Planning*, 11 (3), 8–15.

Schein, E.H. (1985) *Organizational Culture and Leadership*. San Francisco: Jossey-Bass.

Schein, E.H. (1987) *Process Consultation*, Vol. II. Reading, MA: Addison-Wesley.

Schein, E.H. (1988) *Process Consultation*, Vol. I (revised edn). Reading, MA: Addison-Wesley.

Schein, E.H. (1997) 'The concept of "client" from a process consultation perspective: A guide for change agents', *Journal of Organisational Change Management*, 10 (3), 202–16.

Scott-Morgan, P. (1994) *The Unwritten Rules of the Game*. New York: McGraw-Hill.

Sturdy, A. (1997) 'The consultancy process – an insecure business', *Journal of Management Studies*, 34 (3), 389–413.

Tom, P.L. (1987) *Managing Information as a Corporate Resource*. Glenview, IL: Scott, Foresman and Co.

Tsoukas, H. (1991) 'The missing link: A transformational view of metaphors in organisational science', *Academy of Management Review*, 16 (3), 566–85.

Tsoukas, H. (1994) 'What is management? An outline of a metatheory' *British Journal of Management*, 5, 289–301.

Tubbs, M.E. (1986) 'Goal setting: A meta-analysis examination of the empirical evidence', *Journal of Applied Psychology*, August, 474–83.

Van de Ven, A.H. and Drazin, R. (1985) 'The concept of fit in contingency theory', *Research in Organizational Behaviour*, 7, 333–65.

Vroom, V.H. and Yetton, P.W. (1973) *Leadership and Decision-Making*. Pittsburgh: University of Pittsburgh Press.

Wickham, P.A (1997) 'Developing a mission for an entrepreneurial venture', *Management Decision*, 35 (5), 373–81.

Wooldridge, W. and Floyd, S.W. (1990) 'The strategy process, middle management involvement and organisational performance', *Strategic Management Journal*, 11, 231–41.

Wortman, M.S. and Forst, L.I. (eds) *The Academic Consultant Connection*. New York: Kendal-Hunt.

Index